I0131243

The Bottom Line

Unfortunate Side Effects of Capitalist Culture

Arthur McGovern

Nichols College

Vernon Series in Critical Perspectives on Social Science

VERNON PRESS

Copyright © 2017 Vernon Press, an imprint of Vernon Art and Science Inc, on behalf of the author.

All rights reserved. No part of this publication may be reproduced, stored in a retrieval
system, or transmitted in any form or by any means, electronic, mechanical, photo-
copying, recording, or otherwise, without the prior permission of Vernon Art and Science Inc.

www.vernonpress.com

In the Americas:
Vernon Press
1000 N West Street,
Suite 1200, Wilmington,
Delaware 19801
United States

In the rest of the world:
Vernon Press
C/Sancti Espiritu 17,
Malaga, 29006
Spain

Vernon Series in Critical Perspectives on Social Science

Library of Congress Control Number: 2016959069

ISBN: 978-1-62273-244-9

Product and company names mentioned in this work are the trademarks of their re-
spective owners. While every care has been taken in preparing this work, neither the
authors nor Vernon Art and Science Inc. may be held responsible for any loss or
damage caused or alleged to be caused directly or indirectly by the information con-
tained in it.

Table of Contents

Chapter 1

Capitalism and society

Introduction

This book is about the influence of the capitalist economic system on cultural values and rules here and abroad. One basic assumption that informs this work is that the globalized economic system is based on rational, but necessarily amoral goals and values, while the social and cultural world of human interactions is not. For example, remember when you were a child you learned that all human life was precious? Well, how precious? The answer matters and it's not useful to simply claim that it's priceless. For one thing, the value determines how much spending the government will require from businesses in the form of regulations and safety standards to prevent a human death. This value is calculated by many government agencies in the U.S. and varies, but has generally increased over time. In 2011, for example, the U.S. Transportation Department valued a human life at around $6 million to justify new regulations for the automotive industry (Applebaum, 2011). Businesses also make these types of calculations, but often use different valuations and for other purposes. One American car manufacturer, for example, estimated that a human life was worth about $200,000, in the context of a wrongful death associated with their product. In that case, one of the largest American auto manufacturers knew for several decades that the placement of the fuel tank in one particular model created an unreasonable risk of exploding in the event of a rear collision (Geyelin, 1999). Internal memos released into evidence in 1998 showed that the company estimated that deaths resulting from post-collision fuel-tank fires would cost the company $2.40 per car, based on an estimate that each life "has a value of $200,000." Other memos showed that the company had developed an improved design for protecting the gas tank in collisions, but would cost the company $8.59 per car. The company executives decided not to make the improvement.

We recognize that corporations are guided by rational values and tend to make these kinds of quantifiable calculations in order to reduce risk, manage costs, generate profits, and promote growth.

But if unchecked, such analyses suggest a dark and dangerous future when many pro-business advocates argue against any regulations at all. The problem here is not capitalism as an economic system – it is surely the most efficient system for the production and distribution of goods and services. But the economic system has no role to play in the civic, moral, or personal circumstances of human life without degrading those circumstances. The question posed by many scholars like the philosopher Michael Sandel is whether some aspects of human life are immune to economic calculation. In other words, whether there are some things that money can't buy (Sandel, 2012). For example, during the AIDS epidemic in the 1980s, entrepreneurs saw an opportunity to capitalize on the high mortality rates among victims by investing in viatical settlements. Viatical settlements involve the sale of a person's life insurance policy once they become chronically or terminally ill. Basically, an insured victim gets an immediate cash payout by naming the investor as the beneficiary of the policy, and the investor agrees to pay for medical care until the victim's death. In 1989, two investment firms specifically targeted individuals with advanced cases of AIDS for viatical settlements; by 1994, the industry had grown to some 60 firms (Atkinson & Gilkeson, 1998). The risk for the investor was how long the AIDS victim lived; the longer they survived the less profit the investor would realize. In this industry, the inescapable conclusion is that the investor has a financial interest in the prompt death of the insured. "There have been some phenomenal returns, and there have been some horror stories where people live longer," said the president of one viatical company (quoted in Sandel, 2012). My argument isn't with the fact that this happens but that too many of us consider this to be a normal part of life. My concern is that if the market continues to rationalize these sorts of relationships between people, where one person's illness is another person's investment opportunity, then the logical conclusions are harrowing: Free markets for kidneys and other organs, various forms of slavery or indentured servitude, predatory for-profit healthcare. The problem is that the economic marketplace is morally neutral at best, since value is calculated in monetary terms, and this means that the further the market reaches into our civic and personal spaces, the less influence that moral and social values will have. This, I contend, is just one of the unfortunate side-effects of capitalist culture.

I argue in this book that the globalized capitalist economic system has become increasingly efficient in terms of scale and scope, but has also become less humane in many regards; less connected to human needs and concerns. It is an amoral system, and concerned with profits and growth, even when it tries to convince us of its beneficence and humanity. The general premise of this book is that the globalized capitalist economic system, dominated by powerful corporations, is guided by instrumental rather than moral values, largely unconstrained, increasingly intrusive, and socio-politically influential enough to alter our cultural rules and values in ways that are problematic at best. I also emphasize that the blame for these outcomes is not simply due to the capitalist economic system but because of its development alongside a process described as the *rationalization of society*, an evolutionary process that began during the Industrial Revolution and continues today. It is the side-effects of this combination of capitalism and rationalism, the combination of science and technology used to maximize capitalist goals, that are too often damaging for the world and its people. In this book, we will explore these issues and their implications.

Of particular concern is the encroachment of economic interests into areas of human society that traditionally have been free from this type of encroachment, or at least only minimally influenced by profit motives; areas such as scientific research, the justice system, and the personal social spaces in which we live, including even our family relationships. I suggest that there is a slow but steady intrusion into these areas of human life that were once considered off-limits to naked economic incentives and calculations. In a sense, the idea of "mission creep," the gradual expansion of objectives during the course of a military operation or bureaucratic goal, is similar to what I call "market creep," which is the gradual intrusion of economic activity into new "markets" that were previously considered non-economic in nature. This intrusion is the natural result of the economic system's relentless need for expansion and is a completely trivial characteristic of capitalism as such. However, this process does not necessarily involve any concern with social responsibility or public welfare, which means that the economic system is essentially penetrating the cultural barriers that have traditionally separated economic from non-economic realms of human life. This intrusion puts even the idea of America as a free and democratic society increasingly at risk, as economic stakeholders meddle in the political and cultural areas of society in ever more creative ways to further their own enrichment, sometimes at the expense of the public.

Furthermore, the vast capitalist economic system is in many ways increasingly disconnected or disembedded from the contexts and regulations of traditional social relations. Most of us remember when Mitt Romney, the 2012 Republican presidential nominee, claimed that *corporations are people*. I suspect that he was attempting to humanize the face of corporations in general, but his words reminded many of us of the strange situation in which corporations have various rights and privileges but remain relatively free from the corresponding obligations and sanctions that constrain individual human actions. And if corporations are people, then they are extremely powerful people, since the Supreme Court's *Citizen's United* ruling recognized money as speech, allowing corporations to spend virtually unlimited amounts of money to support their preferred candidates in political elections. In fact, the economic power concentrated in the hands of nongovernment economic stakeholders in pursuit of profit creates a number of dangerous problems. According to the Polish sociologist Zygmunt Bauman, for example, we are currently suffering a kind of existential crisis in western societies, one in which power, "the ability to do things," has become divorced from politics, which is "the ability to decide how things should be done" (2013).

> On the one hand, there are powers liberated from political control, while on the other hand, we have politics that is suffering from a chronic shortage of power… power released from political control is capable of guiding itself by its own interests (2013).

These developments lead to the conclusion that the economic system is in some ways fully entangled in our day to day lives in ways that are troubling, but at the same time it is unconstrained by many of our social rules and values. This is not a new phenomenon, and many social theorists have warned about this problem since the time of the Industrial Revolution, but few societies have figured out how to solve this problem without sacrificing either civil liberties or the benefits of technical innovation. The globalized economic system is ultimately made up of individuals exercising their rights around the world, and this freedom has led to remarkable creativity. But in some ways, the economic system has created an alternate reality for itself, where freedom equates to an insatiable quest for profit, and innovation is often aimed at developing more successful forms of influence over an unsuspecting public. As the French sociologist Pierre Bourdieu described it, modern evolution "enabled the economy eventually to be constituted as... a separate universe, governed by its own laws (the laws of self-interested calculation and unfettered competition for profit)" (2005, p. 7).

Market Logic

Worse than a system that is entangled in our lives yet exempt from our social rules and values, however, is one that is *predatory*, entangled, and exempt. Consider, for example, the idea of prison privatization. What would it mean for a country that already imprisons more of its citizens than any other country on Earth to establish a for-profit prison system, where corporations and wealthy investors try to maximize profits by incarcerating as many people as possible while minimizing the costs? Sounds scary, right? But it's already happening, right here in America. The private prison industry has been around since the late 1980s but since then has consolidated to the point that only four companies control over 90% of the business (Fields, 2011). In fact, some critics point out that the market is now effectively an oligopoly. As an example of a growing trend, in 2011 a Cleveland newspaper reported that Ohio had sold one of its state prisons to Corrections Corporation of America (CCA), the largest of the for-profit enterprises (Fields, 2011). As part of the agreement, according to the report, the state guaranteed a minimum occupancy rate of 90% for at least three months or would have to pay stiff penalty fees to CCA. In fact, several states have had similar agreements with these companies, with minimum occupancy rates of more than 90%. What are the implications of a system where states are being confronted with choices such as whether to imprison more people to meet incarceration quotas or pay penalties to private companies? The solution for Ohio was apparently to increase incarcerations. An independent investigation by the Ohio chapter of the American Civil Liberties Union in 2013 found that several courts in Ohio started jailing people when they failed to pay their criminal fines (Alcuohio.org, 2013). This is a modern-day version of debtors' prison, according to the ACLU report. "The use of debtors' prison is an outdated and destructive practice that has wreaked havoc upon the lives of... thousands... throughout Ohio." The conditions in that particular Ohio prison also degraded, possibly due to the revenue-enhancing efforts of the private owners. Within a year of its privatization, according to the ACLU, the prison failed several inspections, and the investigation found broken facilities, overcrowding, and a forty percent increase in violence in the prison (2013).

Even worse, the for-profit prison concept leads to new forms of corruption. What does it say about our society when judges receive millions of dollars in kickbacks from for-profit prison companies for routinely sending children as young as ten to private youth detention centers for "crimes" like trespassing in an empty building or making fun of a school principal via social media? Yes, that happened too. Two former juvenile court judges were convicted in 2009 of racketeering in a case where the judges sent thousands of youth offenders to for-profit detention centers in Pennsylvania in exchange for millions of dollars in illicit payments from the owners of those detention centers (Tavernise & Hurdle, 2011).

The for-profit prison model may represent a particularly extreme form of economic innovation. But as a more mainstream example, consider the for-profit healthcare industry in America. It is well established that Americans pay more for their healthcare than any other country in the world, even though American health outcomes are no better than in other countries (OECD, 2013). The healthcare industry in America can justifiably be called an *illness* industry, since the industry profits from charging sick people as much as possible for medicines and procedures. A New York Times article reported some of the exaggerated prices Americans pay for vital asthma medicines, for example.

> Pulmicort, a steroid inhaler, generally retails for over $175 in the U.S., while pharmacists in Britain buy the identical product for about $20 and dispense it free of charge to asthma patients... Rhinocort Aqua, a prescription drug that was selling for more than $250 a month in Oakland pharmacies last year... costs under $7 in Europe, where it is available over the counter (Rosenthal, 2013).

These price differences may make good business sense, corporations want to increase profits whenever possible, but in the case of healthcare we are dealing with a public good and life-or-death issues for millions of people. In such a situation, putting profits ahead of the public good on such a basic level violates our shared human values and erodes the social bonds that connect us. Recent news coverage has pointed to the dramatic price increases in essential medications like the epinephrine injectors needed by people with allergies, which increased six hundred percent since 2008, and insulin, needed by over six million diabetics in America alone, which has increased 700% in 20 years and has never been sold in generic form. In fact, even doctors who benefit from the American medical model are finding the need to warn against its excesses. For example, in a New York Times op-ed from 2014, two physicians at Harvard Medical School warned, "...financial forces largely hidden from the public are beginning to corrupt care and undermine the bond of trust between doctors and patients" (Hartzband & Groopman, 2014).

Cases like these point to more than simple economic propositions. The fact that many of us would consider the for-profit prison model an acceptable and even "normal" business innovation, or that American businesses sell asthma medications for thirty times more than what people in other countries pay, are indications of a deeper cultural issue. This is an issue of values, cultural resources that we rely on to differentiate right from wrong, and these values can be manipulated and altered by forces antagonistic to our most cherished social goals. In chapter 2 I explore the cultural and psychological components that make these manipulations possible. In Chapter 3 I explore the history of capitalism and the problems inherent with some of its aspects. But I want to be clear that I am not criticizing entrepreneurial success. Earning money through innovative business enterprises clearly is an acceptable and even admirable pursuit. However, those pursuits must be within the various boundaries created by our common values. But both these examples represent predatory economic strategies that allow business interests to profit from the poor, the socially marginalized, and the sick. These "customers' have little if any choice in the matter. Economic enterprises like for-profit prisons and predatory pharmaceutical corporations therefore represent the growing domination of certain cultural perspectives that benefit specific economic interests within society, even as the results of those benefits do harm to the larger community. My point is that the justifications for these economic developments are first rationalized and then normalized within the larger community through the power of mass media, political pressure, and even ideology, so that economic incentives and activities that were once considered unacceptable are now considered equal to or even elevated over other social concerns.

In addition to the perverse incentives and potential harm that specifically predatory business practices represent, there are significant problems with the most basic assumptions of consumption-based economies. The idea that a rising economic tide would lift all boats, to paraphrase John F. Kennedy, requires economic expansion and growth. Consumerism, the celebration of consumption and materialism that has become commonplace in our society, echoes the need for "newer, faster, better," but this is a social phenomenon driven by an economic agenda, despite the fact that the traditional cultural values here in America were based on thrift and self-sufficiency. Later in this chapter, I describe the rise of rationalism and its implications for modern societies in terms of marketing and money. In Chapter 3 I will delve deeply into the processes by which corporate businesses began to transform American society into a society preoccupied with consumption - with comfort and bodily well-being, luxury, and acquisition – by promoting the idea that consumption equated to good citizenship. But for now, we should simply point out that the long-range implications of consumerism in general are a mixed blessing at best, and can be potentially devastating if they are not regulated and counterbalanced. For example, a 1998 report from the United Nations Development Program (UNDP) had this to say:

> Today's consumption is undermining the environmental resource base. It is exacerbating inequalities… If the trends continue without change — not redistributing from high-income to low-income consumers, not shifting from polluting to cleaner goods and production technologies, not promoting goods that empower poor producers, not shifting priority from consumption for conspicuous display to meeting basic needs — today's problems of consumption and human development will worsen (UNDP, 1998, p.1).

Unfortunately, there are few institutions in this country that can offset the power of the powerful economic stakeholders and the consumption patterns that they rely on. Under the banner of free enterprise and liberal capitalism, the economic system in this country and others has become the 800-pound gorilla in our midst, and the joke goes like this: "Q: What's that 800-pound gorilla doing in our living room? A: Whatever it wants."

I am not arguing that some different sort of economic system should replace capitalism, nor am I suggesting that consumption is necessarily bad. In fact, that same U.N. report previously quoted has this to say on the first page: "Human life is ultimately nourished and sustained by consumption. Abundance of consumption is no crime. It has, in fact, been the lifeblood of much human advance" (UNDP, 1998, p.1). I do, however, wish to point out some clear problems with some of the characteristics of the current system. In some ways, I suspect that economic stakeholders like corporations and the marketing industry they rely on, in their efforts to promote consumption, have simply gotten too successful. As the U.N. report clarifies, "The real issue is not consumption itself but its patterns and effects" (1998). And these patterns and effects have ramifications for society that reach psychological and cultural levels.

Modernity and the Rise of Modern Problems

At this point, we should begin to address the "modern" characteristics in our discussion of the globalized economic system, specifically the rise of rationalism and scientific thinking that blossomed in 17th century Europe. I will argue that the type of thinking that leads to decisions like the ones made by the car manufacturer in our earlier discussion, the decision to not repair a safety flaw because the loss of life would probably be less expensive, has its roots in this historic time. Here, I suggest, during the Age of Enlightenment and then the subsequent Industrial Revolution, is where the ideas that support an economic system that is unconstrained, intrusive, and most of all, efficient, take root.

First, it should be noted that the evolution of modern economic practices went hand-in-hand with several other major changes in the world, including the spread of democratic forms of government, scientific advances, and the elevation of education as a public good. Historically, however, the massive changes in the economic systems of industrialized societies since then have been part of a larger, more comprehensive evolutionary process encompassing all of humankind. Significantly, the theories that help explain human social evolution tend to start with the fundamental need for economic activity. In *The Rise of Anthropological Theory* (1968) and *Cannibals and Kings* (1977), for example, the American anthropologist Marvin Harris described a theory of social evolution that was based primarily on human consumption and production and emphasized the power of the economic system to shape human life. According to Harris, long-term social evolution is a continuing process of social action aimed at material adaptation to changing environmental situations. This theory, referred to as *cultural materialism*, suggests that human socio-cultural development is a process of finding the most efficient solutions to biological, psychological, and ecological problems experienced by all human beings and all cultures. Cultural materialism is an expansion on the theory known as historical materialism, first developed by the German philosopher Karl Marx, which argues that the material conditions of a society's modes of production fundamentally determine its organization and development.

> ...life involves before everything else eating and drinking, housing, clothing and many other things. The first historical act is thus the production of the means to satisfy these needs, the production of material life itself. And indeed this is a historical act, a fundamental condition of all history, which today, as thousands of years ago, must daily and hourly be fulfilled merely in order to sustain human life (Marx & Engels, 1970, p. 47).

Initial successes in the production of food and other necessities result in population growth, which results in depletion of resources, which, in turn, requires intensification of production and innovation (Harris, 1968). Periods of growth eventually create new challenges for human groups in terms of organization and production, and, in order to adapt to these changes, more efficient and complex structures and processes must be developed to meet the material needs of the expanding population. Innovation leads to new forms of technological intensification which result in new forms of environmental depletion, and these continuous processes of material adaptation lead to the continual reorganization of social structures.

Like Marx, Harris proposed a model of cultural change within a framework with three distinct levels: infrastructure, structure and superstructure. According to cultural materialism, a society's infrastructure, the material aspects of a society such as technology, the economy and reproductive factors, dominates the development of culture. The structures within a society are the organizational aspects such as kinship systems, and the organization of the political and economic systems, and the superstructure consists of ideological and symbolic aspects of society such as social roles and religion.

From this perspective, the technological and economic factors play the primary role in shaping society, and the values, norms, and practices of that society are determined and altered based on material needs and developments. We can easily see the role of technology behind major historical social changes: the first cultivation of plants and animals, the plow, the steam engine, and the computer chip are the four most obvious innovations. In the earliest tribes of hunter-gatherers, which were often little more than extended families with shared norms and values dictated by the most powerful members of the group and then, eventually, tradition. In these first crude societies, cultures provided social cohesion based on traditional concepts of authority, worship, status, sacrifice, etc. But once these tribes learned how to herd the wild cattle and plant the seeds from the cassava or corn crops that they encountered on their nomadic wanderings, these groups expanded from small, nomadic hunter-gatherer tribes into larger, more stable and complex groups that raised crops and domesticated animals. Surpluses grew and trade became possible. Families expanded and kinship relations became more complex. Permanent settlements became possible since it was no longer necessary for people to follow the food supply. These large settlements expanded much more dramatically after the invention of the plow, which resulted in an even greater abundance of foods and goods, and made large cities possible because it freed some members of the group from being dedicated to the production of their own food. Surplus, in the form of extra food and trade goods, led to leisure time, more division of labor, and issues pertaining to the distribution of resources, which meant the use of policies and practices to organize and manage those resources. As things progressed, political and economic practices associated with the organization of these agricultural societies and their resources became more complex and, in many ways, better.

It is generally agreed that the modernization of industrialized production and the twilight of monarchist political systems ushered in the historical period known as *modernity*, and it traces back to the 17th century, to the beginning of the period known as the Age of Enlightenment and its optimistic view of science and progress. "Since the beginning of the modern era the prospect of a limitless advance of science and technology, accompanied at each step by moral and political improvement, has exercised a considerable hold over Western thought" (in Habermas, 1984, p. v). The concept of modernity and its ramifications is a well-developed area of interest. In fact, many experts in the field of sociology believe that sociology itself began as an effort to comprehend the process of modernization in industrialized Europe. We can define modernity as the patterns of social action linked to the rationalization of society and the industrialization of production. The process of modernization includes general characteristics such as the decline of small, traditional communities and the rise of large cities; the expansion of personal choice and individualism; increasing social diversity; and a future-oriented awareness of time (Berger & Luckmann, 1966). The Canadian psychologist Dan McAdams describes modernity as "the economic, political, and cultural systems spawned in the 19th and 20th centuries by the industrial revolution" and links modernity to the expansion of capitalism and markets, the increasing domination of science and technology, and the rising power of democratic states (McAdams, 1996).

Since about the seventeenth century, scientific progress has been continual. Although the greatest rate of technological progress for the average person occurred around the end of the 19th century when safe water supplies, telephones, automobiles, electric lighting, and home refrigeration developed in short order, we continue to benefit from general advances, especially communications, medical, and environmental technologies. We recognize these benefits as cultural in nature, stemming from a combination of two cultural elements: technology and ideology. As the American biologist and theorist E. O. Wilson suggests,

> In contrast to widespread opinion, I believe that the Enlightenment thinkers of the seventeenth and eighteenth centuries got it mostly right. The assumptions they made about a lawful material world, the intrinsic unity of knowledge, and the potential for indefinite human progress are the ones we still take most readily to heart, suffer without, and find maximally rewarding as we learn more and more about the circumstances of our lives (1998).

But progress involves trade-offs, as we know, and many of these trade-offs have become problematic. In fact, the archaeologist Jared Diamond, in an article titled "The Worst Mistake in the History of the Human Race," claimed that human history over the past million years has not been a history of progress at all, and cites research that suggests that the development of agriculture, "supposedly our most decisive step toward a better life, was in many ways a catastrophe from which we have never recovered" (1987). In particular, he identifies side effects of agriculture such as social and sexual inequality, disease and despotism. We assume that we're better off than our ancestors, and that quality of life for most people has steadily improved throughout history. And we also assume that "our escape from this misery was facilitated only 10,000 years ago, when in different parts of the world people began to domesticate plants

and animals," which marked the beginning of the agricultural revolution (Diamond, 1987). However, the assumption that the lives of
primitive people improved when they switched from gathering to
farming may be false. Hunter-gatherer societies enjoyed a better
diet than farmers who "obtained most of their food from one or a
few starchy crops." Dependence on a limited number of crops
created the risk of starvation if the crops failed. Agriculture led to a
greater abundance of foods and goods, and made large cities possible, but this encouraged people to crowd together, which led to the
spread of parasites and infectious disease. As Diamond's research
shows, societies that fail to maintain effective resource management systems eventually collapse, as have societies that cannot
adapt to changing environmental conditions. Diamond's warnings
are particularly relevant today with the increasing problems associated with climate change becoming more and more obvious.

Yes, economic activity is a basic and necessary need in any society, but our need to push consumption beyond the essentials can
lead to the paradoxical situation where economic success will eventually produce harmful environmental and social outcomes. The
central question, of course, is how to manage these problems. One
answer is to harness our collective will to reduce our levels of consumption, and thereby reduce our environmental impact. But this
solution requires major changes, including cultural, political, as
well as economic changes, and the globalized economic system is
in many ways unconstrained by political will, and also has control
of the media outlets that sway our cultural world. In fact, one of my
major issues in this book is the imbalanced relationships among
our society's cultural, political, and economic systems. This again is
not a new phenomenon, but one that gets less attention than I think
it deserves. The economic historian Karl Polanyi has written extensively about this issue, and his concerns are worth noting. I will
present Polanyi's ideas more fully in Chapter 2, but for now it is
worth noting that, according to Polanyi, one problem with modern
capitalism is that the stuff of economic relationships, money and
commodities, have come to dominate the other domains of human
life, including political and social institutions, leading to increased
risk and instability, and an erosion of well-being (2001). As Polanyi
describes it, Instead of economy being embedded in social relations, social relations are embedded in the economic system (Polanyi, 2001, pg. 77).

This unbalanced relationship between economics and human life is enabled by a transformation of our cultural landscape and is not just an economic issue. As we shall see in later chapters, the modern capitalist economic system promotes materialism and consumption, but psychological research has consistently shown that people who develop strong materialistic values and organize their lives around extrinsic goals such as acquisitiveness and consumption report greater unhappiness in relationships, poorer moods and more psychological problems (Kasser, 2002). Yet this is specifically the message that the economic system sends us, that acquisitiveness and consumption are the paths to happiness.

Worse, the economic imperative of growth drives the search for new markets and new consumers, which means that the influence of the economic system has reached into personal spaces that have long-range cultural consequences. For example, the economic system increasingly influences even the psychological realms of childhood development and personal growth. In a 2005 article in the journal *Childhood*, the psychologist Beryl Langer addresses the effects of consumer capitalism on children's sense of identity. Commercial or popular, culture is an important source of symbolic material for children as they develop a sense of identity and self-concept. The games they play, the fantasies they indulge in, and the identities they mimic are all potential sources of meaning and value to a growing child. Unfortunately, the logic of consumerism means that the globalized economic system can recognize children only as consumers. Thus, according to Langer,

> Children are increasingly socialized into the endlessly recur-
> ring cycle of fashion and obsolescence that fuels economic
> growth… the parameters of what children play and what
> they want to play with are increasingly set by decisions made
> in the design and marketing departments of global corpora-
> tions (p. 267).

The problem is not that consumer capitalism and healthy social development are at odds in principle. However, Langer points out that this promotion of materialism means that "children's sense of sufficiency is thus continuously undermined, in that the moment of possession offers not closure but new objects of desire" (p. 268). Not surprisingly, a meta-analysis of psychological research showed that a negative relationship between materialism and well-being is universal, consistent across all types of people and cultures. Generally, the more people embrace materialistic values, the more they experience unpleasant emotions, depression and anxiety, and physical health problems (Kasser, 2014). In the same way, the more materialistic people are, the less they experience pleasant emotions and feel satisfied with their lives.

The larger point is that this ability to motivate children and adults to participate in the "endlessly recurring cycle of fashion and obsolescence" is part of the evolution of the capitalist economic system, and it means that whatever problems we have now will increase along with the improvements in expertise, information processing, and efficiency of the system's corporate stakeholders. Remember that two of the central tenets of capitalism are the pursuit of profits and expansion. As corporations study us and collect our data, we become increasingly susceptible to their influence. As the American philosopher Brian Epstein put it,

> Increasingly, economic activity turns on collecting and mobilizing information about people... Google—whose business, after all, is directing people to documents written by people and tailoring advertisements to people—has over 35,000 employees, more than twice the 13,000 academic economists in the United States. And the marketing department of Procter and Gamble is larger than the sociology departments of all US universities combined. It is only a slight exaggeration to say that the world economy is transforming into a massive system for doing social science (2015, p. 2).

Technocracy and Instrumentality

The idea that the globalized economic system is transforming into a massive system for doing social science means that there will be increasing knowledge asymmetries and potential for manipulation (and corruption) among powerful stakeholders. Unfortunately, the existing technical requirements of running both complex economic and political systems and the increasingly bureaucratized way these systems work has meant that their administrative functions have already become separated from society's cultural rules. For example, macroeconomic policies could not be understood in the same way that a household budget could be, and this meant that the public might have trouble grasping the details of modern economic issues that involve complexities like global trade or environmental concerns, creating a gap between large-scale economic and political action guided by experts and the day-to-day experiences of the public. For example, the idea that America's welfare outlays are potentially ruinous for the future of the nation is a popular idea among the public, but not among experts. During Obama's first term, for example, Republican politicians recommended cuts in entitlement programs like Social Security and public pension systems, and millions of people were convinced that this was a critical issue. The conservative columnist PJ Ferrara typified these concerns when he claimed,

> The biggest problem facing America is the overwhelming entitlement crisis... If no changes are made, then just 15 years from now, only five federal programs will consume all federal revenues. The five are Social Security, Medicare, Medicaid, interest on the national debt and federal employee retirement. No money would be left for any other federal activity... (Ferrara, 2012).

Yet a study by research fellows from the progressive Roosevelt Institute reveals two empirical findings that go largely unrecognized in mainstream political discourse. First, there are powerful oligopolies in the health care and defense industries, and second, it is *their* excessive costs that play a dominant role in current concerns about the federal budget, and not entitlement spending, especially not transfer programs like Social Security which are self-funding (through payroll taxes) and separated from the actual federal budget (Ferguson, 2012).

In the same way, industrial production techniques rely on scientific advancements that are not well understood by the public, making the regulation of these production techniques a matter for technically trained elites rather than a democratic populace. In many of these cases, the public simply could no longer encompass the rapid advancements within these technical areas and was therefore forced to increasingly rely on the "creative minority," as the historian Alfred Toynbee put it, the technocratic elite that directs the society's complex machinery of economy and state.

Further, it meant that these systems were no longer explicitly guided by the cultural attitudes of the general public but by a small cadre of experts even in the most democratic nations (see Lippmann; Bachrach). This topic will be more deeply developed in Chapter 5, but for now, the point is that increasing complexity is a side-effect of progress, and complexity can often appear alien or mysterious. The German sociologist Max Weber predicted that modern evolution and its emphasis on rational calculation would contribute to a "disenchantment of the world," an alienation from the bureaucracies and institutions that manage so much of modern human life (1946).

However, the greater issue that many social theorists have warned us about is that economic and political systems around the world are increasingly guided by their own *inner* logic, an instrumental logic that has reduced human concerns to calculable variables (see Habermas; Beck). And, of course, the concentration of power within these systems has resulted in a much greater risk for corruption and the formation of autocracies. A major source of theoretical guidance in regard to these issues is the work of the German philosopher Jürgen Habermas. Over the years, Habermas has developed a comprehensive social theory that explains many characteristics of modern rational societies (1984). Communication, or *communicative action* in Habermas' terms, is the essential component of social life, according to his theory, and is governed by a taken-for-granted rationality, in the sense that practical assumptions about human interaction guide communication among people and mediate the exchange of information necessary for social life. Language represents one of the central components of culture, and people fundamentally rely on language to communicate and share their life experiences through both concrete information and also the *meanings* of things.

Society can be described as the culmination of all of the interactive patterns of social interactions that organize large groups of people into a cohesive whole. In other words, any society is essentially a structured social system created through the actions and interactions of its members, guided by needs, desires, goals, rules, and values. Much or our lives consist of informal social interactions like those we experience among our friends and families. But our lives are also filled with more formal social relationships that form social structures and larger institutions. Our individual material needs are generally met through economic means, for example, and we rely on jobs, businesses and industries, and commerce in general for our livelihoods and for the goods that we need in our daily lives. Also, our actions are constrained and our broader social goals are achieved generally through both informal and organized political systems, involving institutions like the various levels of government, the law, and democratic participation. These economic and political aspects of society are all products of social action and interaction, although they take on the appearance of being entities that are separate from us. But they are not "things" that are isolated from human action; they are the *results* of ongoing human action.

Habermas has labeled this idea that we live our lives based on shared understandings and practical assumptions as the *lifeworld,* the world of normal, everyday social interactions and culturally established meanings. The *lifeworld* is essentially the product of all the honest communicative interactions within society. (Incidentally, the *lifeworld* concept was not introduced by Habermas and has been used in social sciences for many decades. In fact, Edmund Husserl introduced the *lifeworld* concept in the *Crisis of European Sciences* in 1936 where he defined it as the state of affairs in which the world is experienced.) Habermas viewed the social integration of the *lifeworld* as a cultural process of normative institutionalization, requiring a combination of socialization and social control. In other words, routine and predictable interactions among people are made possible when culturally shared values are internalized within each individual (socialization) and also institutionalized within society (social control). In this way, the world "out there" is synchronized to some degree with our inner world of ideas and frames of reference.

Thus, the *lifeworld* consists of informal, culturally grounded experiences, and the kinds of interactions that are the basis from which we interpret the world around us. It represents the practical world of social interaction and shared knowledge that we all experience in our day-to-day lives, but rarely acknowledge. As an extreme example, Gallup surveys from 2010 show that over half the people throughout sub-Saharan Africa personally believe in witchcraft. The point is that these beliefs have real implications for the population. The BBC reported on an incident in 2014 where Tanzanian police charged twenty-three people with murder after seven villagers were burned alive on suspicion of witchcraft (BBC, 2014). That same report estimated that around five hundred people are killed annually on suspicion of witchcraft in Tanzania alone. It seems that witches and spells and so on are simply part of the taken-for-granted daily lives for millions of people in that region of the world. On the other hand, belief in witchcraft and other supernatural phenomena is less common in richer, industrialized societies and such things are rarely discussed as a practical consideration. Nevertheless, this "taken-for-granted" aspect of daily life is the essence of the *lifeworld,* according to Habermas.

The philosopher Alistair MacIntyre referred to humans as "storytelling animals." Historically, according to Habermas, the *lifeworld* provides the necessary mechanisms for integrating and maintaining the social cohesiveness and coherence that a society requires to survive. The stories we tell about ourselves are part of our identities, they are the narratives by which we make sense of ourselves and the world around us. And in many ways, the historical narrative that we share to describe the world *is* the world. If we teach our children that there are witches, for example, then witches will exist for them in terms of consequences. This idea ties in nicely with the *lifeworld*, the world of personal interactions mediated by *communication* and *meaning*.

In contrast to the *lifeworld*, however, Habermas describes the *systems world* as the realm of instrumentality, where economic and political activities are governed by technical rationality rather than the practical rules that govern the *lifeworld*. For Habermas, human interaction is always anchored in norms and social institutions. Therefore, effective communication, in general, requires practical observation of society's rules about honesty, openness, and so on. Cultural values and rules work on an individual and institutionalized level to create the predictability and order necessary for successful collective human action. On the other hand, entities within society like political parties, corporations, and government bureaucracies endeavor to maintain and improve their capacities largely through technical rationality and a reliance on logic and calculation rather than on honest and open communication.

Here, however, is one of the biggest contributing factors to the unfortunate side-effects of modern capitalism, namely that technical rationality, logic, and calculation are largely *amoral*. Yet popular modern ideologies and economic stakeholders both increasingly emphasize rational instrumental values over moral considerations. These enable political and economic actors to shrug off the practical but humane rules that the rest of us live by and instead rely more and more on instrumental norms in order to shape collective action and optimize their particular interests. Let's take two obvious but slightly exaggerated examples; that we increasingly accept and even expect that politicians and advertisers make untrue or misleading statements. Not only do politicians and advertisers mislead us, we have grown to expect it, which indicates a normative shift away from honest communication toward a purely instrumental or strategic form of interaction. They say whatever it takes to achieve their goals with little regard to the overarching values of honesty and reciprocity. Consider Arizona's Senator Jon Kyl, who made a false claim during a congressional debate in 2011 about Planned Parenthood's activities (Epstein, 2011). It was soon revealed that the congressman's assertion was false, but when confronted by the news media, Kyl's spokespeople explained that Kyl's claim was "not intended to be a factual statement." This may sound like an attempt at humor, but it was not. People in these circumstances are violating the basic rules and assumptions of the *lifeworld* but are obeying the instrumental rationality of the *systems world*. They lie and misinform us to influence our behavior for their own benefit, even though they expect us to assume that they themselves are actually being honest and adhering to the practical rules of the *lifeworld*. Unfortunately, according to Habermas, these efforts can create a distorted understanding of the world, one that allows the mechanisms of social control to remain hidden from common awareness. In this way strategic manipulation becomes possible.

Consider, for example, the benefits that follow from the fact that modern securities regulations in the U.S. stock market have ensured that shareholders have access to consistent and reliable information from publicly traded corporations. The requirement that companies provide accurate information on a regular basis to shareholders and potential investors helps to maintain the essential functionality of the financial markets, which rely on trust in many ways. Basically, publicly traded corporations are prohibited from lying to the public about their financial circumstances. This requirement is an example of an institutionalized norm that promotes open and honest communication based on practical rationality and is squarely intended to ensure the principles represented by the *lifeworld*.

In the same way, and on a much larger scale, the provision of accurate information on a regular basis to the public in the form of news reports, either via television, radio, newspapers, or websites, helps to ensure the essential functions of a democratic society. Democratic societies, in particular, are completely reliant on a steady flow of accurate information in order to maintain the informed citizens upon which the democratic system of governance relies. As the well-regarded Dutch sociologist Loet Leydesdorff puts it, "Society is defined by its communication network(s)" (2001, p. 160). It is therefore of interest when these communicative rules come under attack since the absence or manipulation of "the news" could have such a profound impact on social integrity and democratic functionality.

As an example of such an attack, consider the efforts of a conservative politician in Canada, in coordination with certain American economic interests, to degrade the accuracy or truthfulness of information provided to the public by allowing falsehoods to be presented as fact. In March of 2011, the conservative government in Canada led by John Harper quietly attempted to do that very thing (Williams, 2011). Members of the government basically attempted to change the longstanding public regulation that prohibits the dissemination of false or misleading news in Canada. The proposed changes would have weakened the definition of "false news" by making it illegal for media outlets who broadcast false or misleading news *only* in cases where it could be proven that the broadcaster knew the news was false prior to broadcast and that reporting it was likely to endanger the lives, health or safety of the public.

Coincidentally, the regulatory change was proposed just in time for the launch of Sun News, a new conservative Canadian television news station, and the brainchild of Prime Minister Harper's former director of communications. The network, nicknamed "Fox News North," was expected to provide vitriolic political rhetoric and right-wing attacks similar to Fox News in America (Williams, 2011). However, public outcry from Canadians forced the Canadian Radio-Television and Telecommunications Commission (CRTC) to abandon the attempted policy changes. Even better, the conservatives' efforts were recognized by a majority of Canadians as an attempt by political ideologues to make it legally acceptable for biased stakeholders to mislead the public, a clear example of instrumental rationality and communicative distortion.

Sadly, that type of amoral, instrumental rationality used by the *systems world* has long been prevalent here in America. In the past, U.S. television networks produced news and educational programs to fulfill strictly enforced Federal Communications Commission (FCC) license requirements. By law, networks had to provide a set amount of public interest and public service broadcasting in order to run profit-making entertainment shows on the public airwaves. News programs made up a good portion of that requirement. However, in 1996 the Telecommunications Act legislation changed the rules. Like all legislation, the Telecommunications Act of 1996 was justified on the basis of the public interest. And as in many legislative processes, commercial stakeholders ended up defining the public interest rather than public policy advocates. The public was likely harmed by these regulatory changes, where efforts to supposedly increase competition among networks actually dismantled the requirements of public interest for communications services. These changes reduced the traditional sources of communication and information necessary for a well-informed public and thus represented another triumph of instrumental rationality over the practical needs of a democratic and open society.

Efforts to mislead the public via slanted or even erroneous information is common in advertising, for example, but political legislation has made it possible, by allowing purported news organizations to do the same thing, for institutions such as the news media to be corrupted by strategic rather than communicative motivations. For example, a poll released by Fairleigh Dickinson University in 2011 found that people who got their news from Fox News know significantly less about current events both in the U.S. and around the world than people who don't watch any news programming at all (Memoli, 2011). Yet Fox News is, and has been, the most popular cable news channel in America for many years, often drawing more viewers than MSNBC and CNN combined.

As far back as the 1950s, in *White Collar* (1951) and *The Power Elite* (1956), the American sociologist C. Wright Mills described the mass media as a socializing force, influencing individual behavior and promoting particular values and norms. But he also warned about the increasingly manipulative power of the media to influence public opinion and strengthen the power of the dominant elites, noting how "the mass media plug for ruling political symbols and personalities." (1951, p. 338). Unfortunately, his warnings did not impede the progress of this manipulative power. For example, a study by the watchdog group Fairness and Accuracy in Reporting (FAIR) found that the Sunday morning news shows on network television have a distinct conservative, white and male skew (FAIR, 2012). The study reports that 70% of politically affiliated guests given one-on-one interviews were Republican, 86% were male, and 92% were white. The broader roundtable segments of the shows were also heavily biased in favor of white male Republicans. This is not surprising given that the Republican Party is known as the party of Big Business, and large corporations own the networks on which these shows are hosted. As a reminder, research has found that Americans with conservative values are more likely to support existing social institutions, more likely to have negative attitudes toward underprivileged groups (Rubin & Peplau, 1975), and tend to assign blame to the individual victims of poverty, crime, and homelessness. Mills identified the pro-business media bias almost sixty years ago and we see that it persists today, in which one political party dominates the major outlets for the framing and promotion of "public" information.

The two basic components of the *systems world* in modern societies are the economic system, where interactions are mediated by *money*, and the political system where interactions are mediated by *power or influence*. Habermas echoes the American sociologist Talcott Parsons when he describes money and power as *steering media*, through which the economic and political spheres interact with the rest of society. These media act as communicative forces. Distorted communication results, however, when instrumental rationality replaces the practical rules that guide the *lifeworld*, and money and power are used in ways that violate the moral assumptions of the public.

Unfortunately, there are many examples where issues of instrumental importance to economic stakeholders are mediated according to technical goals instead of the cultural norms of the *lifeworld*. Reconsider, for example, the idea of a cost-benefit analysis to determine whether a life-threatening problem with a particular batch of automobiles or food products should trigger a recall of those products. Here are a few examples of this type of *systems world* rationality identified by the American Association for Justice on their website: A major tire manufacturer decided to ignore a problem with defective tires that eventually took the lives of at least 271 people and seriously injured many more before they issued the largest tire recall in history in 2000 (Bradsher, 2000). Internal company documents showed that the company had known of the deadly problems since 1997 but chose to do nothing, based on their own internal cost-benefit analyses. The company eventually recalled 6.5 million tires only after the National Highway Traffic Safety Administration (NHTSA) opened an investigation into the problem in 2000. That same year, NHTSA warned the company that over a million more tires had worse problems than the recalled tires but the tire company refused to order another recall. The National Highway Traffic Safety Administration imposed the maximum fine of $925,000, which represented a small fraction of the profits the tire company made selling those faulty tires. In another case, in 2006, executives at a major peanut producer learned that their products were contaminated with salmonella, but continued to ship them to customers for two more years (Zhang & Jargon, 2009). At least nine people died and over seven hundred were sickened before the company finally agreed to recall all the products it had produced in the previous two years.

Examples like the tire recall show that the legal system has in fact normalized many of these kinds of instrumental processes, to the detriment of the public. One obvious problem is that this puts people in danger since economic stakeholders are less likely to obey the cultural norms regarding honesty and transparency and instead follow the short-term logic of economic costs and benefits. Another result, however, is the marginalization of distinctly human patterns of communication and interaction, and the public acceptance of instrumental or manipulative interactions that benefit these economic stakeholders at the expense of the public. Unfortunately, this marginalization is not recognized as such. Instead, it is accepted as "the way things are" or "the way the system works." For another more explicit example of strategic marginalization, consider some aspects of the American legal system. People basically follow the rules and manage to avoid committing crimes even though most of us are generally unfamiliar with the extent and details of all the statutes, prohibitions, and laws actually documented in the "law books." (The framers of the American constitution identified three federal crimes: treason, counterfeiting, and piracy. Today there are over 2700 federal crimes.) This is because most of our laws are related to a set of simple, easy to understand principles that we learn and internalize as children: don't hurt people, respect their property, be fair, be honest in your dealings, etc. Ideally, the law is a codified version of those same principles, enforced by legitimate authority figures, and violations of the law are supposed to result inconsistent penalties.

But here we can draw an unappealing conclusion when we examine the distribution of penalties for violations of the law in America. Penalties are not evenly distributed across the population (at least not as often as we'd think). For example, according to the Bureau of Justice Statistics, African-Americans represent about *thirteen* percent of the general population in the U.S. but they are *forty* percent of the incarcerated population. Drug sentencing disparities are even more lopsided. Illicit drug use is five times as common among white Americans as African Americans, yet African Americans are sent to prison for drug offenses at ten times the rate of

Whites (NAACP, 2013). In fact, although African Americans represent only twelve percent of the total population of drug users, they represent fifty-nine percent of those in state prison for a drug offense (ibid). Why? It is easily argued that these imbalances are due to widespread institutionalized racism. Racial bias is a lingering American value, and racial discrimination is a lingering norm that can be seen in the high incarceration rates among Blacks. This process maintains the marginalized status of these victims of discrimination for generations. According to the legal scholar Michelle Alexander, for example, African-Americans are more likely to be arrested for drug offences mainly because police conduct drug operations primarily in poor communities of color (2010). This is a form of profiling, of course, but it is not often framed in those terms. Worse, once they are arrested, these defendants are "generally denied meaningful legal representation and pressured to plead guilty, whether they are or not" (p. 180). Then, following a conviction, African Americans are routinely marginalized on a relatively permanent basis. Ex-convicts likely will be discriminated against for the rest of their lives, "denied employment, housing, education, and public benefits. Unable to surmount these obstacles, most will eventually return to prison and then be released again, caught in a closed circuit of perpetual marginality" (Alexander, 2010, p. 181). This describes a justice system that follows the technical rules while ignoring the most basic human aspects of the institution, which are centered on decency, fairness, and protection of the innocent.

Colonization by the Capitalist Market

In his writings about the conflicts between the *lifeworld* and the *systems world*, Jürgen Habermas uses the term colonization in the sense that the *systems world* has colonized the *lifeworld*. Theoretical support for the colonizing metaphor used by Habermas comes from many sources, including research in the field of social psychology. In 1992, for example, Alan Fiske, a professor of anthropology, developed a framework he called the Relational Models Theory (RMT) that identified four relational structures that could account for practically all socially significant interactions. The four structures include *communal sharing, equality matching, authority ranking, and market pricing.* Basically, these four ways of relating to one another have been shown statistically to be culturally universal dimensions of sociality or social life. An interesting aspect of Fiske's theory is that these structures permeate all aspects of social life, from how we constitute our own individual relational selves to the way we form groups and relate to others, to notions of justice and political ideologies, and the ways we make decisions. In Fiske's theory "the meaning of tangible things depends on the social relationship in which they are embedded" (1992, p. 691). One particular structure, the *Market pricing* structure is especially problematic because it reduces social action to strategic exchanges within a presumed competitive framework, and is associated with many unfortunate "market-driven" social tendencies such as slavery, prostitution, child labor, economic exploitation of third world countries, and the drugs trade. Unfortunately, Fiske posits that "market pricing is so pervasive in Western societies and so important to Western conceptions of human nature and society" that we generally assume it to be the *only* structure for social interaction, despite the vast research showing humans to be historically oriented toward communal and equality-based relationships (p. 692). Fiske suggests that our modern cultural emphasis on market pricing is the result of the Industrial Revolution and its influence on social life, and this growing influence of rationalized, market-oriented social action is what Habermas means by colonization.

Another colonization example comes from an unlikely source: an American daycare center. In his 2008 book *Predictably Irrational*, psychologist Dan Ariely devotes a chapter to the changes in behavior associated with a change in relational orientation from one guided by what he terms *social norms* to one guided by *market norms*, which is exactly the kind of change that Habermas is referring to when instrumental rationality that governs the *systems world* replaces the practical rationality that guides the *lifeworld*. Ariely based his research on Fiske's earlier work, looking to confirm the differential effects of particular social relation orientations. In Ariely's example, a daycare center is struggling with the problem of parents who arrive late to pick up their children, requiring the center's employees to stay late. The parents would eventually arrive, apologize profusely, and bundle up their kids with promises never to be late again. The center's managers, however, in an effort to reduce this sort of disruptive behavior, decided to impose a financial penalty for late pickups. The logic was that the monetary costs of late arrival would decrease the instances of late arrival. Instead, the opposite occurred; there was a marked increase in the number of times parents were late picking up their children. In addition, the parents were no longer apologetic about their tardiness. The psychological explanation for this is relatively clear – the daycare center had inadvertently switched from a social interaction based on social norms to one based on market norms. Once the parents perceived that the issue was no longer based on the social relationship between parent and care provider and instead was based on an economic relationship between buyer and seller the norms for behavior became very different. The parents were justified in being late because they paid for the privilege, and it didn't take long for that privilege to become a "right." Once the daycare center realized its mistake it attempted to undo the damage by eliminating the late penalty and tried to return to the previous pattern of social interaction but was unsuccessful. Apparently once social relations are rationalized by the economic system, the market norms that are produced remain in effect regardless of further tinkering. This transition from social norms to market norms is precisely what Weber and later Habermas have warned us about, that the technical processes of bureaucracy and rationalization built into modern economic and political systems will eventually alter the social norms in negative ways.

Here's how Ariely describes the difference in his book:

> Social norms are wrapped up in our social nature and our
> need for community. They are usually warm and fuzzy...
> The second world, the one governed by market norms, is
> very different. There's nothing warm and fuzzy about it. The
> exchanges are sharp-edged: wages, prices, rents, interest,
> and costs-and-benefits (2008, p.68).

Money

For purposes of completeness, a general discussion about the role of money is in order, especially given the claim that "market pricing is so important to Western conceptions of human nature and society." One of the most obvious factors in modern societies that typify the rise of the *systems world* is the expanded influence of money. On its own, of course, money is an essential component of market-based exchange systems and has functional dominance over more traditional patterns of exchange such as bartering. Money is both an evaluative criterion and functional medium of exchange in all modern societies, and its use stretches back millennia. On the other hand, when the functions of money seep into systems of cultural exchange like in the previous daycare example, it represents a form of cultural distortion. In such a case the power of money is inflated at the expense of other cultural norms and values.

To be clear, in essence, I am equating cultural distortion to the rationalization of social interaction through pricing mechanisms. This idea is not new. Over a century ago, the German sociologist Georg Simmel, in his essay *Metropolis and Mental Life* described how money, or the modern monetary economy, slowly penetrates and rationalizes all forms of social life. "Money is concerned only with what is common to all, i.e. with the exchange value which reduces all quality and individuality to a purely quantitative level" (1903, p. 325). In line with Ariely's more recent research, about one hundred years ago Max Weber had similar thoughts about the transformation of traditional social relationships into functional relations oriented to money and ruled by calculation.

> Money is the most abstract and 'impersonal' element that exists in human life. The more the world of the modern capitalist economy follows its own immanent laws, the less accessible it is to any imaginable relationship with a religious ethic of brotherliness. The more rational, and thus impersonal, capitalism becomes, the more is this the case (Weber, 1946, p. 331).

Certainly, these side effects of a monetized society; the erosion of ethics of brotherliness and the reduction of human life to calculable, quantitative relationships may be problematic. Along those same lines, according to Simmel, the often-overlooked characteristic of modern capitalism is that it promotes an individualistic and "heartless" worldview. "The whole heartlessness of money mirrors itself in the culture of society," Simmel claimed, "which it determines" (1907, p. 344).

Alienation

Thus, the rise of the *money economy* and the corresponding *market pricing* of what were once excluded social relations can lead to a type of alienation and degradation of human life. Alienation is a social malady associated with the consequences of modernization, and left-leaning social theorists have long argued that it arises as a byproduct of capitalism. The philosophers Georg Hegel and Karl Marx both used the term "alienation" to describe a form of self-estrangement that they perceived in certain segments of the European population in the 19th century. According to Marx, alienation is the condition in which a person's "own act becomes to him an alien power, standing over and against him, instead of being ruled by him" (Quoted in Fromm, 1991, p. 118). More specifically, Marx emphasized that the separation of the worker from the products of his work was a byproduct of industrial labor and had an alienating effect on those workers.

We have already discussed some of the characteristics of modernization: the development of technical and bureaucratic processes that have rationalized major aspects of society; increasing complexity; and the encroachment of economic values into the public and cultural spheres of life. When these processes reach the point where people no longer recognize the structures and processes within society as being a product of their own collective actions, the result is alienation. For example, a Chinese company that manufactures Apple iPads in Taiwan had over 800,000 workers in 2010 (Ramzy, 2010). The workers earned a few hundred dollars per month, working on assembly lines for up to twelve hours each day, six days a week. I am not claiming that this type of factory work should be eliminated. It is of value to our discussion, however, to point out the realities underlying commodity production. This particular company is a poignant example because of reports in the news about working conditions. Proponents can claim that factory workers take pride in their work and experience a sense of accomplishment, but as the Pittsburgh Tribune-Review reported in 2010, at least 10 employees of the factory had committed suicide that year. In the news article, one worker complained that "life is meaningless" and that every day is the same as the last. Another complains, "I have become a machine." These are descriptions of alienation.

It should be noted that alienation does not just affect a worker's relationship with the products of his or her labor; it also negatively impacts the worker's psychological self. In the book *The Sane Society,* the social theorist Erich Fromm has a description of alienation that goes beyond the relationship between worker and work product but touches all relationships.

> The alienated person is out of touch with himself as he is out of touch with any other person. He, like the others, are experienced as things are experienced; with the senses and with common sense, but at the same time without being related to oneself and to the world outside productively (1991, p. 117).

Writing in the 1950s, Fromm believed that the alienating aspects of modern culture in industrialized nations were growing worse as the technical and economic developments increased. The negative side-effects of economic and scientific expansion were pervasive and disfiguring, turning social actors into passive servants of a domineering and soulless economic system.

> Alienation as we find it in modern society is almost total; it pervades the relationship of man to his work, to the things he consumes, to the state, to his fellow man, and to himself... He has constructed a complicated social machine to administer the technical machine he built. Yet this whole creation of his stands over and above him... He is owned by his own creation and has lost ownership of himself (1991, p. 121).

Summary Thoughts

Modernity has led to massive increases in wellbeing around the world, as the forces unleashed by industrialization, scientific advancement, and capitalist enterprises have transformed the globe. On the other hand, here in the U.S., arguably one of the richest countries on Earth, life expectancy rates for the bottom rungs of the social ladder are actually falling, especially among white members of society. One problem with modernity, unfortunately, is that the combination of free-market capitalism and rationalization, while beneficial in many ways, has altered the cultural landscape permanently. By elevating the ideologies and methods of science and logic but coupling them with market-based goals and rules, our societies have expanded and progressed technologically, but at some cost. The dehumanization of the workplace and the domination of consumerism have trapped us in an "iron cage," according to sociologist Max Weber. The effects of instrumental rationality have led to the "disenchantment of the world," and alienation, which are significant cultural costs. The stuff of economic relationships, money and commodities, now dominate political and social institutions that were once guided by public interest, leading to *increases* rather than decreases in risk and instability and an erosion of the quality of day-to-day life.

In the past, economic institutions were secondary to social relationships, which allowed the cultural system to manage the disruptive elements of economic and technological development through political regulations based on cultural values and norms. However, modern economic systems have become detached from the traditional forms on constraint and regulation and have generated disruptive side effects that are often pushed out into the larger social system. As an example, consider the catastrophic future problems associated with climate change, yet many corporations and politicians continue to deny the very existence of this existential threat. In fact, it's been tallied that 72% of Republican senators in the U.S. Congress are deniers, and also staunchly pro-business (Schulman, 2015).

Chapter 2

The Role of Culture

Culture

One major premise of this book is that the globalized economic system has had great success harnessing social science to improve production, distribution, marketing, and advertising, but also the more subtle forms of political and cultural influence that shape public perceptions. Unfortunately, this progress has resulted in the manipulation of mass culture in problematical ways. What follows is a description of the basic aspects of culture and then an exploration of how culture is routinely manipulated.

First, culture includes both symbolic components such as ideologies, values, and rules, as well as material components like art, architecture, language, and technology. Although the particulars of culture may differ from one society to another and even within the same society, culture itself is universal, and all communities develop shared, learned ways of perceiving and participating in the world around them. We often think of culture as synonymous with the fine arts, and the arts are certainly a part of culture. But culture is much more than that. Culture in this particular context is like the mass psychology of a society; the ideas that shape our worldviews, the rules we live by, the interpretations of our experiences that we take for granted. In fact, it is no exaggeration to suggest that the organization of a society is largely dependent on its cultural system.

As previously mentioned, the economic and political aspects of society are all products of social action and interaction, not "things" that are isolated from human action but the *results* of ongoing human action. There is no economic system without producers and consumers; there is no democratic political system without voters and legislators. Furthermore, the economic and political actions of a society are themselves guided by rules and values that are largely cultural in origin, and human experience is the foundation of culture. The rules and values of a society, in fact, are the very things that create the necessary foundations for sustained social integration and human progress. The social psychologist Roy Baumeister, author of the book *The Cultural Animal*, has argued that the success of human evolution has depended on culture.

> Culture is a better way of being social. That is, culture emerged as a strategy for dealing with the social and the physical environments. Ultimately, culture developed because it served the biological goals of survival and reproduction. To be sure, cultures have developed additional ideas, goals, and purposes, but the reason that natural selection created the capacities needed for culture is because some animals found they could survive and reproduce better by making use of culture. (2010, p. 9).

Frames and Ideas

Cultural factors, especially language, create a shared template for human existence. Much of social life is symbolic in nature and mediated by language. As humans, we live in a world of meanings and understandings the same as we live in the physical world, and these meanings and understandings help shape our lives by putting our experiences into human context. Language allows us to express and share our experiences and ideas, and these include frames of reference. Frames are a useful concept for understanding the variations in points-of-view and help explain differences in behaviors, decision-making, and outcomes among people and groups (Small, Harding & Lamont, 2010).

> The basic premise behind the idea of a frame is that how people act depends on how they cognitively perceive themselves, the world, or their surroundings... A frame structures how we interpret events and therefore how we react to them (2010, p. 15).

According to linguist George Lakoff, language significantly shapes our thoughts and actions through the various metaphors that create what Lakoff calls "deep frames" that we incorporate into our thinking and communicating. "People... reason using frames, prototypes, image-schemas, and metaphors — and bring emotion into the mix as an inherent part of rationality" (2006). Lakoff suggests that our conceptual understandings regarding the world and human thought processes in general, are often filtered through metaphorical frames that constitute our moral worldviews or political ideologies. Deep frames, he claims, define one's overall "common sense" (2006).

> The concepts that govern our thought are not just matters of
> the intellect. They also govern our everyday functioning,
> down to the most mundane details. Our concepts structure
> what we perceive, how we get around in the world, and how
> we relate to other people. Our conceptual system thus plays
> a central role in defining our everyday realities (Lakoff &
> Johnsen, 2003, p. 3).

Many of our most enduring social structures are predicated on
deep frames that reach back to our earliest and most primitive
idealizations and have been ingrained in our cultural memories for
millennia (see Lakoff, 1996). Particular assumptions, or frames,
often perpetuate differentials of power, which we can demonstrate
using the example of gender bias (Held & Thompson, 1989). Around
the world, male dominated, or patriarchic, family structures have
been maintained throughout human history, and some argue, long
after the usefulness of that particular structure has expired. According
to historian Gerda Lerner, patriarchy was the "institutionalization
of male dominance over women and children in the family and . . .
women in society" (1986, p. 239), and its roots stretch back to the
Neolithic period. During that period men first began to understand
their role in reproduction and sought control of reproductive
processes to ensure that the children produced were actually their
own and not some rival's. In a related development, around that
same time men established the concept of private property. Lerner
argued that in the transition from early hunter-gatherer societies to
agricultural societies, men began to treat women and their procrea-
tive potential as an economic resource, and over time established
legal rules as well as "ideas, symbols, and metaphors by which patriarchal gender relations were incorporated into western civilization" (p. 10). Historically, then, fathers and husbands have been
granted economic power and political status over the women and
children in their families for millennia. The assumptions and norms
that support this particular structural organization have shaped any
number of practices and world-views that persist today, even when
the actual roles of males in many societies have changed. Think of
the similarities among the family dynamics in which the father is
the dominant figure and the religious and political institutions
dominated not just by men in reality, but by male symbols. Chris-
tianity and Islam, to name two of the world's major religions, are
both organized around a masculine, patriarchal narrative of powerful males (God, Jesus, Mohammed), and these religions are still

dominated by male representatives (priests, the Pope, Imams, etc.). This domination is of a piece with the worldviews and rules promoted by these religions. Thus, patriarchal family structures that stretch back millennia have been perpetuated in the patriarchic social institutions that many of us take for granted in modern times. Unfortunately, one has only to look at the persistence of gender discrimination around the world to see the unfortunate effects that some traditional social structures such as these have had on modern life.

By their nature, these structures are embedded in our deep frames, according to Lakoff, and we often fail to recognize them as the sources of problems. But research shows that economic or political stakeholders can and do often manipulate these frames of reference. For example, consider the idea of torture and the outrage that was sparked by news reports that the American military was engaging in torture during the Iraq War. Research found that if reports of torture perpetrated by Americans military personnel were described to people as a longstanding practice and part of the status quo, people were more likely to accept the practice of torture as justified (Crandall, Eidelmann, et al, 2009). Similarly, surveys show that many more Americans approve of spending public money "to help the poor" than on "welfare," though those terms are practically synonymous. The difference is in the framing – the term "welfare" evokes negative emotions while the generic term "the poor" does not.

The Strategic Use of Framing

Commercially motivated media outlets know these things about framing, and therefore have the power to influence public discourse, which means that economic interests can often sway public opinion by presenting information using specific frames of reference. The ability to change attitudes and behavior by manipulating our frames of reference is actually commonplace, and the mass media fill our everyday lives with manipulated information. Consider the reign of Silvio Berlusconi, who was the Prime Minister of Italy for twelve years despite being almost routinely investigated for a number of serious crimes. Berlusconi was able to maintain political power because he also controlled his own private media empire of television networks that dominated Italian news cycles and was able to use this power to propel his own interests and quash criticism.

Once Berlusconi came to power, journalists on state television were required to adhere strictly to a news formula known as "the sandwich," in which virtually every political story began by stating the government's (or Berlusconi's) point of view, followed by a sound bite or two from the opposition and concluded with a rebuttal from the government. Berlusconi himself occupied an incredible 50 percent of airtime on the state-owned newscasts, while the opposition accounted for barely 20 percent (Stille, 2006).

Berlusconi used his political power to influence the state media outlets, but he used his control of his commercial media outlets as well to manufacture positive images of himself and his policies, including an incident where Italian state TV inserted fake video footage of audience applause for a speech he gave at the United Nations. His manipulation paid off handsomely (Stille, 2006). Research showed that the strongest predictors of political orientation among Italian voters were which television stations they watched and for how long. In general, the more hours a day people watched television, the more likely they were to vote for Berlusconi, and people who tended to watch Berlusconi's channels were also much more inclined to vote for him. Berlusconi's success shows how effective public relations strategies can be when they manipulate the delivery of information to the public. Techniques like these are commonly used for the protection of special interests around the world, and in some cases, our assumptions about the integrity of our sources of information are sadly optimistic.

In June 2011, for example, the Federal Communication Commission published a report that makes clear that serious problems have arisen in the American media markets. "An abundance of media outlets," the report states, "does not translate into an abundance of reporting. In many communities, there are now more outlets, but less local accountability reporting" (Waldman, 2011). This, in turn, has led to increases in problems associated with a lack of accountability, such as government waste, local corruption, poor education outcomes, and other serious community problems. The decline in local reporting has shifted the power to set the news agenda away from citizens and, instead, to government agencies and powerful private economic interests. In fact, according to the FCC, some news outlets are "exhibiting alarming tendencies" to allow advertisers to dictate content. Journalism's "independent watchdog function" necessary for a healthy democracy, the report concludes, "is in some cases at risk" (2011).

Keep in mind that only two parties represent America's political system, and only one of them is known as the party of big business. Advertisers may increasingly dictate media content, but this also means that political agendas can be promoted the same as economic agendas. Current issues may be presented in biased ways or selectively reported to sway public perceptions, and research suggests that that has indeed been happening. According to the American journalism professor Stephen Reese, for example, by framing, or "spinning," the news, small groups of elites that control access to the mass media are able to promote private interests and manipulate public discourse and awareness by emphasizing certain perspectives over others in the information they provide (2007). As an example of this, a study found that network news coverage in the U.S. during the Persian Gulf crisis in 1991 was preoccupied with military affairs rather than diplomatic efforts and was highly event-oriented rather than reflective and context-oriented (Iyengar & Simon, 1993). Not surprisingly, survey respondents who reported higher rates of exposure to television news expressed greater support for a military as opposed to a diplomatic response to the crisis.

A more recent example of this type of framing was the intentional and misleading juxtaposition of the invasion of Iraq and the terrorist attacks of 9/11 (Reese, 2007). Research shows that President George W. Bush and his supporters clearly framed the Iraq invasion in the context of the War on Terror by underscoring a false link between the terror attacks on the U.S. on 9/11 and Saddam Hussein, the leader of Iraq. Vice-President Cheney, for example, during an interview on Meet the Press in September 2003 claimed falsely that success in Iraq would strike a major blow at the "geographic base of the terrorists who had us under assault now for many years, but most especially on 9/11" (2003, quoted in Reese, 2007). Subsequent investigations determined that there was no link between the Iraqi dictator and the terrorists responsible for the 9/11 attacks. Instead, there is a great deal of suspicion that government officials from Saudi Arabia, nominally at least a U.S. ally, were complicit in the attacks, but information about the Saudis' involvement was redacted from the 2002 Congressional investigation.

Worse, the hubris exhibited by political stakeholders when they tried to justify the American invasion of Iraq by framing it in various ways has led to a shocking looseness with concepts like truth and reality. The reporter Ron Suskind very clearly documented this hubris. During the Iraq War Suskind interviewed a senior adviser to

President George W. Bush who said that reporters like him were "in what we call the reality-based community," defined as people who "believe that solutions emerge from your judicious study of discernible reality" (2004). According to Suskind, the advisor went on to explain the administration's power to create reality.

> "That's not the way the world really works anymore," he continued. "We're an empire now, and when we act, we create our own reality. And while you're studying that reality -- judiciously, as you will -- we'll act again, creating other new realities, which you can study too, and that's how things will sort out. We're history's actors . . . and you, all of you, will be left to just study what we do" (quoted in Suskind, 2004).

More recently, Reese and colleagues attempted to explore the widespread acceptance of the "war on Terror" frame even by professional journalists. Their study showed that the War on Terror was a powerful organizing principle and, because journalists shared that framing in their reports and analysis, it created a favorable news discourse climate for military action in Iraq (Reese & Lewis, 2009). Reese and his colleague warned that this internalization of the frame by journalists, "short-circuits democratic debate by allowing little space for deliberative scrutiny from citizens and meaningful action by elected officials. We need to understand better how dominant frames become so with the active participation of the news media" (p. 792).

Another technique used by media outlets to sway public opinion is called *agenda setting*. Agenda-setting allows the media to influence public opinion based on the frequency, depth and importance of coverage associated with certain issues. For example, during the 1991 Persian Gulf War the level of network news coverage matched the proportion of Gallup poll respondents naming the Gulf crisis as the nation's most important problem. Public perceptions about the importance of the war increased as more reporting increased (Iyengar & Simon, 1993). This suggests that media coverage helps determine the level of engagement the public has with such issues.

The biases in media messaging and the steady decline in independent watchdog journalism are therefore even more problematical because accurate information is essential to the concept of an informed citizenry in a democratic nation. In fact, freedom of the press is enshrined in the First Amendment to the U.S. Constitution, but freedom is not the same as commercial sustainability. As far back as the 1950s, in *White Collar* (1951) and *The Power Elite* (1956), the American sociologist C. Wright Mills described the mass media as a socializing force, influencing individual behavior and promoting particular values and norms. But he also warned about the increasingly manipulative power of the media to influence public opinion and strengthen the power of the dominant elites, noting how "the mass media plug for ruling political symbols and personalities." (1951, p. 338). Unfortunately, his warnings did not halt the progress of this manipulative process.

Incidentally, Mills also warned that entertainment programming is also an especially powerful instrument of social control because "popular culture is not tagged as 'propaganda' but as entertainment; people are often exposed to it when most relaxed of mind and tired of body; and its characters offer easy targets of identification, easy answers to stereotyped personal problems" (Mills, 1956, p. 336). For example, advertisements aimed at children are considered problematical since they do not have the cognitive maturity to distinguish the inherent bias of advertising, and therefore tend to interpret the claims and appeals as accurate and truthful information (APA, 2004). Yet the American Psychological Association in 2004 estimated that advertisers spend more than $12 billion per year on advertising messages aimed at the youth market, and the average child watches more than 40,000 television commercials per year.

From a historical perspective, Mills described the shift from a community-based social order, in which individuals participated in public debate and collective action, to a society characterized by a non-participatory "mass" of consumers dominated by media. This shift replaced a communication system of shared public opinion with a system that simply provides public opinion, resulting in a one-way flow of information that minimizes feedback, negates public action, and reduces or even eliminates the ability of the public sphere to generate and share the discourse necessary for democratic functionality.

Ideologies

One final aspect of culture that is significant to our exploration of modern society is the notion of ideology or shared and organized world-views. Here is one definition of what ideologies are by a group of social psychologists:

> Specific ideologies crystallize and communicate the widely (but not unanimously) shared beliefs, opinions, and values of an identifiable group, class, constituency, or society... Ideologies also endeavor to describe or interpret the world as it is—by making assertions or assumptions about human nature, historical events, present realities, and future possibilities—and to envision the world as it should be, specifying acceptable means of attaining social, economic, and political ideals (Jost, Federico, & Napier, 2009, p. 309).

The German philosopher Karl Marx claimed that the domineering class in any modern society legitimated its power first through ideas: "The ideas of the ruling class are in every epoch the ruling ideas, i.e. the class which is the ruling material force of society, is at the same time its ruling intellectual force" (Marx & Engels, 1970, p. 64). Additionally, an appeal to the general public welfare, what the German social theorist Jürgen Habermas calls *generalizable interests*, is fundamental to any effort by the ruling elite to make their power seem legitimate, though their stated justifications may not necessarily coincide with the true aims of the ruling party. These efforts were well understood by the European socialist intellectuals like Karl Marx and his colleague, Josef Engels, authors of the *Communist Manifesto* and *The German Ideology*. According to them,

> A certain type of ruling ideas is necessary to justify a ruling position. In other words, a ruling class is compelled, merely in order to carry through its aim, to represent its interest as the common interest of all the members of society (Marx & Engels, 1970, p. 65-6).

The use of ideology as a political tool can be traced back to Machiavelli and his claim that power either can be maintained through the use of force or through ideological control and the manipulation of social discourse (Sidanius, Levin, et al, 2001). The use of force may be common in the early stages of social organization, but its continuous use is often counterproductive. Members of dominant groups are better served by convincing subordinates (and themselves) of the moral and intellectual legitimacy of the existing social order. In fact, research in the area of social dominance shows that members of a dominant group who have a stake in preserving an existing hierarchy naturally attempt to justify their motives through socially acceptable principles, which includes any number of ideologies that reinforce the status quo. "What unites these ideologies is ... their tendency to preserve rather than undermine social arrangements marked by dominance and subordination" (Hanson, 2012, p. 365). Social dominance theory argues that societies universally exhibit three universal forms of group-based hierarchy, one based on age in which adults have disproportionate power over children, a gender-based hierarchy in which men have disproportionate power compared to women, and a form of hierarchy based on some arbitrarily defined distinction that provides a mechanism for further dominance. The theory also confirms the integrative and nature of what some researchers call *legitimizing myths*. Decisions and behaviors at the individual level contribute to the formation of new social practices and the operations of institutions but the normalizing influence also feeds back from the institutional level back to the individual because each level is shaped by consensually held values and beliefs, in other words, the dominant cultural ideologies. One contentious example of this arbitrary set is the development of racism in the colonial American South. The importation of slaves, the argument goes, began as an economic necessity in order to keep up with the expansion of farming and processing of commodity goods. More and more workers were required and the agricultural producers were forced to import workers from overseas. This opportunity coincided with the expansion of the slave trade in Africa by Portuguese traders, creating an economically beneficial opportunity for the colonial landowners. Over time, the severe social inequalities experienced by the slaves needed to be justified, or legitimated, and this need for legitimation led to the development of a racial ideology that justified the discrimination against blacks by defining them as inferior. In essence, economic actions *preceded* the creation of the beliefs that would be required to justify those actions. Southern capitalists needed workers, bought slaves, and only then began to develop a moral justification of slavery based on notions of racial superiority.

The ideologies associated with neoliberal capitalism, in particular, are promoted via the mass media and tend to help justify current conditions around the world as normal or natural, despite the potential unfairness of the *status quo*. Neoliberal capitalism will be much more deeply explored in Chapter 2, but for now, we need to recognize that these ideologies legitimate current conditions partly by minimizing the effects of any questioning or critical stance to the status quo. In a capitalist system, especially a neoliberal one, contradictions develop between a society's cultural system of norms and values that cannot explicitly permit exploitation and a market-oriented economic system that does exactly that, allowing the "privileged appropriation of wealth." Ideology solves, at least temporarily, the problem of how socially produced wealth may be inequitably, and yet legitimately, distributed (Habermas, 1973). One way that the moral issues associated with growing power imbalances and economic inequality can be nullified is through an appeal to nationalism or some other seemingly legitimate justifications. In 1953, for example, President Eisenhower nominated the head of General Motors, Charles Wilson, for Secretary of Defense. During the hearings, Wilson claimed that he couldn't imagine a situation where he would ever have to choose between national interests and the interests of his company, "because for years I thought what was good for the country was good for General Motors and vice versa." Over time this statement transformed into a widely accepted truism supporting the notion that "what's good for business is good for America." In this way, criticisms of labor relations or distribution of profits at auto plants during the 1950s could be construed as attacks on society itself and dismissed as un-American or unrealistic. Thus, the existing social order could be maintained despite the labor inequalities at the time "by falling back on traditional world-views and a conventional civic ethic" (Habermas, 1973, p. 19).

Just as language is a socially created system that is internalized by members of society, beliefs and values that make up our ideologies are also shared symbolic components of culture that become internalized by members of society through education, socialization, and social interactions. Values represent general and abstract goals, tend to be stable over time, and often influence individual choices. When certain values are widely held within a community, these shared assumptions about the world lead to similarities in attitudes regarding what is true or imaginary, desirable or undesirable, good or bad, beautiful or ugly. There are different types of values, of course, and the differences are related to differences in the goals people seek to attain. *Intrinsic values* are those we uphold regardless of the external benefits or costs, and these often are ethical or moral values that reflect our sense of identity and self-worth. Intrinsic values include a sense of community, affiliation to friends and family, and self-development, for example. In contrast, *extrinsic*, or instrumental, values are directly beneficial to us and reflect our own self-interests. These include money, social status, and fame.

If intrinsic values are simplified as *moral* goals and instrumental values as *rational* goals, the two types are not mutually exclusive and may often coincide. We may accumulate wealth, for example, not just because we benefit directly but also because we can share it with our families. But rational goals that are motivated by simple profit, may be potentially harmful, yet these actions can be legitimated or made acceptable and even normal through the force of ideologies that value individual freedoms over social responsibility. For example, even today financial speculation is accepted as a legitimate source of wealth production despite the risk of enormous social costs. Speculation in the commodities markets often drives up the costs of basic goods, especially food grains, and this results in making food less affordable for poor communities and increases levels of malnutrition and even starvation in the poorest regions of the world. Generally, therefore, the increased efficiencies associated with profitable economic action like commodity speculation is a potential problem for some segments of global society and must be managed by the cultural system. Pope Francis, the head of the Catholic Church, for example, has consistently criticized financial speculation and the wealth made from it. "It is increasingly intolerable that financial markets are shaping the destiny of peoples rather than serving their needs, or that the few derive immense wealth from financial speculation while the many are deeply burdened by the consequences," the Pope said in June 2014. He added, "Speculation on food prices is a scandal which seriously compromises access to food on the part of the poorest members of our human family" (quoted in Pullella, 2014). Yet the influence of a cultural icon like the head of the Catholic Church may be insignificant in the face of corporate political power and supportive ideologies like the sanctity of free markets and the superiority of rational individualism. According to social scientists Jon Hanson and John Jost,

> Social systems achieve their highest degree of stability under conditions of widespread "false consciousness"—that is, when dominant and subordinate groups alike come to believe in culturally palatable principles that bolster a preference to maintain the status quo (Hanson, 2012, p. 365).

Capitalism as Ideology

One of the most dominant ideologies in the modern world is free-market capitalism, and in America its principles are clearly palatable. In modern America, where polls show that 40% of the public identifies as conservative, there is an arguable connection between conservative political values and a preference for free-market economic principles over state regulation and "big government." The conservative-liberal distinction has a lot to do with the competing values of freedom and equality, and research confirms that supporters of left-leaning political parties and policies place much greater emphasis on the value of equality than supporters of right-wing political parties and policies. The psychologist Milton Rokeach, for example, found that supporters of free-market capitalism as an ideology tend to place a higher value on individual freedom than on equality (in Sidanius & Pratto, 1999). This is basically the reverse of supporters of communism, for example, who tend to place high value on equality but low value on individual freedom, or socialists who place a high emphasis on both values. These differences in values influence both economic and political preferences, and we can see how they may contribute to economic inequality here in America. Research shows that Americans with conservative values are also more likely to support existing social institutions, more likely to have negative attitudes toward underprivileged groups (Rubin & Peplau, 1975), and tend to assign blame to the individual victims of poverty, crime, and homelessness.

Therefore, the persistence of social and economic inequality is at least partly connected to the power of *the idea* of capitalism and its institutionalized norms, which reflect the cultural preference of freedom over equality. Yet right-wing political parties are not popular simply for the rich. Indeed, many right-wing constituents are middle-class and working-class and support a party that often does not have their best economic interests in mind. The implications of this situation will be more deeply explored in Chapter 4, but for now I will note that many political scientists see this as an example of the false consciousness that promotes the status quo despite the possibility of changes that would benefit those same people.

Historically, the ideological principles of capitalism have been well integrated into American society and their influence is persistent. Indeed, we have seen the recurrent rise and resurrection of modern capitalism to the level of ideological dominance in the U.S. The reputation of liberal capitalism has risen and fallen over the last hundred years; each fall prefaced by an economic catastrophe, and yet has risen again. Surprisingly, this influence remains politically powerful even now in the aftermath of the latest U.S. financial meltdown, which further demonstrates the power of an ideology firmly rooted in cultural life. Echoing the ideas of Charlie Wilson, who believed that what was good for GM was good for America, the economist and former International Monetary Fund chief Simon Johnson puts it this way,

> In a society that celebrates the idea of making money, it was easy to infer that the interests of the financial sector were the same as the interests of the country—and that the winners in the financial sector knew better what was good for America than did the career civil servants in Washington. Faith in free financial markets grew into conventional wisdom—trumpeted on the editorial pages of The Wall Street Journal and on the floor of Congress (Johnson, 2009).

Individualism

Another fundamental influence on cultural norms in the United States is rooted in the values associated with individualism. In fact, the goals of capitalism and individualism go hand in hand. American values emphasize the principles of the free market and individual achievement, and the distribution of economic benefits based on individual abilities and effort. This can be thought of as an ideology of individualism (Castillo, 2011). Individualism has resulted in high levels of achievement for society as a whole, according to sociologists like Talcott Parsons, and the social structure of American culture emphasizes freedom of action for individuals and subgroups rather than an emphasis on equality or collective effectiveness. Parsons in the 1950s referred to this phenomenon in modern societies as *institutionalized individualism* (1951).

Yet the benefits of individualism here in America have not been universally praised. The French historian Alexis de Tocqueville toured America in the early 19th century and produced a comprehensive analysis of American society, noting that "equality of conditions" was a fundamental aspect of American culture. Although many fine aspects of American culture flowed from this, there were potential problems associated with the kind of isolated independence that resulted from that equality of conditions. In fact, De Tocqueville introduced the term "individualism" in Democracy in America (1840), which he described as "a novel expression, to which a novel idea has given birth." He differentiates individualism and egotism, suggesting that egotism is "a passionate and exaggerated love of self," "originates in blind instinct," and "is a vice as old as the world." Individualism, on the other hand, is

> A mature and calm feeling, which disposes each member of the community to sever himself from the mass of his fellow-creatures; and to draw apart with his family and his friends; so that, after he has thus formed a little circle of his own, he willingly leaves society at large to itself (p. 140).

Individualism, however, according to De Tocqueville, was not a positive thing. He wrote that it "proceeds from erroneous judgment" and "originates...in the deficiencies of the mind." Most importantly for our purposes, however, is his assertion that individualism "is of democratic origin, and it threatens to spread in the same ratio as the equality of conditions" (p. 140). Thus the weaknesses associated with individualism are inherent in the democratic ideals that are so celebrated in the United States. Individualism, liberty, and democracy are integrated, De Tocqueville suggests, and we have a tough time separating out the negative aspects of these lofty values from the positive. In fact, we know that soon after De Tocqueville's American visit, by the late 19th century, a small number of powerful families had assumed a great deal of political control, as powerful business interests like the railroad tycoons came to control and manipulate the country's economically essential rail traffic, the media, and a great deal of legislation, until public outcry finally forced the federal government to intercede. In fact, before the Pendleton Act of 1883, which established that positions within the federal government should be awarded on the basis of merit instead of political affiliation, political administrative positions for both state and local governments were mostly filled based on political patronage and cronyism.

Thus, individualism has led to the reduction of the social cohesion created by shared interests since it tends to isolate the individual from the social system. This makes concepts like "the common good" meaningless, since motivations are reduced to simple individual self-interest. Another result of this is to create and concentrate the divisions between the "haves" and "have-nots," since resources are unlikely to be evenly distributed, and over time the inequalities that are created are supported and strengthened by the perpetuation of these same ideals.

Paradoxically, research shows that legitimation of the existing social order is sometimes strongest among those who are most disadvantaged by it (Jost & Major, 2001). A recent psychological framework called System Justification Theory provides support of the tendency to maintain the status quo, and suggests that people form attitudes, beliefs, and stereotypes about groups and individuals to justify the way things are, so that existing social arrangements are perceived as fair and legitimate, even natural and inevitable (Jost & Banaji, 1994). The theory shows that people are motivated to believe that the world they inhabit is legitimate, rational, and fair, because otherwise, they would live in an unpleasant state of psychological discomfort. This means that there is a general bias among the public in favor of the status quo. Other research has demonstrated that people who are more socially and physically deprived develop the strongest needs to justify their own suffering, in order to reduce the mental discomfort associated with the schism between their beliefs about the world and their own experiences (Festinger, 1957). Thus, those who suffer the most within society are those who have the most to explain, justify and rationalize. This can explain, for example, the research finding that there is a negative relationship between income and ideological support for authority (Jost, Pelham, et al, 2002). In essence, this research confirms that people with the least economic power are often the most likely to accept external rules and sanctions (Haines & Jost, 2000).

Additionally, when inequality in America rises, other studies find, the public responds with increased conservative attitudes regarding redistributive policies even though this conservative response produces more economic inequality (Kelly & Enns, 2010). This conservative shift in sentiment occurs among both the rich and the poor. In fact, the preferences of both the wealthiest and the poorest Americans move in tandem and respond to economic inequality similarly over time. From a larger perspective, recent sociological research suggests that, in general, countries with the highest inequality are the ones that most strongly support individualism as a dominant ideology (Castillo, 2011). Unfortunately, this suggests that a society's cultural values may contribute to its own social problems by accepting economic conditions that are directly at odds with the material well-being of its people.

Homo Economicus: The Ideal Man

The ideology of individualism, the rise of rationalism, and the capitalist economic system have contributed to an ideal conception of man as a calculating agent possessing all necessary knowledge and motivated purely by rational self-interest. This represents the latest in a line of dominant character ideals over the ages. Phillip Rieff, in his introduction to Freud's *Therapy and Technique* (in Freud, 1963), describes several character ideals that have emerged over the course of Western civilization. These ideals embody the taken-for-granted aspects of social values and norms that constitute the culture's traditional world-views and are reproduced through socialization. Historically the character ideal that has persisted the longest is *religious man,* which stretches back to the beginning of human evolution and is still with us today. For example, the German social theorist Max Weber's most famous book was an analysis of the influence that Protestantism had on the development of capitalism. But the evolution of social organization gave rise to another ideal millennia ago, that of *political man,* documented in the writings of Plato. According to Plato, the health and stability of a person is analogous to and dependent upon the health and stability of the political order. Thus, the ideal political man has always participated rationally and responsibly in the processes of public decision. In the 18th century, however, another character ideal developed: *economic man,* or *Homo economicus.* Economic man was fearful and suspicious of public life and assumed that a focus on his own private needs would automatically generate a general satisfaction of public needs in (Freud, 1963). This led to a moral revolution that elevated private interests over the public good, or as Max Weber put it, the retreat of ultimate values from public life. This transformation of our cultural character occurred exactly in harmony with the development of modernity, fueled by rationally organized and abstract, universal standards, capitalist industrial systems, and bureaucratic forms of authority. This *homo economicus* character ideal has been institutionalized in Western culture to the point that it is a universally accepted, legitimated conceptualization of human action. As the theoretical physicist Mark Buchanan wrote in an online op-ed,

> The idea that biological competition favors the greedy, creating the ultrarational and incentive-driven Homo economicus, remains at the core of the models economists use to understand the world. It is taught to millions of students

and informs the decisions of the planet's most powerful policy makers (Buchanan, 2013).

However, later in that same article, Buchanan claims, "Problem is, the "hard-headed," supposedly scientific take on human behavior bears little relation to reality. An overwhelming body of research demonstrates that helping behaviors are the norm in human interactions around the globe" (2013). Nevertheless, the idea that humans are motivated by pure, rational self-interest remains as popular as ever.

Summary Thoughts

From a cultural standpoint, modern economic development has triggered a change in relational orientation within our communities from one guided by *social norms* to one guided by *market norms,* which is what Habermas meant when he warned that the instrumental rationality that governs the *systems world* is replacing the practical rationality that guides the *lifeworld.* Simmel also warned that the cohesive relationships of society are eroded as capitalism becomes more rational and thus impersonal.

Further, modern economic systems are increasingly mediated according to their own technical needs, not the cultural norms of the lifeworld. As the instrumental ideas that emerge from the economic sphere gain communicative power, via methods such as advertising campaigns or financial punditry, people are more likely to accept the resulting consensus as normal. This results in the slow transformation of cultural rules and expectations, the "colonization of the lifeworld by the system," and the marginalization of distinctly human patterns of communication and interaction. These claims lead us to a deeper analysis of the systems world, especially aspects of the global economic system and its particular characteristics and ramifications.

Chapter 3

The Power and Problems
of Capitalism

In this chapter, I present a brief review of the various incarnations of capitalism and the cultural implications that flow from each of its variations. Specifically, I wish to draw attention to the unstable nature of unfettered liberal or neoliberal capitalism, but also to the instrumental market values that typify what might be called the *logic of capitalism* and the harm that flows from its logical conclusions. The Miriam-Webster online dictionary defines capitalism as an "economic system in which most of the means of production are privately owned, and production is guided and income distributed largely through the operation of markets." It may be safe to claim that no economic system in the history of the world has been as successful as capitalism, yet by no stretch of the imagination can it be considered optimal. Although our modern capitalist economic systems are assumed to be the "best possible" systems of production and exchange, and therefore taken for granted, they are also blighted by historical failures that have consistently done great harm to societies.

Winners and Losers

One major problem is the inequalities that a market-based economic system produces. The emphases on competition and the pursuit of profits will, by definition, produce winners and losers, and the losers are often marginalized or even preyed upon by the winners. These less successful segments of society will also have fewer resources to cope with the challenges produced by a competitive environment. For example, the U.S. has the highest teenage birthrate in the developed world, about seven times the rate in France (Porter, 2015). Also, more than 25% of American children lives with one parent, the largest percentage by far among industrialized nations, and more than a fifth live in poverty, sixth from the bottom among industrialized nations. Finally, the incarceration rate is more than five times the in most other rich democracies (Porter, 2015).

These problems have often required political intervention in various forms, such as government programs to insure basic living standards among the less successful or resourceful members of society, regulatory agencies that constrain economic actors from putting the public or the environment at risk, and bailouts of key industries during what are often self-induced financial crises. Unfortunately, however, the government programs that attempt to promote safety, competitive fairness, and public welfare are often attacked and even dismantled by the very stakeholders that most benefit from our democratic political systems and market-based economies. This is partly due to the basically amoral and market-based values that capitalism promotes, where actions like taking advantage of loopholes or taking advantage of competitors' or customers' lack of knowledge, or "bending the rules," or "tilting the playing field" are considered acceptable and even praiseworthy. I'm reminded of the recent presidential debate when Donald Trump was accused by his opponent of not paying taxes for twenty years. "That makes me smart," he replied. It is also partly due to the political influence the corporate stakeholders have over government policies. For example, despite many egregious examples of oligarchic or even monopolistic economic power concentrated in the hands of the few (Standard Oil, Microsoft, etc.), the current economic landscape is one in which concentration of power continues to grow largely unhindered. In a recent report from the Council of Economic Advisors, several industries were identified in which market concentration was increasingly oligopolistic: hospital markets, wireless providers, and railroad market concentration, to name a few. The report also found that consumers were stuck with less choice and higher prices as a result of these concentrations (CEA, 2016).

At the corporate level, things are even more lopsided, since corporations are in the enviable position of being "people" in terms of having freedoms and rights, but not in the sense that any particular corporate representatives are responsible for the actions of the organization. In fact, recent corporate malfeasance has been notoriously immune to criminal prosecution. For example, since the financial crisis of 2008, accusations of corporate white-collar crime are commonplace both here and abroad, with new financial scandals uncovered almost routinely. Apparently, banks, mortgage lenders, hedge funds, and a number of other financial institutions have been engaged in various forms of fraud, bid-rigging, insider trading, and manipulation of key interest rates for personal profit for years. The point is that these extremely profitable criminal acts committed by financial industry executives, crimes that may have contributed to that global financial crash, are often explained as the results of a particular *culture* within the financial industry. In effect, many of these unethical and sometimes blatantly illegal actions are excused by relegating them to the level of corporate culture, as though a corporation could act independently of its executives and employees. The journalist Matt Taibbi describes a speech by the U.S. Attorney General Eric Holder in 2014, who suggested, "that, in the corporate context, sometimes bad things just happen without actual people being responsible." That sounds like an absurd justification for his department's lack of prosecutions for the financial crimes committed by major corporations. But Holder reportedly explained that "Responsibility remains so diffuse, and top executives so insulated, that any misconduct could again be considered more a symptom of the institution's culture than a result of the willful actions of any single individual" (Taibbi, 2014). As Taibbi summarized it, "In other words, people don't commit crimes, corporate culture commits crimes." This view is popular in other countries as well. In Britain, Sir Mervyn King, when he was the Governor of the Bank of England, was quoted as saying that excessive levels of compensation, shoddy treatment of customers, and deceitful manipulation have typified the U.K. banking industry, and that the problem was *cultural.* "We can see that we need a real change in the culture of the industry. And that will require two things, one is leadership of an unusually high order and [the other is] changes to the structure of the industry" (quoted in Aldrick, 2012). The implication of Sir Mervyn's description of the banking industry is that they are operating under a different set of rules and principles than the rest of us, essentially they are a rogue subculture that needs to be straightened out and constrained by a new, more honest, more moral cultural orientation.

Perhaps ironically, Britain's Serious Fraud Office initiated an investigation of the Bank of England itself in 2015 for improprieties during the financial crisis, the first time that the central bank has been implicated in a criminal inquiry since the Serious Fraud Office was set up in 1987 (BBC, 2015). I suggest that Sir Mervyn's description of corporate culture is partly right, but misses the major point, which is that the banking industry has *not* been failing to abide by the tenets of our dominant cultural rules and values. I contend that a better way of understanding the problem is that many institutions of society, including the financial industry, are obeying an *economic* set of rules that are rational, successful, and firmly entrenched here in the U.S. and elsewhere. The actions of the financial industry are simply an example of the colonization of whole segments of society by the values and rules of the economic system, the adoption of rational, instrumental but also amoral values that are justified by the system itself rather than the public.

Historical Context

Industrial capitalism unrestrained by regulation will produce problems, and this fact has a great deal of historic support. In the second volume of Democracy in America, originally published in 1840, for example, the French historian, diplomat, and political scientist Alexis de Toqueville already recognized the cultural threat posed by the rise of an American economic aristocracy, made possible by the power provided to business elites through the mechanism of industrial capitalism. "The object is not to govern that population, but to use it" (p. 172). Unlike the aristocracies of the past, these modern oligarchs would have no obligations to their "subjects." Instead, they would view the working classes as disposable. "...[T]he manufacturing aristocracy of our age first impoverishes and debases the men who serve it, and then abandons them to be supported by the charity of the public" (p. 172). De Tocqueville warned us to be wary of this new "aristocracy," which represented a significant threat to democratic principles and posed the risk of a "permanent inequality."

Despite De Tocqueville's reservations, free-market, or liberal, capitalism was widely celebrated in the 19th century. From the beginning of the Industrial era European societies and then the U.S. were dedicated to the imperatives of economic growth and expansion. The social theorist Max Weber found the roots of capitalism in the Protestant work ethic, which eschewed conspicuous consumption and glorified thrift and investment (Weber, 1905). This can be traced back to the Reformation and to the idea that people can achieve religious salvation through worldly pursuits. Although development requires the presence of rational, instrumental values as well as intrinsic values such as salvation, piety, or prestige, it was the intrinsic values of Protestantism that Weber identified as the source of capitalism's success. His conception of capitalism was that of a rational system of economic enterprise, but motivated by the moral benefits of work rather than the selfish pursuit of worldly goods. However, Weber recognized that competitive advantage in a market might result in a problematical accumulation of resources. Protestant values of thrift and charity were popular, but capitalism could potentially condemn workers to the necessities of thrift while rewarding the wealthy capitalists with the luxury of charity. Naturally, the competitive advantage enjoyed by owners and management who had control over productive resources led to risks like the unequal distribution of surpluses and the potential exploitation of workers. As the worker created surplus value, this value was transferred to the capitalist owners and investors but not necessarily to the worker, and the condition of the worker often remained stagnant or could even deteriorate. Thus, even though labor became much more productive in industrial forms of capitalism than in earlier economic systems, productivity gains did not necessarily translate into higher wages for workers and instead could be turned into profits for the owners. This seems to describe our current circumstances as well, where corporate earnings in America have risen over twenty percent *per year* since the global financial crisis of 2008, while the disposable income of workers has barely increased at all over the same period (Schwartz, 2013).

While no economic system is without potential risks and inherent problems, capitalism *per se* is not the major issue in terms of our social problems. Rather, it is the disconnection between economic actions in the capitalist system and the social values of the larger cultural system that is the problem. Historically, economic activity has been integrated into the broader social system and economies have reflected the cultural values of the societies in which they were situated. These cultural values elevated social relations far above market relations and were crucial to the survival of the society. The economic historian Karl Polanyi described the historic role of economic activity as being largely "non-economic" and "submerged in social relationships" (Polanyi, 2001, p. 65). According to Polanyi, economic action had always been integrated within the cultural system and "embedded in long-range relations implying trust and confidence" (p. 65). While recognizing that economic action is necessary in any society, Polanyi's point is that the dominance of non-economic cultural values and norms were historically a source of stability and guidance, while the market system as a self-regulating and independent aspect of social life was a relatively new and disruptive ideology.

No society could, naturally, live for any length of time unless
it possessed an economy of some sort; but previously to our
time no economy has ever existed that, even in principle,
was controlled by markets. In spite of the chorus of academic incantations so persistent in the nineteenth century, gain
and profit made on exchange never before played an important part in human economy (Polanyi, 2001, p. 43).

Traditionally, economic relationships were not only determined
by individual motives and beliefs but were influenced by social and
cultural patterns of interaction. The idea of *embeddedness* refers to
the ways that social and cultural relations guided economic interaction in ways that reflected and strengthened those relations (Granovetter, 1985). Echoing the claims made by other historians, Polanyi also argued that historically people engaged in economic
action not simply for individual acquisitive goals, but in order to
achieve social goals. Polanyi argued that in traditional economic
systems, local markets were subordinate to long-range relations of
trust and confidence among participants, which minimized the bila-
teral character of economic transactions and strengthened the existing social bonds within and between communities (Polanyi, 2001).

He does not act so as to safeguard his individual interest in
the possession of material goods; he acts so as to safeguard
his social standing... Neither the process of production nor
that of distribution is linked to specific economic interests
attached to the possession of goods; but every single step in
that process is geared to a number of social interests ... (Polanyi, 2001, p. 65).

The Oxford Dictionary of British History describes the transition
from medieval to modern economic systems as characterized by a
progressive removal of restrictions on individuals and groups in
favor of the operation of market forces. Enlightenment-era liberal-
ism was the guiding philosophical framework for these changes and
was emancipatory on many levels because of the associated increases in
personal autonomy and social justice. It was accepted that some
state power would be necessary to ensure optimal functioning of
society, but state power would be kept at a minimum and individual liberty and rational self-interest would be emphasized. The Scottish philosopher John Stuart Mill defined the minimum level of
state intervention necessary for the greater good back in 1849,
which included the power to enforce contracts and secure property

rights, the administration of justice, the right to tax in order to provide public goods such as sanitation and public health, and state-supported education (Mill, 2004).

By the middle of the nineteenth century, however, the idea had solidified that an economy was somehow separate from society, a collection of markets with its own principles and logic, and this idea led to significant changes in the ways that capital markets operated and how they were perceived (Polanyi, 2001). It resulted in a transformation in which the economic system took charge of the larger sociocultural system, in essence, "the running of society as an adjunct to the market" (p. 77). Market-based integration resulted in a transformation in which the role of traditional social exchanges was diminished while the market-based exchanges of the economic system were elevated to a dominant position.

> Instead of economy being embedded in social relations, social relations are embedded in the economic system. The vital importance of the economic factor to the existence of society precludes any other result. For once the economic system is organized in separate institutions, based on specific motives and conferring a special status, society must be shaped in such a manner as to allow that system to function according to its own laws (Polanyi, 2001, pg. 77).

This concept, that the economy was a collection of markets with principles and goals that were separate from society, was not a discovery but an invention, and shifted the locus of economic activity from Habermas's *lifeworld*, where it had been situated in the past, to the *systems world*. It also coincided with the elevation of a new type of human ideal, *homo economicus,* the view that people were rational, calculative, and responsive to the material incentives of the marketplace. This cultural ideal arose from the scientific optimism of modernity but also has contributed to pessimism and poverty, environmental degradation, and misery. Tania Singer, the Director of Neuroscience at the Max Planck Institute, has argued,

> Economies, both crisis-stricken and thriving, are failing to eliminate poverty, improve the provision of public services like education, and maintain and allocate collective goods... effectively and equitably. At the same time, societies are increasingly fragmented, with perceived loneliness and stress-related illnesses on the rise. And existing governance structures are inadequate to improve the situation... The concept

of homo economicus... has dominated political and economic thinking since the 1970's. But... it is not conducive to
overcoming today's most pressing global issues (2013).

Further, scientific literature supports the idea that much of the
traditional kinds of social interactions associated with ideals like
love, community, and faith have been replaced by rational, less
personal economic exchanges in industrialized societies like the
U.S. For example, research shows that modern individualistic cultures tend to exchange universalistic resources like money, information, and goods much more often than the resources like love,
status, and service that are emphasized in traditional cultures. In
modern societies, parents give money to their children more frequently but show love and give individual attention to children's
needs less frequently (Triandis & Bontempo, et al, 1988, p. 324).

Market versus State Capitalism

The popularity of liberal capitalism's doctrine dramatically waned
in the late 20th century, when it proved inadequate to deal with the
social and economic problems caused by war on an industrialized
scale. The First World War led to a collapse in international commerce and investment, and in the aftermath, classical liberal capitalism failed to reestablish itself as it had been. Political circumstances had changed dramatically, and the emerging European
states carefully guarded their economic autonomy, while the working classes empowered the political left and politicized macroeconomic policymaking for the first time. In the 2001 edition of Polanyi's *Great Transformation,* Fred Block wrote of the impossibility
of disembeddedness, and also of the staying power of its ideological
foundation.

> The efforts of free market theorists to disembed the econo-
> my from society are doomed to fail. But the very utopianism
> of market liberalism is a source of its extraordinary intellec-
> tual resilience. Because societies invariably draw back from
> the brink of full-scale experimentation with market self-
> regulation, its theorists can always claim that any failures
> were not the result of the design but of a lack of political
> will in its implementation. The creed of market self-
> regulation thus cannot be discredited by historical expe-
> riences; its advocates have an airtight excuse for its failures
> (2001, p. xxxiv).

According to social theorist Jürgen Habermas, the failures of the classical liberal economic system were a legitimation failure. By the mid-20th century, U.S. and European policymakers began to recognize that the attempt to disembed the markets had been politically unsustainable because international societies did not accept the resulting dislocations and inequalities produced by liberal capitalism. In other words, the freedoms demanded by capitalist stakeholders were no longer seen as legitimate by those who represented the public. Influential American economists like John Maynard Keynes suggested that regulation and government intervention were needed in order to provide equity and stability for the postwar economic redevelopment. This led to the "Keynesian" model of development that formed the foundation for rebuilding the international economic system after World War II.

The European nations saw the benefits of social provisions such as healthcare, education and so on, as did the U.S. under the leadership of President Roosevelt and his New Deal policies. After World War II, claims that the market should be allowed to make major social and political decisions, that the state should reduce its regulatory role in the economy, or that trade unions should be curbed and citizens given less rather than more social protection were utterly foreign to the spirit of the time. Regulations were seen as necessary and important, because when they "are effective and effectively enforced, they have the potential to stop corporations from harming and exploiting individuals, communities and the environment" (Bakan, 2004, p.150). Even heads of corporations and wealthy individuals were in agreement with the necessity of ensuring the general public welfare.

The resulting "double movement" described by Karl Polanyi, where the results of deregulation created social crises followed by an attempt by the state to "tame" the economic system in reaction to those crises, has been a common pattern in national and global economies. The social disruptions that resulted from economic crises such as the Great Depression of the early 20th century here in America were increasingly managed through the establishment of social welfare structures among industrialized nations. What resulted was a merger between a political orientation focused on protections for the public welfare and the capitalist economic model. This merger was often referred to as state capitalism, which managed to temper the socially disruptive effects of markets without eliminating the benefits of the marketplace. This new state capitalism generated both better long-term economic performance and more effective social protections than its laissez-faire predecessor. The regimes in Europe that created welfare states and the New Deal policies in the U.S. created a wildly successful era of economic and social development during most of the twentieth century. The strength of the state-regulated capitalist system's legitimacy was based on the argument that basic civil liberties guaranteed freedom for all its citizens, including freedom from economic oppression. The existence of social structures that would limit the arbitrary exercise of power by economic actors through protective social institutions like trade unions and regulatory agencies, and processes like collective bargaining and arbitration, helped capitalism regain legitimacy in the minds of the public and the workforce. Thus, the legitimation of advanced capitalism involved a compromise between a free-market economic system and the cultural demands of the populace, for example in the ways that it permitted labor to organize and bargain collectively so that workers could share in the productivity gains enjoyed by capital owners. For several decades following WWII, this development worked, producing what is sometimes called capitalism's "Golden Age."

> The great boom in wages that began with World War II had lifted tens of millions of Americans... from urban slums and rural poverty to a life of home ownership and unprecedented comfort. The rich, on the other hand, had lost ground. They were few in number and, relative to the prosperous middle, not all that rich... As a result, there was a striking sense of economic commonality: Most people in America lived recognizably similar and remarkably decent material lives (Krugman, 2009).

Neoliberalism, or the Sad State of American State Capitalism

There are several issues here that need to be addressed, however. A new cultural norm began to emerge based on the idea that political action would help compensate for the inequalities and dislocations created by economic activity. The result was the widespread social acceptance, at least for several decades, of the status quo in which the working classes did not revolt against the wealth and power that was accruing among the wealthiest or politically connected because the social institutions available to the working classes generated steady improvement in their own welfare.

However, by the mid-1970s, this social arrangement came to an end. Margaret Thatcher's attitude about society is particularly interesting since she, along with Ronald Reagan in the U.S., embraced the notion of neoliberalism as an economic solution to social problems. Neoliberalism was in most ways a resurgence of the laissez-faire free-market model of capitalism so popular in the 19th century and involved privatization of the management of public sector resources. Thatcher became one of the industrialized world's most enthusiastic promoters of neoliberal policies, not only for Britain but also for the entire world. And so it came to pass, with the World Bank and International Monetary Fund helping to spread the neoliberal agenda promoted by America and Britain throughout the developing world during the latter part of the 20th century. State involvement in the economy was reduced, government enterprises were privatized, trade barriers were eliminated, and restrictions on foreign investment were lifted. The result, according to researchers at the Brookings Institution, was the opposite of what those proponents expected.

> In the world's poorest region, sub-Saharan Africa, the poverty rate remained above 50 percent throughout the period, which, given the region's rapid population growth, translated into a near doubling in the number of its poor. Similarly in South Asia, Latin America and Europe–Central Asia there were more poor people in 2005 than there were a quarter of a century earlier (Chandy & Gertz, 2011).

The neoliberal agenda was a disaster for the developing world, and it is only now recovering from its effects. Even Britain itself was rocked by the privatizations, labor disruptions, and service cuts implemented during Thatcher's rule. Health disparity research has also shown disastrous social impacts from the neoliberal policies enacted there. In fact, alcohol- and drug-related deaths, suicide, violence, widening health inequalities, unemployment, poverty, and income inequality all rose during the heyday of neoliberalism in Britain, or "Thatcherism," as it came to be called there (Scott-Samuel et al., 2014).

Yet neoliberal values continue to weave themselves into the social fabric in ways that conflict with the intended purposes of democratic society. Today in the U.S., the belief of shared economic progress is no longer seen as valid, and many members of society are recognizing that American families are economically worse off now than they were thirty years ago, despite decades of productivity increases and corporate profits. Consider some of the facts reported by the U.S. Bureau of Labor Statistics in recent years: Since the 1970s worker productivity has risen steadily but pay has not. Average real wages in the U.S. stopped rising around 1974 and have been flat ever since (BLS, 2011). Since 1980, however, the incomes of Americans in the top quintile (top twenty percent) have doubled while those in the middle and at the bottom have remained flat for over the last thirty-five years. More than forty million people are currently living in poverty in America. More than forty-five million people use food stamps in order to provide enough food for their families to eat. Over thirty million workers are unemployed or under-employed. On the other hand, according to a report by the Economic Policy Institute, "from 1978 to 2012, CEO compensation increased about *875 percent* (Mischel & Sabadish, 2012). Also, in 2012 the top twenty-five hedge fund managers in the U.S. earned a total of twenty-five billion dollars in compensation, an average of one *billion* dollars each (Vardi, 2013). Or consider that Ken Lewis, the outgoing CEO of Bank of America, received more than $53 million in pension benefits and stock when he retired at the end of 2009, not long after his company was loaned $45 billion in taxpayer dollars in an effort to save his bank from financial collapse due to misguided investments (Gomstyn, 2009).

These unappealing facts point to a flaw in the notion that the current status of state capitalism in the U.S. provides a successful strategy for managing the problems of a market-based economy. As previously mentioned, one outcome of modernity is the rationalization of economic and administrative systems to the point where these systems, especially the economic system, become at least semi-autonomous and follow a systems logic separate from, or alien to, the cultural foundation within a given society. In the U.S. and other industrialized cultures, the combination of individualism as a dominant ideology and an increasingly alien capitalist economic system has led to persistent pressure to allow for "freedom" of economic action (the actions of the system) despite the risks and negative side effects of such freedom on social actors (the actual people affected by the economic system). Extremes of social inequality and environmental degradation are two of many side effects.

One possible reason that social inequalities are on the rise is because state capitalism as a model of political economy has been normalized to represent a balance between the political efforts of the state to provide for the general welfare and to smooth over the problems created by capitalist economic action. Rather than regulating economic activity, however, the solution seems to be to stretch tax revenues enough to help ameliorate the damage done by the economic system, thus tacitly reinforcing the disembeddedness of economic actors from the cultural *lifeworld*. Some have taken to describing this situation as the "privatization of profits, socialization of losses." At the same time, state capitalism has been persistently attacked and undermined, and the resurgent ethos of liberal capitalism has led to the persistent popularity of neoliberalism.

Furthermore, there is a persistent idea that industries can successfully regulate themselves, and voluntary self-regulation is often promoted as an efficient and satisfactory form of risk management. Neoliberal economic ideology asserts that free markets without government interference are the most efficient and socially optimal method for the allocation of resources, therefore deregulation is necessary to allow market forces to function as self-regulating mechanisms. Yet many examples of regulatory failure spring to mind from recent years. For example, the financial crisis of 2008 was in large part a failure of banking regulations, especially the repeal of the Glass Steagall legislation that kept risky investment banking separate from savings and loan banking, which led to frozen credit markets and the worst recession since America's Great Depression in the 1930s. In another industry, the oil drilling disaster in the Gulf of Mexico was partly due to the fact that the energy industry was allowed to write and enforce its own regulations as to the safety requirements for offshore deepwater drilling. These examples suggest that self-regulation by corporate entities, entities whose fiduciary obligations are to maximize profits by any legal means available, is not a reasonable expectation and that the economic system needs rules to regulate behavior and interactions the same way that any community needs rules, in order to limit harm. But somehow the belief in Smith's "invisible hand" leads to exemptions for powerful economic actors. According to Canadian law professor Joel Bakan,

> No one would seriously argue that individuals should regulate themselves, that laws against murder, assault and theft are unnecessary because people are socially responsible. Yet oddly, we are asked to believe that corporate persons...
> should be left free to govern themselves (Bakan, 2004, p.110).

Karl Polyani wrote similarly decades ago in *The Great Transformation,*

Our thesis is that the idea of a self-adjusting market implied a stark utopia. Such an institution could not exist for any length of time without annihilating the human and natural substance of society; it would have physically destroyed man and transformed his surroundings into a wilderness (2001, pp. 3-4).

It should also be noted how hypocritical the notion is that markets need to be free of state interference. The development of capitalism necessarily required preconditions such as a state bureaucracy that enforced a predictable legal system that granted corporations extensive rights and protections. Consider, for example, the corporate entity itself. Corporations are not new; they have been around since the 18th century. They are economic entities, and in modern form represent the results of both the institutionalization and bureaucratization of economic action. A corporation is by design tasked "to pursue, relentlessly and without exception, its own self-interest, regardless of the often harmful consequences it might cause to others" (Bakan, 2004, p.1-2). One of the peculiarities of the corporation legal structure is the joint stock, limited liability form, which allows individuals to organize themselves in order to take collective action in their own self-interests but limits their personal liability for the acts that are carried out. Furthermore, corporate law provides the organization with an artificial legal personality that creates the possibility that the corporation may be punished for crimes rather than the individuals who make up the corporation, thus protecting the corporate leaders from legal sanctions. These privileges that corporations enjoy, in fact their very existence as a legal form, are the product of state action. According to Bakan, the corporation has always needed the state to exist. Only the state can create a corporation and grant it "essential rights such as legal personhood and limited liability" (2004, p.153). The state "raises police forces and armies and builds courthouses and prisons (all compulsorily paid for by citizens) to enforce corporations' property rights – rights themselves created by the state" (p. 153). And, ironically, only states are able to create the legal institutions that in turn limit those same states from regulating the corporations that they themselves created.

Based on these observations, it must be acknowledged that the capitalist economic systems of industrialized nations require a great deal of political intervention, yet the political systems of many industrialized nations are particularly susceptible to financial pressure aimed at reducing oversight and responsibility. Currently in the U.S., there is a growing feeling that the increases in economic inequality and the resulting social problems are partly the result of public policies that are shaped by a political system colonized by market forces, such that the oligopolistic sectors of the economic system are protected at the expense of other areas of the economy. Consider the health care industry, where health insurers are consolidating their market power across the nation (Dafny, 2012). In 2012, sixty percent of the nation's largest metro areas, the two largest health insurers had a combined market share of *seventy percent* or more, and one insurance carrier controls nearly half of all metro areas. The report also found that *ninety-nine percent* of health insurance markets in the U.S. are "highly concentrated." At the same time, an article in the Oregon Law Review in 2011 plainly spells out the fact that monopoly power in the hands of health services or products providers is more harmful to both consumers and the general welfare than monopolies of other kinds, yet the antitrust agencies and courts tasked with regulating these monopolies have done little to curb these consolidations. Specifically, "U.S.-style health insurance greatly enhances the pricing freedom of firms possessing market power in health care markets, resulting in much larger monopoly profits and much greater redistributions of wealth" (Havighurst, 2011, p. 850). This is bad news for consumers. Higher prices stemming from hospital mergers that took place between 1997 and 2006 alone added twelve billion dollars to annual health care costs, according to one study (Capps, 2009).

There are, in fact, a growing number of oligopolies around the world, and especially in the United States. Some recent examples include national mass media, where 90% of U.S. media outlets owned by six corporations: Walt Disney, Time Warner, CBS Corporation, Viacom, NBC Universal and News Corporation. Just two companies, Apple iOS and Google Android dominate Smartphone operating systems, while computer Apple and Microsoft have cornered the computer operating system markets around the world. There are only three leading auto manufacturers in the United States, Ford, GMC and Chrysler, and only four major cell phone service providers, Verizon, Sprint, AT&T, and T-Mobile. Even toothpaste (yes, toothpaste) production is controlled by just two firms, Procter & Gamble and Colgate-Palmolive, who together control more than eighty percent of the market (Linn, 2010).

Capitalism and Social Justice

The "double movement" described by Polanyi has resulted in [yet] another drift toward a state-capitalist system in response to the failures of liberal and neoliberal economic systems. Yet the current system is by no means ideal, and practically every day we see failures of state intervention to curb economic risks and excesses. In addition to the subtle legitimation of the social inequalities inherent in our system of state-regulated capitalism, there is a constant and powerful pressure on the political system to drift more toward the neo-liberal models of capitalism. The inherent social problems in a liberal (laissez-faire) capitalist system are well understood and the consistent pressure toward a "free market" is powerful and often successful. For example, taxes and social welfare spending are the main mechanisms of wealth redistribution in pursuit of the broad social policies that societies use to ensure shared prosperity and protect against the emergence of a wealthy and socially disruptive elite. The usual argument against wealth redistribution policies made by the wealthy members of society is couched in terms of fairness. It is unfair and disincentivising to take an economically successful individual's earnings and give them to those who didn't have the skills, motivation, or make the effort to earn for themselves, the argument goes. Not only does this argument ignore the massive resources provided by the larger society that must be paid for by those who benefit the most, but it also inflates the likelihood that the wealthy individual's success is due to skill, motivation, and effort. For those with wealth, further economic success is often simply a matter of luck.

Another problem is that concentrations of wealth tend to siphon income away from the rest of the country's wage earners. Taxes and social spending are the mechanisms by which the political system distributes the country's wealth. It is the Robin Hood part of the social equation, where the government takes from the rich and gives to the poor to maintain basic standards of living for the populace and limit the economic and political power of the elite. Every developed nation has such a transfer system. However, in the U.S. those taxes that would limit the concentration of wealth, taxes like the capital gains tax on investment income for private individuals, corporate earnings taxes, or even more importantly the estate taxes that limit intergenerational concentration of wealth within families, have been reduced over time and are now no longer effective mechanisms of wealth redistribution. Furthermore, the spending part of the equation is also consistently attacked and increasingly undermined by politically powerful wealthy interests. The result is predictable – more and more wealth concentrated in fewer and fewer hands.

Externalities

In 1971, in *Theory of Justice*, the philosopher John Rawls argued that state intervention should work to correct market imperfections, protect public resources, and ensure the background conditions essential to distributive justice, but today this goal often goes unmet in the American system. Consider the issue of negative externalities. The top four tobacco manufacturers generated around $30 billion in profits in 2008, selling roughly 16 billion packs of cigarettes, 12 billion cigars, and 120 million pounds of smokeless tobacco (Callard, 2010). Today about one in five Americans smoke and, according to the U.S. Centers for Disease Control (CDC), and smoking is the leading cause of premature death in the United States; an estimated 438,000 Americans die as a result of smoking or exposure to secondhand smoke each year (CDC, 2013). In addition, for each person who dies from a smoking-related disease, about 20 more are living with an illness attributable to smoking. These are some of the negative externalities of tobacco use, and the deaths and illnesses place a terrible burden on society, including economic costs. During 2000–2004, for example, the CDC estimated that cigarette smoking was responsible for $193 billion in annual health-related economic losses in the United States, $96 billion in direct medical costs and approximately $97 billion in lost productivity (2013).

Based on these statistics, the CDC estimates that the total economic costs (direct medical costs and lost productivity) associated with cigarette smoking would be $10.47 per pack of cigarettes sold in the United States (2013). In other words, the government would need to apply a tax of over $10 per pack to recoup the public costs arising from the private use of tobacco products. But the federal government only taxes cigarettes at $1.06 per pack, and the states tax no more than double that amount. New York State has the highest tax rate, with a state tax of $2.75 per pack, and tobacco friendly Missouri adds only a 17 cent state tax on each pack. But this means that the combined state and federal taxes leave, at best, over 60% of the social costs of tobacco use unaccounted for by either the consumers or producers of tobacco products. The top three tobacco companies generated over $477 billion dollars in revenue in 2014,

according to the non-profit Action on Smoking and Health organization (ASH), which is more than most national GDPs around the
world, and continue to be taxed as lightly as any other industry in
America.

Tobacco use is one example of the negative externalities associated with economic activity, but there are many others, such as
the side effects associated with oil exploration, especially the
process known as "fracking" for natural gas, the byproducts of the
chemical industries, the coal industry, and so on. The general pattern in the U.S. is to pass off the costs of the various types of externalities onto the general public rather than the economic actors
themselves. Therefore the American people suffer from a lack of
social justice because of the continuing dominance of the liberal
capitalist framework driven by wealthy individuals and powerful
corporations within our putative welfare-state system.

A Global Issue

The global expansion of these economic systems poses an even
larger problem simply because of scale. The concept of globalization is controversial and can be defined in a number of ways. For
our purposes, I will limit the definition of globalization to represent
the spread of capitalism, particularly seen in the expansion of cross-
border flows of capital (i.e., investment and trade) and labor around
the globe, and the growth of multinational corporations supported
by international political protections and legal rights. Globalized
capitalism also includes the ability to locate production facilities in
low-cost areas around the globe, a process facilitated by financial
and technological developments. This gives a new significance to
capital mobility and threatens long-standing social and economic
arrangements together with the political and institutional frameworks that accompanied those arrangements. As the political historian Christopher Lasch put it, "In the borderless global economy,
money has lost its links to nationality" (1995). Incidentally, the
historic French icon Napoleon Bonaparte said something similar
two hundred years ago, "Money has no motherland; financiers are
without patriotism and without decency; their sole object is gain."

Modern social theorists like Immanuel Wallerstein argue that the
Western world has been integrated into a single "world system"
through a process of economic organization that began centuries
ago and has resulted in a globalized capitalist economic system
based on political protection without political oversight or inter-

vention. According to Wallerstein, the world-economy is a large geographic zone within which there is a division of labor and hence significant internal exchange of basic goods as well as flows of capital and labor. The role of the political system is recognized in this conceptualization, but not any *single* political system. "A defining feature of a world-economy is that it is not bounded by a unitary political structure... Rather, what unifies the structure most is the division of labor which is constituted within it" (1974, p. 348). Unlike Adam Smith's classic view that capitalism is a system based on the noninterference of the state in economic affairs, Wallerstein argues that the success of capitalism *requires* the interventions of various state actors but it must remain *unbounded* by any specific political or cultural restrictions.

> Capitalism is based on the constant absorption of economic loss by political entities, while economic gain is distributed to "private" hands... capitalism as an economic mode is based on the fact that the economic factors operate within an arena larger than that which any political entity can totally control. This gives capitalists a freedom of maneuver... It has made possible the constant economic expansion of the world-system, albeit a very skewed distribution of its rewards (1974, p. 348).

Wallenstein suggests that the freedom enjoyed by multinational corporations allow them to leverage various political systems around the globe to their own advantage. Unfortunately, the competitive nature of capitalism suggests that there will be losers as well as winners, and often these corporations make rational decisions that benefit themselves but at the expense of entire regions of the world and the people in them. Consider that, while the blatant colonization of "third world" nations by the industrialized Western nations ended after the Second World War, the appropriation of resources and labor in these regions by the West persists, and is still seen as exploitative, so corporations have become clever in how these exploitative arrangements are created (see Prasad, 1996; Darby, 2007). For example, one way that industrialized nations form economic relationships with other countries is through financial aid. Foreign financial aid allows industrialized nations to maintain extensive economic involvement in developing countries. In return for compliance with strict economic regulations, funding and capital investment are provided to poor peripheral countries.

However, these financial interventions put those countries, situated in South-East Asia, Latin America, and Africa, under the firm control of the economically strong core states. Often the peripheral nations build up massive external debts to entities like the IMF and World Bank, who end up having a strong influence on the country's economic policy. These indebted countries are forced to allow foreign intervention on government policy decisions and often result in massive privatization of existing national resources, especially raw materials like oil and natural gas, minerals, and metals, and the opening up of internal markets to foreign competition. These policies allow foreign corporations to buy land and agricultural resources in these poor countries, and to buy rights to other essential natural resources at discounts or even obtain monopolies on the extraction of these commodities. It is not difficult to see this process as one of neo-colonial exploitation (Chandy & Gertz, 2011).

The characteristics of a global world economy also predict the need for expansion. In the past, transportation and other transaction costs discouraged investment in places where people were poor, industrial activity was limited, and local demand was low. Lack of investment, in turn, slowed the development of human and industrial capital and kept consumption demand low, and those constraints often reinforced a vicious circle of poverty. This feedback process partly explains why the benefits of industrialization have not spread evenly around the world, and why some regions remain mired in poverty while others enjoy ongoing prosperity. Improvements in communications, manufacturing, and transportation technologies, however, have made the poor regions of the world much more attractive to economic entrepreneurs, because globalization allows existing capital to take advantage of low priced productive labor, land and raw materials in these impoverished areas, which justifies capital investments such as factories or extractive infrastructure. The implementation of these investments creates new feedback loops that increase employment opportunities in these regions, create new localized opportunities for development and eventually reduce levels of poverty. Geographically, it is inevitable that more and more regions of the world will be absorbed by the *world-economy*. The desire for ever-expanding wealth requires ever-expanding markets and materials.

Historically, organized capitalist ventures like the English East India Company and the Dutch East India Company in the 17th and 18th centuries thrived on low-wage labor and sources of raw material extracted with the backing of colonial guns and legislation. But by the late 19th century the problem with capitalist expansion and perpetual growth was revealed: it required a ready supply of raw materials, an increasing demand for goods, and ways to invest profits and capital. European and American power expanded into areas like Africa and Asia that had remained relatively untouched by capitalism. Nineteenth-century colonialism expanded markets, increased opportunities for investors, and ensured supplies of raw material. This imperialist expansion converted far-flung communities around the world into producers of export crops while millions of subsistence farmers were forced to become wage laborers producing for the international markets. Ideally, according to liberal capitalists, these markets would be free of borders, boundaries, and cultural constraints. As Wallerstein pointed out, liberal capitalism requires freedom from regional cultural or political restraints and be allowed to follow its own logic and values, *but* it also requires state intervention on a number of fronts such as in terms of the rule of law for the enforcement of contracts and property rights.

> [T]he capitalist system requires a very special relationship between economic producers and the holders of political power. If the latter are too strong... their interest will override those of the economic producers and the endless accumulation of capital will cease to be a priority. Capitalists need a large market... but they also need a multiplicity of states so they can gain the advantages of working with states but can also circumvent states hostile to their interests (Wallerstein, 1974, p. 24).

In the current stage of capitalism, the predictable side effects of a globalized system are becoming more obvious and confounding. Productive industrial economic power has become concentrated in certain major industries and their global reach has expanded as large national corporations turn into larger international corporations and then into multinational conglomerates. It is common knowledge that many of the world's largest economies are corporations, not nations. Investment and local development in underdeveloped areas of the globe would seem like a clearly beneficial arrangement, a "win-win" situation for all of the stakeholders, and indeed, many underdeveloped regions of the world have benefitted economically from the process, although the cultural benefits of this process in these areas are much more controversial. Yet globalization results in contradictory consequences for these societies.

According to Wallerstein's world-system theory, among the most important structures of the current world economy is a power hierarchy between core and periphery nations, in which powerful and wealthy "core" societies dominate and exploit weak and poor peripheral societies (1974). Technology is a central factor determining whether a region is in the core or the periphery, thus advanced or developed countries are the core, and the less developed are in the periphery. One outcome of the arrangement is that peripheral countries are structurally constrained to experience a kind of development that reproduces their subordinate status. Another controversial byproduct of labor globalization is related to the problem of labor movement constraints. The creation of wealth through the use of foreign labor resources allows industrialized societies to maintain high levels of domestic consumption but often contributes to decreases in domestic production. Since labor costs are so much lower in the foreign labor markets, prices can be kept low so that goods remain affordable to domestic consumers.

Thus, as primary production processes migrate from wealthier core nations to poorer peripheral nations, the economies of developed countries like the United States continue to become less production based and more focused on consumption. This leads to a dramatic falloff in industrial employment and an increase in service sector employment. In fact, the state of the U.S. labor market has never been more fragile and precarious. According to the Bureau of Labor Statistics, manufacturing jobs in the United States have been declining for decades, sliding from a postwar peak of sixteen percent of total employment to the current low of around five percent (2012). In the years from 1998 and 2008, U.S. corporations "outsourced" over 2.4 million jobs to foreign workers overseas, including more than 525,000 white-collar positions, according to the country's largest union, the AFL-CIO (2008). These patterns of labor distribution will probably intensify in the future and is simply an economic reality in today's globalized environment.

This redistribution of productive labor across the globe has resulted in stagnant wages, a dramatic decrease in labor union membership and as a result, an equally significant decrease in political power among workers here in America. Even worse, however, is that the stagnant earnings and decreased political power among workers here in the U.S. and other developed nations are not necessarily offset by broad increases in wealth and power among the workers of the developing world. For example, in 2011 Indian political scientist Zoya Hasan warned that economic growth had made India one of the fastest-growing economies in the world, but the concentration of economic power in the corporate sector was actually increasing inequalities within the country (The Hindu, 2011). She mentioned the "disequalising" patterns of wealth concentration, intensified by large-scale corruption, and "the open business-politician-bureaucrat collusion bordering on the corporate takeover of government, and the growing plunder of natural resources" in her speech. All these problems are arising in a democratic country in which previously marginalized groups have become part of the political process. Unfortunately, political inclusion has not resulted in either equitable power sharing among stakeholders or any significant distribution of wealth and income in India.

Perhaps one of the most insidious effects of globalization and the neoliberal economic paradigm is that they have given rise to market inequalities that seem largely disconnected from any cultural moorings. Just as the historian Emmanuel Wallerstein suggested, capitalists have a peculiar influence on the various political powers around the world that has allowed economic expansion and "a very skewed distribution of its rewards." Consider the aftermath of the global financial crisis of 2008. In Europe, many people recognize that the crisis was due to a combination of circumstances. Capital inflows into European countries during the last ten years created a housing bubble and investment boom. Banks lent too freely, people borrowed too much, and when the boom went bust the banks were left with bad loans, investors were at risk of losing value, and the public was left with too much consumer debt. Governments decided to bail out the banks to protect investors, essentially nationalizing many of the private debts of large banks into sovereign debts. At the same time, the public reduced demand, investment dried up, and this resulted in reduced economic growth and increased unemployment. This, in turn, led to increased spending on welfare programs at the same time that tax revenues fell. Reduced growth hurt the banks even more, and sovereign debts continued to increase. Thus the crisis was a matter of sovereign debts, bank debts, and economic recessions among many of the European countries like Greece, Spain, and Italy, and it persists today, especially for Greece which in 2016 is still undergoing the ultimate in debt crises: closed banks, capital controls, and limited access to emergency funding.

Oddly, many observers point out that the solutions to this broad economic crisis promoted by the "experts" and policy makers of

Europe tend to favor the well-being of the banking industry, especially the banks' bondholders, at the expense of the general public. This is not surprising when one recognizes how colonized the policymaking institutions are by members of the economic elite in Europe. For example, in 2010, Greece's prime minister resigned and was replaced by a former European Central Bank official. In Italy, Mario Monti, an economist and a senior adviser at the Goldman Sachs investment bank, one of the largest investment banks in the world, became the prime minister in 2010 by appointment rather than through election by the Italian people, and many saw his appointment as a violation of democratic principles. "By imposing rule by unelected technocrats, [Italy] has suspended the normal rules of democracy, and maybe democracy itself, " it was reported at the time (Foley, 2011). More recently in 2015 Alexis Tsipras, newly elected leader of the radical-left Syriza government in Greece, was dealing with the stalemate between Greece and its creditors and warned that the eurozone's dominant stakeholders like Germany, the International Monetary Fund, and the European Central Bank, were "by degrees bringing about the 'complete abolition of democracy in Europe' and were ushering in a technocratic monstrosity with powers to subjugate states that refuse to accept the 'doctrines of extreme neoliberalism'" (Evans-Pritchard, 2015). Yet there is the continued promotion of the supposed technocratic experts in the mass media, experts who have shown themselves unable or unwilling to protect the public welfare or even solve the pressing issues associated with the various ongoing crises like the situation in Greece. Some argue that the fact that these technocrats show a clear bias in favor of corporations and the wealthy represents an ongoing effort among the global elite to reduce the power of the public and increase the power of elite administers over matters of public policy and national sovereignty. As the popular philosopher Slavoj Žižek recently warned,

> This passage from politics proper to neutral expert adminis-
> tration characterises our entire political process: strategic
> decisions based on power are more and more masked as
> administrative regulations based on neutral expert know-
> ledge, and they are more and more negotiated in secrecy
> and enforced without democratic consultation (2015).

These issues point to a tendency for elite stakeholders to promote economic expertise to solve political and social problems. The economist Simon Johnson has observed that here in the U.S. the large banking corporations are so influential in government deci-sion-making that the country is effectively an oligarchy run by the leaders of the financial industry, where politicians are "bought and paid for" by corporations. In Europe, however, it is less blatant and mercenary but still driven by the ideological orientations popular with the banking industry and other powerful economic actors. "What you have in Europe is a shared world-view among the policy elite and the bankers, a shared set of goals and mutual reinforce-ment of illusions" (Johnson, quoted in Foley, 2011).

Just as Wallerstein described it in 1974, modern capitalism is de-pendent on "the constant absorption of economic loss by political entities, while economic gain is distributed to 'private' hands." Present circumstances allow corporate special interests to external-ize risks, damages, and costs onto the social system, largely the political system, in a way that increases corporate profits while at the same time degrading the social fabric and material environ-ment. Because capitalism as an economic system operates within an arena larger than that which any political entity can totally con-trol, capitalists are structurally unrestrained. Unregulated capital moves around the globe at will seeking increased profit and accu-mulation, and, in the process, often disrupts established labor pat-terns, thereby disrupting and straining the lives of the working classes. Yet the costs of these labor disruptions are left for the politi-cal system to manage, which is itself strained by growing limitations and crises. In essence, the economic systems are offloading their responsibility for the social problems they create onto the backs of those most affected, pushing risk down to the level of the individual while manipulating the political system to reduce or eliminate any penalties for "white collar" crime or mismanagement. In a variation on this theme, the sociologist Ulrich Beck (2007) suggests that the current neoliberal capitalist economic system consists of a global capital-state coalition where the political system is complicit in maintaining the power and profitability of the economic system. Around the world, governments provide subsidies and tax breaks to multinational corporations and thus contribute to the conse-quences of investment decisions made by globalized capital, de-spite the tendency of economic actors to externalize risks, destabil-ize markets, disrupt access to vital commodities, and contribute to the uncertainty of modern economic life. Neoliberal capitalism has been increasing global risks in the form of climate change, pollu-tion, etc. for many years, and pushing the costs of those risks downward onto less powerful peripheral parts of the social system.

At the same time, the neoliberal political state attempts to optimize and legitimize the interests of capital worldwide and surround itself with an aura of self-regulation and self-legitimation.

Perverse Industries

The neoliberal tendencies of the capitalist system inadvertently perpetuate painful social inequalities, but it also produces outcomes that are simply inimical to human welfare as well. As previously mentioned, corporations and other stakeholders of the economic system are often governed by instrumental rationality, or *market norms,* rather than practical rationality, or the *social norms* that guide the *lifeworld.* These differences in normative guidance and motivation lead to seriously maladaptive practices within the economic system because the values of profit and reduction of overhead costs are often at odds with the traditional human values such as the sanctity of life, fairness, and compassion, for example. The result is that these value differences create perverse situations within our modern societies, especially here in America. Perverse incentives, a term first coined by Edgar Allan Poe in his short story, *The Imp Of The Perverse,* are incentives that have unintended results contrary to the interests of the incentive makers. A few examples from Wikipedia: In Vietnam, a program intended to promote the extermination of rats paid people a bounty for each rat pelt they handed in, but this led to the farming of rats. Nineteenth-century paleontologists in China paid peasants for each fragment of dinosaur bone that they found, but peasants dug up whole bones and then smashed them into multiple pieces to maximize their payments. Because the penalty for murder is no worse than for kidnapping, kidnappers may be more likely to murder their hostages, since both crimes carry the same penalty. These are all examples of perverse incentives.

It is well established that capitalism itself embraces a variation of perverse incentives in certain areas of the economic system in general, in which the logic of capitalist markets are at odds with the preservation of maximum human welfare, activities in which the benefits of economic success come at a significant social expense. One simplistic example of this market logic is that an insurance company makes a profit by either collecting more in premiums than they would ever need to pay out for claims or simply by collecting premiums and then finding ways to avoid paying out for claims. The same logic is inherent in the American healthcare industry, which relies in no small part on growing numbers of sick people to prop up profits and growth, and especially in the for-profit prison industry, which relies on growing numbers of prisoners for its success. There are in fact a number of industries that seem to be more and more influenced by these perverse incentives. The following section identifies three of the most egregiously perverse industries.

The Illness Industry

In an article published in *The New England Journal of Medicine*, the journalist Robert Kuttner pointed out that U.S. health care expenditures in 2008 exceeded $2.1 trillion, or more than $7,000 for every man, woman, and child in America at the time (Kuttner, 2008). This average is the highest in the industrialized world. But Kuttner did not attribute the problem of such high healthcare costs to the traditional reasons - the aging population, the proliferation of new and expensive technologies, poor diet and lack of exercise, excessive litigation and defensive medicine, etc. Instead, Kuttner claimed that the "extreme failure of the U.S. to contain medical costs results primarily from our unique, pervasive commercialization" (p. 549). It is the profit-maximizing behaviors of insurance and pharmaceutical companies themselves that are a major reason for high medical costs, and they also distort public resource allocation. "Profits, billing, marketing, and the gratuitous costs of private bureaucracies siphon off" almost a quarter of the $2.1 trillion spent each year, Kuttner claimed, and suggested that an even bigger problem was "the set of perverse incentives produced by commercial dominance of the system" (p. 549). As previously mentioned, the American Medical Association itself reported in 2010 that the two largest health insurers in over half of the nation's largest metro areas had a combined market share of *seventy percent* or more, and one insurance company controls nearly half of all metro areas in the country (Dafny, 2012). These insurance companies are just one set of corporations in the healthcare industry that are tasked with maximizing profits by any legal means possible, and also represent what many would describe as a *de facto* oligopoly in those regions.

In what might be an even worse situation, not only is the medical industry distorted by pervasive commercialization to the point that healthcare services and products are increasingly expensive even while their actual benefits are often negligible, but commercial interests are also increasingly corrupting the scientific research

efforts of the medical industry. Consider the words of Marcia Angell, an editor of The New England Journal of Medicine for over
twenty years, "It is simply no longer possible to believe much of the
clinical research that is published, or to rely on the judgment of
trusted physicians or authoritative medical guidelines. I take no
pleasure in this conclusion, which I reached slowly and reluctantly
over my two decades..." (Angell, 2009). Angell's declaration in 2009
is well supported by investigations into the clinical drug trials sponsored by the major pharmaceutical companies. Consider the recent
research of Charles Seife, from the Carter Institute of Journalism at
New York University. Seife sought to investigate whether published
clinical trials in which a Food and Drug Administration inspection
found significant evidence of violations are mentioned in the peer-
reviewed literature. According to Seife, the US Food and Drug Administration (FDA) inspects several hundred clinical research sites
every year and occasionally finds evidence of research misconduct.
"However, the FDA has no systematic method of communicating
these findings to the scientific community, leaving open the possibility that research misconduct detected by a government agency
goes unremarked in the peer-reviewed literature" (Seife, 2015).

Seife's investigation found numerous studies for which the FDA
determined there was significant evidence of fraudulent or otherwise problematic data that was never mentioned in the relevant
published literature. According to Seife, the FDA does not typically
make any announcement intended to alert the public about the
research misconduct that it finds, which makes it "usually very
difficult, or even impossible, to determine which published clinical
trials are implicated by the FDA's allegations of research misconduct" (Seife, 2015). His investigation identified only three out of
seventy-eight published articles (4%) in which the FDA found significant violations and actually mentioned the violations, and "no
corrections, retractions, expressions of concern, or other comments
acknowledging the key issues identified by the inspection were
subsequently published."

The irony, of course, is that medical professionals all over the
world rely on the integrity of these types of medical studies to determine which drugs are safe and effective and which are not. Unfortunately, the failure of the government agencies tasked with the
oversight of such studies puts lives at risk while giving the pharmaceutical industry something like a free pass when their drug research is found to be fraudulent or tainted. This suggests that there

is a perverse incentive at work to minimize the economic risks to pharmaceutical makers while tainting the integrity of scientific research in general and increasing the healthcare risks for the entire world of pharmaceutical consumers.

This type of corruption of the scientific process also leads to the seemingly perverse notion of *disease mongering*. For example, the pharmaceutical industry provides solutions for various health problems, but they also increasingly define and popularize new medical conditions as part of their production process, essentially creating new illnesses. Unfortunately, expanding the definitions of existing illnesses and creating new ones can lead to profits for the industry, but at the expense of the general public. An article in the British Medical Journal described the manipulation of expertise in what the authors called the *corporate construction* of disease. "There's a lot of money to be made from telling healthy people they're sick. Some forms of medicalising ordinary life may now be better described as disease mongering" (Moynihan, et al, 2002, p. 886). There are indeed organized efforts by groups of pharmaceutical manufacturers, doctors, and patient groups to widen the boundaries of treatable illness in order to expand markets for the industry (Moynihan, et al, 2002). This process of disease mongering is accomplished by providing the news media with reports and other information designed to create fears about particular conditions or diseases and draw attention to the latest treatments. Company sponsored advisory boards supply the "independent experts" for these stories, consumer groups provide the "victims," and public relations companies provide media outlets with the positive spin about the latest "breakthrough" medications (2002, p. 888). The authors point out that many of the professionals involved may have honorable motives, but "campaigns are orchestrated, funded, and facilitated by corporate interests, often via their public relations and marketing infrastructure" (p. 887).

Big Pharma and Little Kids

A specific example of how potentially perverse incentives influence medical decisions can be found in the field of psychotherapy. The American Psychiatric Association's Diagnostic and Statistical Manual of Mental Disorders (DSM), often referred to as the bible of psychiatry, has recently released its fifth edition. Historically, there had been a number of conflicting diagnostic systems for classifying and treating mental disorders here in the U.S., and a real need for a classification system that minimized confusion, created consensus among mental health practitioners, and helped professionals communicate using a common diagnostic language. The DSM-I was first published in 1952 and featured descriptions of 106 disorders. In 1968, the DSM-II was only slightly different from the first edition and increased the number of disorders to 182 (Wen, 2010). The DSM-III was published in 1980 and included 265 diagnostic categories. It should be noted at this point that the most often prescribed treatment for these mental disorders is drug therapy, and the pharmaceutical industry generates over fourteen billion dollars a year in antipsychotic drugs alone. Psycho-pharmaceuticals are the most profitable sector of the pharmaceutical industry, and Americans, less than five percent of the world's population, consume *sixty-six percent* of the world's psychoactive medications (Wen, 2010). The DSM-V, the new fifth edition, includes 365 different mental disorders, a new record number of diagnoses for mental illness. Interestingly, *over half* of the members of the task force charged with producing the latest version of the DSM had substantial financial ties to the pharmaceutical industry.

In the last decade, the desire to sell pharmaceutical solutions for mental problems have unfortunately pushed healthcare professionals into risky and even lethal decisions, and the medical and pharmaceutical industries in the last few years have had an infamous run of bad publicity relating to drug treatments. Unfortunately, their behaviors can easily be attributed to the economic system's instrumental rationality, where market norms and values trump values like public safety and the general welfare. Many doctors are influenced by pharmaceutical companies to use their drugs, and often these drugs are used inappropriately. In one egregious example, in December 2006, a four-year-old child died in a small town near Boston from a combination of two anti-psychotic drugs, along with a powerful antiseizure medication, which she had been prescribed to treat ADHD and Bipolar Disorder— diagnoses she received when she was *two years old* (Wen, 2010). None of the three drugs she was prescribed was approved by the U.S. Food and Drug Administration to treat ADHD or for long-term use in bipolar disorder, and none was approved for young children. More recently, a major drug maker agreed to plead guilty and pay three billion dollars to resolve criminal and civil charges that it illegally marketed off-label uses for prescription drugs and failed to adequately report safety data. The settlement, a record for a U.S. health fraud case, includes a criminal fine of almost one *billion* dollars. The company pled guilty to misdemeanors for marketing two of its depression drugs for unapproved uses and for failing to report some clinical data on one of its diabetes drug. For years, according to the court records, the company failed to report data showing that their diabetes drug increased the risk of heart attack by as much as forty percent. In the case of one of its depression drugs, the company promoted the drug for use by children and teenagers, despite the U.S. Food and Drug Administration not approving it for patients under 18. In fact, a clinical trial had found that the drug made adolescents *more* likely to attempt suicide. The company also erroneously claimed its other depression drug was beneficial for weight loss and treating sexual dysfunction, although neither claim was supported by data. Whistleblowers said that the company gave doctors lavish trips and spa treatments in order to persuade them to prescribe the drug for unapproved uses, and also hired a company to write a medical journal article downplaying the risks.

The number of big drug companies that have been caught acting illegally is actually quite astonishing. A quick look at the newspaper headlines provides many examples. In January 2009, for example, according to NBC News, the American pharmaceutical giant Eli Lilly agreed to pay almost one and a half billion dollars for illegally promoting the drug Zyprexa. In September 2009, according to the New York Times, the drug maker Pfizer Inc. paid $2.3 billion dollars for improperly marketing thirteen different drugs, including Viagra. In April 2012, according to the New York Times, Johnson & Johnson and a subsidiary were ordered to pay more than one billion dollars for minimizing or concealing dangers associated with the antipsychotic drug Risperdal. And in May 2012, Abbott Laboratories settled for $1.6 billion dollars for false marketing of the antiepileptic and mood-stabilizing drug Depakote. And recently, in 2013, China detained several GSK executives for what the Chinese authorities claim is a pattern of bribery. These facts paint a picture of seriously flawed corporate incentives, according to Dean Baker, co-director of the Center for Economic and Policy Research.

> They are doing the calculation ... and it comes out in their favor that you might as well take the risk here. There is an enormous incentive for them to lie, cheat, steal, whatever, try and push these drugs (Baker, 2013).

For-Profit Law Enforcement

Another industry with perverse incentives is the for-profit prison industry, an industry that contracts with state and federal governments to provide incarceration facilities and services. Consider the following statistics from the 2011 Justice Policy Institute Report: Approximately 129,000 people were held in privately managed correctional facilities in the U.S. as of December 31, 2009 (JPI, 2011). This represents over 16% of federal and almost 7% of state prison populations. In the last ten years private prisons, especially the two largest private prison companies, Corrections Corporation of America (CCA) and GEO Group, have increased their share of the market by approximately 120% for federal prisoners and 33% for state level prisoners, even while the total number prisoners increased less than sixteen percent during this same period. Between 1997 and 2007, annual spending on corrections rose to a record seventy-four billion dollars. CCA and GEO Group alone generated almost $3 billion dollars in revenue in 2010. That is big business.

Remember that all economic stakeholders are motivated by the instrumental values of profit and the reduction of overhead costs, but for-profit prisons take it further than many would see as reasonable. Convict labor, for example, is an appealing way for private companies to lower the costs of doing business, especially labor costs. CCA and GEO, along with a third smaller operator, G4S (formerly Wackenhut), provide inmate labor to Fortune 500 corporations like Chevron, Bank of America, AT&T, and IBM at significantly reduced costs (Fraser & Freeman, 2012). Currently, nearly a million prisoners are working in areas such manufacturing, customer service call centers, and agriculture, while getting paid at subminimum wages, somewhere between one and five dollars per day. These workers are easy to control, stripped of political rights, and subject to martial discipline.

From an economic point of view, the perverse incentives in this particular industry take two forms. First, public prison employee unions exert a powerful influence for tough sentencing policies that lead to larger prison populations requiring additional prisons and personnel, which goes against the public good (we already imprison more citizens than any other country on earth; increasing that number does not improve society), and for-profit prisons may be even more efficient and effective than unions in lobbying for policies that would increase prison populations. Second, they will also naturally try to maximize the spread between the amount billed and the actual cost of delivering services. Privately owned, for-profit prison companies present themselves as more cost-effective and efficient than traditional, publically funded prisons run by state employees. However, these companies have a history of prison management problems, including failures to provide adequate medical care to prisoners; to control violence and escapes; and a high degree of criminal activity on the part of employees, including the sale of illegal drugs to prisoners. These problems are largely due to business incentives relating to resource costs and profitability, since for-profit prisons try to minimize staffing, training, benefits, and pay for their employees while maximizing the number of "beds" and the associated revenue.

Unfortunately, local governments are also seeing incarceration as a revenue generating option. First, local officials around the country have implemented a policy where indigent or poor defendants are jailed to help generate government revenue. According to the LA Times, for example, a particular jail in Benton County, Washington, had an average of 88 prisoners a day serving time for fines they couldn't pay, which equated to about 28% of the jail population (Anderson, 2016). Defendants are often given a choice between sitting in jail and joining a work crew, and the county would profit either way. Either the county was paid $70 a day for each jail cell occupied by a prisoner sitting out his or her fine, or the county would benefit from the free labor of the work crews doing landscaping, janitorial jobs and so on.

Another contentious practice is the use of civil forfeiture laws that allow police to seize cash, cars, and real estate, even if the owner is never charged with a crime. This practice has become so egregious that a rare moment of agreement between the two political parties has emerged: both Republican and Democratic parties have recently endorsed forfeiture reform. In the words of the Democratic Party platform, reform is necessary to "to protect people and remove perverse incentives for law enforcement to 'police for a profit.'" Unfortunately, pressure from law enforcement lobbyists has stopped any reform as yet. And the amount of money is staggering. For example, a recent Institute for Justice report found that total annual forfeiture revenue across 14 states for which the Institute for Justice could obtain forfeiture revenues for an extended period more than doubled from 2002 to 2013 (ILJ, 2015). Two specific examples in Arizona are particularly stunning. In one case law enforcement agents seized a house from a property owner who was later acquitted of criminal charges yet she still lost her house. In another example, police arrested a man for stealing auto parts and seized the truck he was driving, but the truck belonged to the man's mother, who had done nothing wrong (ILJ, 2015, p.0 18).

Beyond the obvious questions about private property laws and constitutional rights, this is troubling for a number of reasons. First, it presents law enforcement agencies with a financial stake that distorts law enforcement priorities, promoting the pursuit of property over the impartial administration of justice and also provides a way for these agencies to fund operations without approval or even knowledge of municipal commissions and legislatures (ILJ, 2015). Second, it makes the process too easy for law enforcement agencies and much too difficult for those victims who try to fight back. In most jurisdictions, police only need "probable cause" to seize cash, cars or other property. And once assets are seized, the owners will face long and costly litigation before they get it back.

In all of these examples, we see the perverse incentives of a society that allows predatory practices to grow despite the harm these practices inflict on society as a whole. What kind of society has towns partly funded by incarcerating people for being poor or homeless; government agencies that finance themselves through seizures of assets from people never arrested for a crime; private prisons that benefit private shareholders at the expense of the marginalized and poor?

Summary Thoughts

Economic activity is primarily an effort of adaptation to environmental realities, a network of productive structures and processes made up of capital, labor, production, and entrepreneurship through which members of a society provide for their material needs. Over time these development efforts improve the functional abilities of the economic system, and this expansion of functionality thereby increases the general welfare of society's members. However, by the middle of the nineteenth century, the idea that an economy was somehow separate from society had solidified, and this idea that markets had their own principles and logic led to significant changes in the ways that capital markets operated and how they were perceived. One result was that the economic systems within many modern societies developed an inappropriate ability to influence the larger sociocultural systems, in essence, "running society as an adjunct to the market" to paraphrase the historian Karl Polanyi.

The negative side-effects of capitalism are embodied in Habermas's distinction between the *systems world* and the *lifeworld*. With capitalism and its associated ideologies and values, the *systems world* can produce new social norms through the power of its wealth-producing economic system. As in the previous examples where corporations engage in cost-benefit analyses that calculate the value of human life in terms of legal risk, the market values of the system become normative as the system dominates the lives and livelihoods of its participants. Thus the "colonization of the lifeworld by the system," results from the marginalization of human patterns of work and interaction based on social values by the instrumental and manipulative interactions appropriate to the capitalist economic system and its market values.

Thus, modern society's economic systems have become alienated from the day-to-day lives of its members due to the same elements of modernity that have greatly improved the general welfare. The resulting economic power can have unintended consequences or perhaps not so unintended, yet perverse. For example, legislators in Arizona made efforts to *increase* incarceration rates for the for-profit prison by drafting laws written by a lobbying group whose major function is to advance private corporate interests.

The principles of capitalism have been well integrated into American society and their influence is persistent. Indeed, we have seen the recurrent rise and resurrection of neoliberal capitalism to the level of ideological dominance in the U.S. As we have already discussed, the reputation of free-market capitalism has risen and fallen over the last hundred years, each fall prefaced by an economic catastrophe, and yet has risen again. Surprisingly, the influence of financial capital remains politically powerful even now in the aftermath of the latest U.S. meltdown, and this suggests the power of an ideology firmly rooted in cultural life. According to Michael Ignatieff, former leader of the Canadian Liberal Party and now a scholar at Harvard,

> From 1945 to the early 1970s we lived in a Bretton Woods world in which sovereigns exerted control over the movement of capital; beginning in the Seventies and Eighties we dismantled that regulatory structure. We did more than that: we created an ideological dogma that government was invariably the problem and markets invariably the solution (2014).

Chapter 4

Consumption Problems

Any economic system requires both producers and consumers to function, and this need for consumers is certainly powerful in the United States, where personal consumption accounts for up to *seventy percent* of the economy, the highest in the industrialized world (worldbank.org). Therefore, many American business interests rely on a dependable and expanding customer base. In the field of economics, the notion of consumer sovereignty asserts that the desires and needs of consumers control the output of producers and sellers, and this implies that the purchasing habits of the public dictate the form and scope of economic activity in any capitalist society. However, one look at the introduction of my old undergraduate economics textbook reminds me that the general consensus is that human wants and desires are *unlimited*. This suggests that consumer sovereignty is a myth; if human wants are unlimited then the producers and sellers of goods have the power, not consumers.

One major cultural development in this regard has been the steady rise of consumerism or materialism that is presented as a kind of ideology, which not only promotes consumption but also legitimizes it. Consumerism is the belief that a person's wellbeing and happiness depends to a very large extent on the level of that person's consumption, particularly the purchasing of material goods. In a consumerist society people devote a great deal of time, energy, and thought to material goods, and globally, consumption is increased by the expansion of this ideology around the world. In many respects, however, the power of the economic system and its associated ideologies has made consumption into a cultural phenomenon, connecting material goods with cultural meaning. The sociologist Don Slater suggests that consumer culture is a social system in which the relations between the *lifeworld*, the lived experience of everyday life, and the material resources upon which our everyday lives depend are now mediated through markets, and that "all social relations, activities, and objects, can, in principle, be exchanged as commodities" (Slater 1997, p.10). According to anthropologist William Mazzarella, this diffusion of consumer culture is "at one and the same time, ideology and social process, as something continuously made and remade through constantly shifting relations, practices, and technologies" of the market (2004, p. 355).

The dominance of consumer culture is impossible to ignore today and represents a triumph of economic interests that have strategically influenced the cultural landscape here and abroad. Indeed, the historian Peter Stearns claims, "we live in a world permeated by consumerism" (2001, p. ix). And, although many stakeholders argue that the economic system simply responds to consumer demands, it is clear that the capitalist economic system attempts to elevate consumption and materialism over other social values. In fact, many scholars argue that consumerism has replaced the social or political ideologies of the past and has become an almost universal orientation to the world. In the words of Paul James, an expert on globalization and cultural diversity,

> In the almost complete absence of other sustained macro-political and social narratives – concern about global climate change notwithstanding – the pursuit of the 'good life' through practices of what is known as 'consumerism' has become one of the dominant global social forces, cutting across differences of religion, class, gender, ethnicity and nationality (James & Szeman, 2010, p. x).

Permissive Politics

The prevalence of consumer capitalism has significant social and political implications but also has a direct effect on health and wellbeing. Research clearly shows that materialistic values are associated with unpleasant emotions, depression and anxiety, and physical health problems (Kasser, 2014). In fact, some of the most unfortunate side-effects of consumer capitalism involve an insidious pattern: the creation of problems by certain economic stakeholders, problems caused by easy credit, smoking, overeating, gambling, and so on, and then the development of products or services that propose to help with those same problems by other economic stakeholders. Instead of solving the problems, however, the stakeholders create a symbiotic and parasitical system whereby the social problems often worsen but the economic outlook for those stakeholders expands. In an online article in 2012, for example, the economist Kenneth Rogoff pointed out a problem in Western capitalism that results when lax regulatory oversight by the political system is combined with profit-driven efforts by corporations. This situation, which he refers to as an "unhealthy political-regulatory-financial dynamic," allows for troubling and deleterious effects within a society based largely on the promotion of consumption as a social good, but without regard to the social costs that result from consumption. He cites the food industry as an example, and its connection to the troubling statistics about obesity here in America and abroad. One-third of all adult in the U.S. are obese, and one-sixth of all children. Rogoff's point is that, even though society as a whole bears the costs of obesity-related problems, specific economic stakeholders connected to the problem thrive.

> Big agriculture gets paid for growing the corn (often subsidized by the government), and the food processors get paid for adding tons of chemicals to create a habit-forming – and thus irresistible – product. Along the way, scientists get paid for finding just the right mix of salt, sugar, and chemicals to make the latest instant food maximally addictive; advertisers get paid for peddling it; and, in the end, the health-care industry makes a fortune treating the disease that inevitably results (Rogoff, 2012).

Given the health risks and quality of life issues associated with obesity, the political system has paid little attention to this issue, especially since there are a number of direct and indirect economic ramifications related to this epidemic problem. Many of the costs of this epidemic are externalized, meaning that society bears the costs (in terms of health care costs, lost productivity, etc.) but the corporations that actually contribute to the problems, such as those in advertising and food production, retain the profits. And, since investors can share in the profits generated by these public organizations, the stock market benefits as well. The problem becomes both political and educational since politicians increasingly are seen as viewing business interests as the more important constituents in their legislative efforts. Members of the food industry and agribusiness make substantial donations, and "politicians who dared to talk about the health, environmental, or sustainability implications of processed food would in many cases find themselves starved of campaign funds" (Rogoff, 2012).

But the problem becomes even more unfair because the political system limits the necessary educational initiatives to combat the problem. Rogoff claims that consumers are habitually misinformed by advertising campaigns, but this misinformation is not effectively countered by the more reliable sources of public information such as schools, libraries, or health campaigns. Children are particularly at risk in this system since they watch so much television. There is limited high-quality public television programming, and children are more likely to be exposed to the misleading advertising found on the commercial television channels and not exposed to any critical evaluation of those advertisement claims. Although it went unmentioned in his editorial, Rogoff was echoing the ideas presented by social critics like Jürgen Habermas 40 years ago, who claimed that the economic system subjects people to its imperatives, consumerism and possessive individualism, and the media-induced desire for things becomes a social norm. But this is accomplished in a way where the public is subtly influenced to keep the economic system going without reflection or scrutiny.

From Puritanism to Consumerism

As previously mentioned, traditional American values were based on thrift and self-sufficiency, and the process of elevating the consumption of goods to the level of a public good has a long and interesting history. The Protestant culture of nineteenth-century America emphasized both economic activity and moderation and frugality. Charity, thrift, and hard work were the signs of God's favor, but so was the accumulation of capital, of wealth. The sociologist Max Weber argued that "the earning of more and more money, combined with the strict avoidance of all spontaneous enjoyment of life" was one of the highest ideals of Protestantism, and this methodical attitude about the acquisition of wealth was partly responsible for the modern social evolution that had begun with the Industrial Revolution (1946, p. 53).

However, by the late 19th century, the Protestant values of moderation and thrift were increasingly antithetical to the needs of the capitalist system. Modern economic systems were no longer interested in simply producing and building. As the production advances of the Industrial Age continued to accelerate, manufacturing interests became concerned about consumption capacity. Goods were being produced more efficiently and more cheaply, but those goods had to be purchased and consumed if the expansion of the capitalist system was to continue. It wasn't enough anymore to work hard, produce, and prosper; now people were required to consume in order to fulfill the economic system's imperatives. This new task required a change in cultural values, and values are not easily modified.

In general, during the 19th and early 20th century, people generally purchased only household necessities like food, clothing, and appliances, and only the wealthy elite engaged in frivolous, conspicuous consumption. Values like thrift and discipline were integrated into the fabric of public discourse and perpetuated generationally through the socialization of children by parents and teachers. Self-reliance and simplicity were celebrated in American arts and literature and enshrined in our most cherished doctrines.

Nevertheless, industrial producers realized that the public would need to be persuaded to consume at higher levels than were strictly necessary, and to that end pushed to transform American and European culture into what most scholars today recognize as a global consumer culture. The extent of this transformation is nowhere more salient than in the advice to the public that President George W. Bush gave immediately following the monumental terrorist attack in NYC in September of 2001. Confirming the dominance of the economic system at the heart of national interests, he entreated, "I ask your continued participation and confidence in the American economy." More cynical members of the press reduced his comments to "keep shopping."

In the historian William Leach's book, *Land of Desire*, he suggests that by the turn of the twentieth century, "American corporate business, in league with key institutions, began the transformation of American society into a society preoccupied with consumption, with comfort and bodily well-being, with luxury, spending, and acquisition, with more goods this year than last, more next year than this." (1993, xiii.) According to Leach, Protestant frugality was, in a sense, delegitimized, and replaced with "acquisition and consumption as the means of achieving happiness; the cult of the new; the democratization of desire; and money value as the predominant measure of all value in society" (pg. 3). This new consumer culture supplanted the long-standing Christian traditions and values that had dominated American society since its founding, instilling the notion that happiness would be achieved through the consumption of material goods rather than through productive enterprise and the traditional Christian values of thrift and moderation. As a result, the rise of consumer culture "diminished American public life, denying the American people access to insight into other ways of organizing and conceiving life, an insight that might have endowed their consent to the dominant culture with real democracy" (Leach, 1993, xv.). In a similar vein, the historian T. J. Lears suggests that, by the early twentieth century, the United States and parts of Europe underwent a transformation of values from those that emphasized "perpetual work, compulsive saving, civic responsibility, and a rigid morality of self-denial" to those that sanctioned "periodic leisure, compulsive spending, apolitical passivity, and an apparently permissive (but subtly coercive) morality of individual fulfillment" (Lears 1981, pg. 3).

In fact, consumption was promoted as a civic virtue after World War II. Americans had to be prodded, however, to participate after the effects of a devastating depression in the 1930s and the scrimping required of them during the war. Despite resistance, however, "business leaders, labor unions, government agencies, the mass media, advertisers, and many other purveyors of the new postwar order conveyed the message that mass consumption was ... a civic responsibility designed to improve the living standards of all Americans" (Cohen, 2004, p. 236). According to historian Liz Cohen, consumption would drive prosperity, create more well-paying jobs, and stoke the economy (Cohen, 2004). Apparently in the late 1940s Bride magazine made this explicitly clear when it told its readers that, through consumption, "you are helping to build greater security for the industries of this country... What you buy and how you buy it is very vital in your new life—and to our whole American way of living" (Harvey 1993, p. 110, cited in Cohen, 2004).

Some scholars rightly point out that human beings have always sought material comfort, and the spread of consumer culture is a natural aspect of social evolution with obvious and significant advantages. In an online article at Reason.com, James Twitchell, a professor of English and Advertising at the University of Florida, while not a staunch defender of capitalism, makes the point that capitalism provides goods and services because people demand them. "Getting and spending have been the most passionate, and often the most imaginative, endeavors of modern life" (Twitchell, 2000, p. 4). He is dismissive of the notion that consumers are manipulated dupes, victimized by a predatory economic system, a view he refers to as "Marxism-Lite." Further, he points out that consumption is largely a symbolic process:

> The idea that consumerism creates artificial desires rests on
> a wistful ignorance of history and human nature, on the
> hazy, romantic feeling that there existed some halcyon era of
> noble savages with purely natural needs. Once fed and shel
> tered, our needs have always been cultural, not natural. Un-

til there is some other system to codify and satisfy those
needs and yearnings, capitalism--and the culture it carries
with it--will continue not just to thrive but to triumph (2000).

Yet in the same article Twitchell admits that consumerism has
many drawbacks: it is wasteful and focuses only on the present
without care for the future. "It overindulges and spoils the young
with impossible promises. It encourages recklessness, living beyond
one's means, gambling ... It is heedless of the truly poor who cannot gain access to the loop of meaningful information that is carried
through its ceaseless exchanges." In an even more telling comment,
he admits, "On a personal level, I struggle daily to keep [consumer-
ism] at bay" (2000).

The Symbolism of Consumption

The idea that markets mediate the relationship between the lived
cultural experience of everyday life and the material and social
resources upon which we depend has serious implications, and
therefore a brief history of the symbolism of consumption is in
order. The evolution of consumption as an element of social status
is a topic well described by Thorstein Veblen, an American economist and sociologist, and critic of capitalism. In his book *The Theory
of the Leisure Class*, written in 1899, Veblen addresses the evolutionary roots of the division of labor, the class system, and the resulting differences in consumption behavior.

The evolution of the class system, according to Veblen, and the
emergence of a leisure class is the result of an ancient distinction
between worthy employments, "those which may be classed as
exploit," and unworthy, "those necessary everyday employments
into which no appreciable element of exploit enters" (Veblen, 1934,
p. 7-8). These distinctions corresponded to the superiority of exploit
and the inferiority of drudgery, drudgery being the menial but necessary work of daily life. Historically, the earliest hunter-gatherer
societies were simple and egalitarian, and everyone did what they
could to help the tribe survive. There were long periods of time that
allowed for peaceful coexistence. However, occasional competition
for scarce resources eventually led to a more predatory social environment in which skirmishes and raids against neighboring tribes
became more necessary and common, and this contributed to a
change in values within these early human communities. Social
differentiation among hunter-gathers became possible through a
process that Veblen calls "invidious comparison." An invidious

comparison is "a comparison of persons with a view to rating and grading them in respect of relative worth or value... An invidious comparison is a process of valuation of persons in respect of worth" (p. 25). The result was that the "activity of the men more and more takes on the character of exploit" and the acquisition and display of booty and trophies became valued as tangible evidence of prowess and strength.

> Aggression becomes the accredited form of action, and boo-
> ty serves as prima facie evidence of successful aggression. As
> accepted at this cultural stage, the accredited, worthy form
> of self-assertion is contest; and useful articles or services ob-
> tained by seizure or compulsion, serve as a conventional
> evidence of successful contest (p. 14).

One result of this elevation of exploitive action is a dramatic decrease in the value of mundane productive work. The valuable and necessary work performed in areas like farming, tending, and building are suddenly seen as undignified and "labour becomes irksome" (p. 15).

These changes in values led to two very significant cultural developments, the ownership of property and the extension of ownership to include the ownership of women (and the products of their industry) through an exploitative and coercive form of marriage. Both of these developments arose from the desire of successful men to advertise their prowess by "exhibiting some durable result of their exploits." This is a very insightful observation that Veblen makes, that the concepts of private property and wealth have their origins not just in the usefulness of those things or the material benefits of their accumulation but in the symbolic meanings that those goods represent to others. Property and other forms of wealth provided a way of differentiating their owners from less successful men, allowing the invidious comparisons to be made between their possessor and the enemy from whom they were taken, and also to distinguish their possessor from other members of the group.

Thus, according to Veblen, the entire institution of ownership and the development of "all those features of the social structure which this institution touches" are based on the simple fact that "the possession of wealth confers honour" (1934, p. 20). As the cultures and material circumstances of those early human communities advanced, wealth came to be valued less as a symbol of prowess and more as a form of distinction among others within the community. The possession of wealth became a way to elevate oneself and one's family within the community in terms of honor and esteem, and it was no longer important whether the wealth was "acquired aggressively by one's own exertion or passively by transmission through inheritance from others." Either way, wealth became "intrinsically honourable." Where property and trophies were once evidence of prowess and strength, now the possession of wealth was a "meritorious act" all on its own, and families could perpetuate their wealth through inheritance without losing any of the symbolic honor associated with it.

As Veblen suggested, "the motive that lies at the root of ownership is emulation," the desire to compare oneself positively against a competitor or opponent, and the accumulation and display of wealth is how those "invidious comparisons" are judged. This type of differentiation based on wealth represents a clear basis for evaluations of people in terms of "class" in the symbolic sense of "low class" and so on, and Veblen ties this type of "class" distinction to psychological factors like self-perception and social comparison, and how they contribute to what we now call class envy. Veblen makes the astute psychological claim that "only individuals with an aberrant temperament can, in the long run, retain their self-esteem in the face of the disesteem of their fellows" (1934, p. 22). In any community, a certain standard of wealth and ability, a baseline of respectability, is necessary for acceptance and wellbeing. Anything in excess of this baseline is considered meritorious and a reason for justified pride, and those who fall below this baseline "suffer in the esteem of their fellow-men; and consequently they suffer also in their own esteem, since the usual basis of self-respect is the respect accorded by one's neighbours" (p. 25).

The idea that large and obvious discrepancies in wealth among members of a community have significant psychological effects on those members, especially on the way those who have the least wealth are viewed by themselves and the rest of the community is undisputed today. For example, research on workplace dynamics has shown that sharing salary or wage details is still one of the great taboos in America. In fact, the Institute for Women's Policy Research found that almost half of all workers in the U.S. "are either contractually forbidden or strongly discouraged from discussing their pay with their colleagues" (Hegewisch, et al., 2011).

For the wealthy elites, those in "the superior pecuniary class," however, wealth must be displayed at all costs in order to secure the esteem of others and the resulting self-esteem.

> It is not sufficient merely to possess wealth or power. The wealth or power must be put in evidence, for esteem is awarded only on evidence. And not only does the evidence of wealth serve to impress one's importance on others and to keep their sense of his importance alive and alert, but it is of scarcely less use in building up and preserving one's self-complacency (Veblen, 1934, p. 26).

Thus, there is a basic desire for conspicuous consumption and leisure. As has been true throughout the history of human development, the possession of wealth must be displayed in order to derive the symbolic benefits of it, and an abundance of wealth can be displayed most clearly in the wasteful spending of money and time in extravagant consumption and leisure that wealth affords.

Veblen's observations remain relevant and insightful even in today's global culture, and every branch of the social sciences recognizes the fact that consumer goods have a symbolic value as well as utility value: they can symbolize distinction, taste, lifestyle orientation, and social status. Behaviors, including consumer behaviors, are perceived within the context of their shared symbolic meanings. The meaning of any behavior is subjective, but socially defined behaviors become significant as they take on consensual meaning, and this is exactly what the advertising and marketing industries do. Terms like "branding" and other marketing techniques are attempts to attach and promote particular positive meanings to consumer commodities in an effort to make those commodities more desirable. This is the same for human social interaction where symbolic meanings are communicated among people via style and quality of dress, hairstyle, and language use. So, for example, a luxury automobile like the Italian-made Maserati can be both useful and valuable as a vehicle, but a Maserati also has a symbolic status within society, signifying wealth, good taste, and social distinction.

From a more modern perspective, the French philosopher Jacques Baudrillard asserts this same conclusion in *The Consumer Society*, that consumption functions as another language by which humans communicate and interact with one another. However, this language is based on commodities, which are not simply defined by their use, but also, and mainly, by what they signify. "And what they signify is defined not by what they do, but by their relationship to the entire system of commodities and signs" (1970, p. 7). Consumption is laden with symbolic meaning, and objects are symbols of happiness or misery, affluence, or poverty. "We are at the point where consumption is laying hold of the whole of life" (p. 29).

Consumer Identity as Social Identity

Social relations have changed significantly over the course of the last century and consumerism has been responsible for many of those changes, partly by integrating cultural norms and values so tightly with the world of objects. It is no stretch of the imagination to claim that consumer commodities have colonized even the psychological systems of modern humans, altering their sense of "self" and the world around them. Today, it is widely accepted that individual identities are bounded and informed by the symbolic language of *things*. However, this language is based on commodities, which are not simply defined by their use, but also, and mainly, by what they signify. "And what they signify is defined not by what they do, but by their relationship to the entire system of commodities and signs," according to Baudrillard (1970, p. 7). Consumption is laden with symbolic meaning, and objects are symbols of happiness or misery, affluence, or poverty. Unfortunately, many of the identities promoted by the capitalist system are antithetical to happiness and well-being.

Identity is described as an individual's internalized self-representation based on the meanings attached to that individual's statuses and functions within a given social structure. Following the work of sociologist G.H. Mead (1934), who claimed that society, through the process of socialization, shaped the development of the individual, the self can be understood as a multidimensional construct that reflects the characteristics of the social system from which it emerges. In our current consumption-based societies, commodities have become tools for the formation of identity and the establishment of social relations. Individuals buy and use certain products as communicative mechanisms to create, develop and maintain their identities, and purchase various product brands for the same reasons (Escalas & Bettman, 2005). Consider one of the most ubiquitous forms of consumer advertising, the promise of creating a new "self." Advertising offers the image of the transformed self and consumption offers the means of effecting that transformation. One example of this transformational offer is the idea of the "makeover."

A 1985 subscription solicitation for the women's magazine Glamour offered the following: "If you'll give me just a few minutes of your time now, I honestly believe that I can help you change almost anything about yourself that you want to..." (Stromberg, 1990). These types of magazines promise the opportunity to create a new self through the careful selection and use of products like clothing and makeup, and the opportunities are made more plausible, more desirable, and more necessary by the articles and advertising within them.

This concept, the idea of managing and even changing one's identity through consumption behavior, is widely accepted in today's marketing industry. This view is in accord with sociologist J.B. Thompson's argument that individuals are "symbolic projects" (1995, p. 210). According to Thompson, individuals utilize available symbolic materials including those associated with consumption to actively construct a coherent identity. Marketing expert Russell Belk has developed a similar concept he calls the *extended self,* suggesting, "we are what we have" (1988, p.160). The extended self-involves possessions and, more importantly, the experience attached to those possessions. Thus, various aspects of consumer behavior, including buying, giving, or disposing of possessions are major contributors to and reflections of self-identity.

The rise of symbolic consumption behavior can be traced back to the nineteenth century when economic and social instability increased as industrialization and imperialism created new opportunities for the rising middle-classes (Fromer, 2008). Rising standards of living and cheaper mass-produced commodities created a fragmented range of groups that differed in occupation, religious affiliation, and political views but were unified by their levels of income, spending power, and a shared consumer culture (p. 6). Social categories, statuses, and identities were evolving. Consumption practices produced new identification categories and new hierarchies of status, new ways of identifying oneself and one's status. Since then, consumption choices are often driven by symbolic outcomes rather than practical needs, such as the desire to make statements about oneself in relation to others, or to differentiate themselves from others (Kadirov and Varey, 2006). For example, research shows that items such as sunglasses and fashion clothing, particularly those brands regarded as being of high status, are conspicuously consumed, and specifically intended to project a certain self-image or to maintain acceptance in particular social groups (O'Cass & McEwen, 2004). A study of British consumer behavior in regard to automobiles found that cars were used as symbols of identity and social status, especially high-status brands such as BMW or Jaguar or Mercedes (Froud et al., 2005). A brand is a complex set of manufactured elements designed to create the promise of differentiation in the mind of the consumer (Okazaki, 2006). These "self-brand connections" assist in "actively creating one's self-concept, reinforcing and expressing self-identity, and allowing one to differentiate oneself and assert individuality" (Escalas & Bettman, 2005, p. 378).

There are potential problems with this type of object-based identity construction, however. First, stable internal sources such as personal capacities and relationships with others are much better foundations to a stable sense of self than are objects and their associated brand images that we purchase and consume. Secondly, these connections are being pushed onto younger and younger members of society and there is a great deal of potential harm in pressuring children to develop a self-image based on guidance from the marketing departments of global corporations.

Economic intrusions

In many ways, the strategic marketing and product expansion efforts signify an incursion of the *systems world* into the *lifeworld,* incursions that rely on rational, *but alien,* norms and values to manipulate the most sacrosanct areas of human life. In fact, one major theme of this book is that economic values and norms that emphasize consumption are fully integrated into cultural institutions that were historically free from economic intrusion, like child-rearing and education. For example, companies like Disney Corporation have long targeted children as customers, and, according to the New York Times, Disney has recently succeeded in turning the "Disney Princess" suite of dolls and costumes, marketed to preschoolers, into a $4 billion dollar a year profit source by tying together TV and cinema programming with merchandise (Applebaum, 2014). But preschoolers aren't the youngest targets at Disney. Since 2011, they have been pushing products like Disney Baby bodysuits for *infants.* Disney and other companies have also aggressively marketed "Baby Einstein" videos for infants, manipulating parents with the hope of giving those children a competitive edge in life. The "kidvid" educational video industry is vast, and many of the products focus on infants. But there was no evidence that they actually work, and Disney at one point was forced to provide refunds to some customers. In fact, a study published in the Journal of Pediatrics in 2007 found that infants aged 8 and 16 months who regularly watched Baby Einstein and Brainy Baby videos showed language development *deficits* compared to infants who did not watch them (Zimmerman, et al., 2007). Even worse, the deficits increased the more time infants were exposed to the videos. The point is that economic actors like Disney and hundreds of others have inserted themselves into an area of family life that was once non-economic, and are actively trying to turn even the youngest children into consumers.

There are a number of unfortunate side-effects associated with these efforts. According to the cultural scholar Henry Giroux, American society has experienced a major change in cultural attitudes related to the lives of children during the last thirty years, marked by a major transition from innocence and social protection to commodification and manipulation. This undermines the ideals of a secure and happy childhood and exhibits what Giroux calls the "bad faith" of a corporate system more interested in profits than in the well-being of the public (2001). Many scholars recognize that the United States has become the most "consumer-oriented society in the world" (Schor, 2004). But more significantly, children are now at "the epicenter of American consumer culture," because of their value as consumers and their ability to influence the spending habits of their parents, and this makes them major targets of powerful corporate marketing forces (Schor, 2004, p. 20).

The issue is a much deeper one than toys and products, and psychological research confirms the effect that these incursions have on the development processes of children themselves. The American social scientist Beryl Langer has done a great deal of research in this particular area. Specifically, Langer addresses the effects of "a media-saturated society" in which the socialization process is "no longer exclusively generated by face-to-face relations in everyday life" (2005). Instead, the mass media and its relentless promotion of materialism have become significant sources of cultural information. Now, writes Langer, children are socialized in relation to "a social form that depends on the reproduction of desiring selves whose longing for purchasable pleasures is continuously stimulated by an ever expanding market" (p. 259). Her particular emphasis is on the logic of consumer capitalism and its effect on children's sense of identity. Commercial, or popular, culture is an important source of symbolic material for children as they work on "their projects of self." The logic of the global economic system, however, means that "the symbolic resources for children's self-formation are increasingly 'commercial' in origin, and children's capacity for spontaneity and creativity is exercised within a commercially constituted life world" (p. 262).

According to Langer and others, material culture in the industrialized nations has been transformed in the last quarter century, and one of the largest changes as been in the production and marketing of children's goods. Langer warns that children are being taught that material acquisitiveness is "the primary activity of consumer capitalist personhood" (Langer, 2005, p. 267). The result of this transformation is that children are now being socialized into a repeating cycle of fashion and obsolescence that fuels economic growth and profits. Consider that a survey by the Kaiser Family Foundation found that children between the ages of 8 and 18 spend on average 53 hours per week using media devices such as laptops, cell phones, and TVs through which they are routinely exposed to advertising (Rideout et al., 2010). An older version of the survey revealed that almost thirty percent of two- to three-year-olds had TV sets in their bedrooms and forty-three percent had them by age four (Rideout, et al., 2006). And consider that the Federal Communication Commission (FCC) deregulated advertising to children way back in 1984, around the time that these broad transformations began.

Growing up in a media-saturated social environment that celebrates materialism and individualism presents a particular set of problems for children in terms of identity formation, and consumption-based marketing often exacerbates those problems. As the social theorist Anthony Giddens explained, "A self-identity has to be created and more or less continually reordered against the backdrop of "shifting experiences" of day-to-day life and the fragmenting tendencies of modern institutions" (2003, p. 198). Advertising and marketing campaigns normalize consumption as a way of life, and this has its own problems, but the symbolic messages of advertising present a deeper issue, striking at the development of identity in the most vulnerable members of society. For example, research shows that a person's sense of self may be distorted or impaired by the ubiquitous idealized techniques and images used to sell products.

Consider the promotion of the pervasive "ideal body" and sexualized female imagery so common in contemporary advertising. Women's issues scholar Jean Kilbourne and psychologist Diane Levin identify this imagery as a form of societal peer pressure that contributes to the development of eating disorders and other un-healthy behavior in adolescent girls (Levin & Kilbourne, 2009). Many scientific studies bear this out. A study by Anne Becker, direc-tor of research at the Eating Disorders Center of Harvard Medical School, for example, found a sharp rise in eating disorders among young women in Fiji soon after the introduction of television to that particular culture. Her team interviewed two groups of secondary school girls in Fiji, first in 1995, one month after satellites began beaming television signals to the region, and again in 1998. By 1998, the researchers found that girls who said they watched television three or more nights a week were fifty percent more likely to de-scribe themselves as "too big or fat" and thirty percent more likely to diet than girls who watched television less frequently (Becker, et al., 2002).

The sexualization of young girls has also become more common in advertising and more extreme. For example, padded bras and thongs for seven-year-olds are now sold in major department stores. *Age compression* is the popular term that describes how younger children are doing what older children used to do. Accord-ing to a Canadian Broadcasting Corporation broadcast in 2005, age compression is a marketing strategy in which adult products and attitude are pushed on younger kids.

> The media, the toys, the behavior, the clothing once seen as appropriate for teens are now firmly ensconced in the lives of tweens and are rapidly encroaching on and influencing the lives of younger children. There is a blurring of bounda-ries between children and adults, as demonstrated by the similarities in clothing marketed to both by the fashion in-dustry (Levin & Kilbourne, 2009).

Especially since the deregulation of advertising to children in the U.S. in 1984, according to the cultural scholar Henry Giroux, child-hood had become completely exploited by corporate interests who transformed childhood into "a market strategy and a fashion aes-thetic used to expand the consumer-based needs of privileged adults who live within a market culture that has little concern for ethical considerations, non-commercial spaces, or public responsi-bilities" (2001, p. 18). This means that the increasingly sophisticated marketing campaigns and media-linked product offerings are a major force in children's development, but a force that children often barely understand. For instance, when young children see advertising or product-based programs, they focus on the most graphic, concrete aspects of what they see, but cannot put the product they see in a meaningful context (Levin & Carlsson-Paige, 2006).

Unfortunately, girls do learn to see themselves and other girls as objects and start evaluating each other based on their appearances. Boys learn to judge girls in the same way, as objects (Levin & Kilbourne, 2009). This objectification is easily recognized in fashion advertising, where children are regularly shown in sexualized situations and positions. In fact, Giroux asserts that "sexualizing children may be the final frontier in the fashion world" (2001, p. 60). For example, ABC news in August 2011 reported that a model on the cover of a current issue of French Vogue was only ten years old at the time (Moisse, 2011). As girls are taught from an early age that their sexualized behavior and appearance are often rewarded by society, they're often encouraged to view their own behaviors as an active choice, a declaration of empowerment, and a component of their own identity. But in 2007 the American Psychological Association reported that girls exposed to sexualized images from a young age are more prone to depression, eating disorders, and low self-esteem. Also, perhaps coincidentally, the United States has the highest rate of teen pregnancy and sexually transmitted diseases in the developed world (APA, 2007).

Marketing and Manipulation

There is a deep irony at the heart of this consumerist ideology, exemplified by writers like Twitchell who celebrate consumerism even as they struggle to keep it at bay in their own lives. In some ways, the economic system has harnessed the powerful techniques associated with science and rationality to induce an *irrational* pattern of behavior within the social system. Behavioral psychology, market research, and the ability of economic interests to "mine" the personal data generated by millions of people when they use communications technologies like the Internet, are all popular sources of insight used by economic actors to influence social behavior. Thirty years ago, the social theorist Jürgen Habermas warned that the capitalist economic system subjects private households, employees, and consumers to its imperatives, consumerism and possessive individualism. Those imperatives lead to competition and social comparison, which give them the power to shape human actions and interactions (1984). He also suggested that the influence of commercial media on social life promotes an antagonistic "hedonism freed from the pressures of rationality" (p. 325). Wanting things becomes a norm; it becomes practically our duty to keep the system going without too much reflection. So, while society itself becomes increasingly administered via rational and bureaucratic methods, members of society are compelled, in their roles as consumers, to be irrational in their consumption habits, to become "desiring ma-chines," as the philosopher Gilles Deleuze put it.

There is a concept in psychology known as *the hedonic treadmill* which describes the tendency of humans to constantly seek new forms of pleasure and satisfaction because the psychological in-creases in happiness and satisfaction that we experience when we attain some new product or service are temporary, and eventually return to a baseline level. We have been convinced that we can be happier, so we seek this heightened happiness even though time and time again we find ourselves back where we started. This is partly a product of the ongoing scientific revolution, according to historian Christopher Lasch (1991). Scientific inquiry served,

> … as a model for the distinctive conception of history asso-ciated with the promise of universal abundance. Just as each advance accomplished by the critical intelligence was des-tined to be superseded by the next, so the definition of hu-man needs and wants was thought to expand as those needs and wants were progressively satisfied" (p. 328).

A general historical assumption about consumption trends has been that once scarcity is eliminated, once the population could meet their daily needs for food, shelter, and so on, consumption would level off because wants would have been satisfied. However, decades ago the American economist John Kenneth Galbraith identi-fied corporations as a powerful force for shaping wants, and their advertising efforts are able to influence behavior on several levels. Incidentally, he also declared that the myth of the corporation as the puppet of the market, the powerless servant of the consumer, is one of the devices by which economic power is perpetuated in a capitalist society. In *The Affluent Society* (1958), Galbraith claimed that con-sumer behavior in affluent societies was significantly shaped by cor-porate manipulation, and that firms are less preoccupied with *satisfy-ing* want than with *creating* it. One of his main points was that the productive capacity of a society affected the cultural values of that society, and the desire for status and identity linked to goods and services increased as productive power increased.

> The urge to consume is fathered by the value system which
> emphasizes the ability of the society to produce. The more
> that is produced the more must be owned in order to main-
> tain the appropriate prestige. The latter is an important
> point, for... the production of goods creates the wants that
> the goods are presumed to satisfy (Galbraith, 1958, p. 121).

Galbraith suggested that ever increasing productive capacities of the economic system would influence the cultural values and norms regarding consumption so that, instead of tapering off, our desires would be relatively boundless, and he further pointed out that these consumer desires could be "synthesized by advertising, catalyzed by salesmanship, and shaped by the discreet manipulations of the persuaders" (Galbraith, 1958, p. 123). In *The New Industrial State* (1967), Galbraith's main argument again was that producers and the market were no longer simply responsive to the consumer but were actively engaged in shaping consumer behavior:

> The unidirectional flow of instruction from consumer to
> market to producer ... is no longer a description of the re-
> ality and is becoming ever less so. Instead the producing
> firm reaches forward to control its markets and on
> beyond to manage the market behavior and shape the so-
> cial attitudes of those, ostensibly, that it serves (Galbraith,
> 1967, pp. 211-212).

The integration of material goods with the psychologies of individuals has also created new and complex relationships. The sociologist Karin Knorr-Cetina writes about the "ways in which major classes of individuals have tied themselves to object worlds" (1997, p. 1). According to Knorr-Cetina, "the demise of community and traditions also leaves the individual in the lurch – without the psychological means to deal with the great freedom of choice or the contingency of contemporary life" (1997, p. 4), and so individuals engage in what she calls an "object-centred sociality," which is the creation of object-centered environments that "situate and stabilize selves, define individual identities just as much as communities or families used to do, and promote forms of sociality that feed on and supplement the forms of sociality studied by social scientists" (Knorr-Cetina & Breugger, 2000, p. 141). In fact, some of these theorists suggest that we may have reached a "post-social" point in our evolution.

One distinctive characteristic of the contemporary scenario
could be that perhaps for the first time in recent history it
appears unclear whether, for individuals, other persons are
indeed the most fascinating part of their environment — the
part we are most responsive to and devote most attention to
(p. 142).

Think of ATM machines and the demise of teller-based banking
interactions. "When person-to-person services are replaced by
automated electronic services, no social structures at all need to be
in place – only electronic information structures" (Knorr-Cetina &
Breugger, 2000, p. 6). The social and material relations in modern
culture have therefore changed significantly. Consider the role of
Twitter, a broadcast-type communication system that allows impersonal communications to reach a broad audience. Or consider
users of Facebook and their tally of "friends," many of whom are, in
fact, strangers with which the user has had no interaction.

Commodifying Culture

The term "culture industry" was perhaps used for the first time in
the book *Dialectic of Enlightenment*, written by the left-wing philosophers Theodore Adorno and Max Horkheimer in 1947. In it, they
described how the capitalistic economic system had subverted
cultural production and made it into a tool for perpetuating the
domination of capitalism over the masses. Capitalism accomplished this through the commoditization of cultural goods and the
subsequent promotion of commodity fetishism for those goods.

However, there is a potential problem when mass markets produce and sell cultural goods. To Adorno, modern popular culture
consists of cultural products like film, popular music, books, video
games, magazines, radio, soap operas, television shows, fashion,
and so on. The major problem with the mass production of cultural
commodities by the economic system is that it strips out the individuality, freedom, and creativity of these cultural products, in order
to achieve a broader, more inclusive audience. Cultural products
are commoditized and standardized for greater mass appeal, but at
the expense of the very things that make those goods valuable in the
first place. The rationalization process allows cultural production to
become an integrated component of the capitalist economy, turning it into a technical process, the production of commodities, but
it accomplishes this by de-emphasizing the qualitative aspects of

culture, the meaning of things, and instead emphasizing their exchange, or money value, or more simply, price.

Adorno recognized that the immediacy and originality of cultural expression are some of its most valuable characteristics, whether music or film, or any other cultural good. "But they nevertheless simultaneously fall completely into the world of commodities, are produced for the market, and are aimed at the market" (1991, p. 278). Thus, the products of culture, the ideas and values, the ideologies and technologies, are "repackaged" and promoted as consumer based commodities through a rationalization process that interprets cultural goods in economic or consumption based terms. For example, think of the effects of the consumer industry on our conceptions and norms of "love." Valentine's Day means we buy flowers and chocolate, engagements aren't authentic unless a diamond ring is involved, and so on.

The rationalization processes that are applied to cultural goods lead to two main effects. First, it produces a standardization of life experiences. Adorno and Horkheimer claimed in the 1940s that "Culture now impresses the same stamp on everything" (1991, p. 120), and that "Culture today is infecting everything with sameness" (p. 94). Second, the standardization leads to socialization effects that are at least partially driven by alien economic interests, and the influence that the culture industry exerts is organized and purposive: "Film, radio, and magazines form a system. Each branch of culture is unanimous within itself and all are unanimous together" (p. 94).

> Television isolates and standardizes. On the one hand, it removes people from traditionally shaped and bounded contexts of conversation, experience and life. At the same time, however, everyone is in a similar position: they all consume institutionally produced television programs, from Honolulu to Moscow and Singapore. The individualization — more precisely, the removal from traditional life contexts — is accompanied by a uniformity and standardization of forms of living (Beck, 1992, p. 132).

Why is it, do you think, that marriages in our society almost always include diamonds? How did diamonds become the cultural symbol for romantic love? The answer is, of course, a combination of production management, marketing, and the integration of diamonds into popular culture through the media. In comparison, what monetary value would you place on a poem or a book of poetry? Poetry is difficult to value in monetary terms because individual preferences and responses are so different among people. A poem that resonates with me may be meaningless to you. This is partly why the popularity of poetry is low compared to other forms of literature because the economic system has a hard time reducing it to exchange-value and therefore does not integrate it into cultural marketing efforts. Against this organized system of influence, the argument goes, the masses have little power. Consumers can exercise choice and make decisions about what they purchase but are subject to a variety of pressures, including manufacturing, retailing, and marketing strategies that are integrated and coercive.

> In all its branches, products which are tailored for consumption by masses, and which to a great extent determine the nature of that consumption, are manufactured more or less according to plan (Adorno, 1991, p. 98).

Adorno suggests that freedom of choice within the cultural sphere is being "colonized," to use Habermas's term, by the economic system bent on reducing the lifeworld to a predictable, structured commodity market, turning citizens into consumers regardless of the non-economic consequences.

> The culture industry intentionally integrates its consumers from above. To the detriment of both it forces together the spheres of high and low art, separated for thousands of years. The seriousness of high art is destroyed in speculation about its efficacy; the seriousness of the lower perishes with the civilizational constraints imposed on the rebellious resistance inherent within it (Adorno, 1991, p. 99).

Consider the evolution of rap and hip-hop music, which were once the raw artistic expressions that emerged from the poverty and racial oppression of African American experience, now standardized, packaged and promoted as a commodity like any other. The offensive and crude lyrics that shocked and alienated the rest of the country in the early days of rap are now one of its major selling points, the more misogynistic the better for the white, suburban, middle-class male customers eager to bask in the reflected "authenticity" of poor urban blacks. Or consider the ancient and timeless themes of human drama that were represented in the tragedies and comedies from ancient Greece and Shakespeare, now standardized and reproduced in prime-time television shows in such formulaic ways that it is hard to tell some shows apart. The authentic expressions of human experience via Art are varied and complex and are a major component of a community's cultural system, but those do not interest the economic system. Instead, it simply is interested in producing and managing the aspects of the cultural system that can be commoditized.

> Thus, although the culture industry undeniably speculates on the conscious and unconscious state of the millions towards which it is directed, the masses are not primary, but secondary, they are an object of calculation; an appendage of the machinery. The customer is not king, as the culture industry would have us believe, not its subject but its object (Adorno, 1991, p. 99).

Anomie

A question arises about why people would accept this encroachment of an alien, exchange-based economic system into their lives, lives generally guided by social values and meanings. The philosopher Theodore Adorno suggests that the masses adopt exchange-value orientations to cultural goods because consumer capitalism sucks away anything else. "It corresponds to the behaviour of the prisoner who loves his cell because he has been left nothing else to love" (1991, p. 38). "The same thing is offered to everybody by the standardized production of consumption goods" (p. 38), so people actually sacrifice individuality, and accommodate the industry's push for conformity. There is only the "pretence of individualism which necessarily increases in proportion to the liquidation of the individual" (p. 38).

The issue further resonates with Habermas's views in that the economy today promotes a consumption-based ideology, exerts tremendous power within society, but without any need for legitimation. There are no justifications given for standardization and commoditization, no explanations provided about the benefits of a consumption-oriented lifestyle, all this is simply glossed over through the advertising and marketing arms of the industry. As Adorno describes it, "the power of the culture industry's ideology is such that conformity has replaced consciousness. The order that springs from it is never confronted with what it claims to be or with the real interests of human beings" (1991, p. 104). This suggests that the economic system influences our social lives in unusual ways without any need for legitimating its power, nor does it need to take responsibility for its effects. While the industry claims to help people make wise choices, it actually "deludes them with false conflicts which they are to exchange for their own. It solves conflicts for them only in appearance, in a way that they can hardly be solved in their real lives" (Adorno, 1991, p. 104). The social theorist Erich Fromm has something similar to say in his book, *The Sane Society*.

> Actually, he is not free to enjoy "his" leisure; his leisure-time consumption is determined by industry, as are the commodities he buys; his taste is manipulated, he wants to see and to hear what he is conditioned to want to see and to hear; entertainment is an industry like any other, the customer is made to buy fun as he is made to buy dresses and shoes. The value of the fun is determined by its success on the market, not by anything which could be measured in human terms (1991, p. 132).

The sociologist Emile Durkheim, in his classic book *Suicide: A Study in Sociology*, identified the causes of a broad social unhappiness, or what he termed *anomie*. Originally published in 1897, in *Suicide* Durkheim poses a fundamental question about human needs: "But how determine the quality of well-being, comfort, or luxury legitimately to be craved by a human being? Nothing appears in man's organic or psychological constitution which sets a limit to such tendencies" (p. 208). In answering that question, Durkheim identifies a particular flaw in human nature, our boundless ability to desire:

> Unlimited desires are insatiable by definition and insatiability is rightly considered a sign of morbidity. Being unlimited, they constantly surpass the means at their command; they cannot be quenched. Inextinguishable thirst is constantly renewed torture (p. 208).

Over one hundred years ago, Durkheim suggested that, left unchecked, these desires create a multitude of psychological and social problems, "to pursue a goal which is by definition unattainable is to condemn oneself to a state of perpetual unhappiness...the more one has, the more one wants, since satisfactions received only stimulate instead of fulfilling needs" (1897, p. 209). For Durkheim, individuals have no way of limiting their own needs, so an external force is necessary. According to Durkheim, society in the form of the cultural *lifeworld* provides the crucial regulative framework for human desire, the force that limits our passions:

[S]ociety alone can play this regulating role, for it is the only moral power superior to the individual, the authority of which he accepts. It alone has the power necessary to stipulate law and to set the point beyond which the passions must not go (p. 209).

However, under exceptional circumstances, society becomes incapable of regulating the passions, and individuals slip into a state of anomie. This was how anomie became a chronic phenomenon over a century ago because regulation of the economic sphere was almost completely absent. "For a whole century, economic progress has mainly consisted in freeing industrial relations from all regulation" (p. 214).

The effects of anomie, like alienation, are grim, and further weaken the options for people to meaningfully engage the world while further strengthening the economic system that produces the anomie and alienation:

To sum up, the vast majority of the population ... sell their physical, or an exceedingly small part of their intellectual capacity to an employer to be used for purposes of profit in which they have no share, for things in which they have no interest, with the only purpose of making a living, and for some chance to satisfy their consumer's greed. Dissatisfaction, apathy, boredom, lack of joy and happiness, a sense of futility and a vague feeling that life is meaningless, are the unavoidable results of this situation (Fromm, 1991, pp. 287-88).

Summary Thoughts

It can easily be argued that the pursuit of the *good life* through consumerism has become one of the dominant global social forces, one that overrides differences of religion, class, and nationality and instead attempts to homogenize the social world into predictable and stable consumption-based markets. The philosopher Jacques Baudrillard warns of the growing dominance of this consumer-based ideology. "We are at the point where consumption is laying hold of the whole of life", he declared (1970, p. 29). Historically, America emphasized moderation and frugality, charity, thrift, and hard work. However, by the late 19th century, the economic system became concerned about consumption capacity and so people were suddenly pressured to consume in order to fulfill the economic system's imperatives. Since then the economic system has had crises and periods of stability, but overall, lax regulatory oversight by the political system combined with profit-driven efforts by corporations leads to an "unhealthy political-regulatory-financial dynamic," to quote the economist Kenneth Rogoff, and allows for troubling and deleterious effects within society (2012). For example, critics like the social theorist Laura Cerni warn that the constant marketing that perpetuates the ideology of consumer capitalism has significant social pitfalls (2007). It glosses over the unproductive character of consumption and promotes an alienated relationship between producers, products, and consumers without any higher purpose other than perpetuating the treadmill of consumption. According to Cerni, the result of this consumption-based relationship is a hollowed out existence, a "lived experience as a succession of isolated and superficial encounters that have no transcending aim" (2007, p. 11). The promotion of consumption as a social good, without regard to the social costs that result from consumption, has had and will continue to have significant negative side-effects. Further, consumption practices are now increasingly the basis of social status and even identity.

Thus, the economic system in its efforts to promote consumption has "colonized" previously protected areas of life and transformed them into markets. Always, according to the economic system, the answer to our needs and desires is some object, some information, some drug or other commodity, rather than the benefits we receive in relationship with other people, or the sense of fulfillment generated by our capacity to work or create, or in any other way find satisfaction in our lives in the absence of consumerism. Additionally, the economic system constantly seeks new markets within the lives and livelihoods of its participants. The historian Christopher Lasch described this process of expansion in his book, *Haven in a Heartless World* (1977). He explains that one of the key aspects of modern social development includes the assertion of social control by the capitalist economic system over activities once left to individuals or families. In essence, Lasch is describing a process that depends on the transformation of personal concerns and social relations into economic activity.

> During the first stage of the industrial revolution, capitalists took production out of the household and collectivized it, under their own supervision, in the factory. Then they proceeded to appropriate the workers' skills and technical knowledge, by means of "scientific management," and to

bring these skills together under managerial direction.
Finally they extended their control over the worker's private
life as well, as doctors, psychiatrists, teachers, child guidance
experts, officers of the juvenile courts, and other specialists
began to supervise child-rearing, formerly the business of
the family (1977, p. xxi).

The sexualization of girls, the marketing efforts to provide infants
with branded products to better snare them into a lifetime of brand
loyalty, and the *irrational* patterns of behavior promoted by economic interests are all examples of the colonization of the *lifeworld*
by the *systems world* that Habermas warned about, and the resulting anomie may help explain some of the widespread depression
and anxiety disorders that affect over sixty million Americans, twenty percent of the population, in any given year (CDC, 2012).

Chapter 5

Manipulation, Mass Media, and Democracy

As previously stated, the globalized capitalist economic system is very efficient in terms of scale and scope, but is amoral and much more concerned with profits and growth than social responsibility or equality. Dominated by powerful corporations, guided by instrumental rather than moral values, largely unconstrained, increasingly intrusive, and socio-politically influential, the side-effects of modern capitalism, coupled with popular ideologies like materialism and neoliberalism, lead to far-reaching problems across the human spectrum. In this chapter, we will explore one of the most significant problems, the political entanglements of the modern capitalist system, especially the neoliberal economic ideology shaping so much of the world's political efforts.

Margaret Thatcher, while Prime Minister of England, once famously declared during a magazine interview, "There is no such thing as society." The context of the quote was her view that people in Britain had developed an unreasonable expectation that "society" would help them cope with their problems through government largesse, an expectation that she discouraged. She went on to describe her view on the primacy of personal responsibility for our own well-being and the well-being of others,

> There is living tapestry of men and women and people and the beauty of that tapestry and the quality of our lives will depend upon how much each of us is prepared to take responsibility for ourselves and each of us prepared to turn round and help by our own efforts those who are unfortunate (1987).

I argue, however, that there is indeed such a thing as society, and that it can be understood in terms of its underlying cultural characteristics. In fact, the most basic definition of society is a group of people with a shared territory and culture. It is sometimes used as a synonym for the idea of a nation or state, but this definition fails in some cases if it refers simply to a geographical entity with established physical borders. Consider the Kurdish people, for example. Historically, Kurdish society had been centered in Kurdistan since the 12th century. But because of the somewhat arbitrary reconfiguration of the Middle Eastern states after the First World War, Kurdistan no longer exists and the Kurds are now spread across four different states: Turkey, Iran, Iraq and Syria. The Kurdish people in these various states still maintain the same cultural traditions and values, like linguistic dialects and religious practices, despite their geographic differences. Kurdish society, then, is no longer clearly geographically bounded but still culturally intact. The term society, therefore, must also include the shared traditions, values, and shared social meanings within a particular group, which represent cultural characteristics that differentiate the group from others.

Clearly, very few nations are culturally homogenous, and certainly, the largest are culturally diverse and pluralistic. But the concept of society includes the dominant cultural characteristics within those national boundaries. When we talk about American society, for example, we are actually referring to a broad mix of ethnic, political, and religious orientations. Yet there are overarching cultural elements that dominate the entire nation, and these elements are embodied in the national institutions that produce stable and consistent characteristics over time. While the specific role of a particular type of government can be debated, for example, the fact that a national government is one of the defining institutions of a nation cannot be denied. The sociologist Talcott Parsons used the U.S. Constitution as an example of the institutionalized cultural values and rules that still shapes our views and expectations of government here in America and abroad.

> Thus, in a broad sense, the American Constitution has remained a stable reference point over a period of more than a century and a half. During this time, of course, the structure of American society has changed very greatly in certain respects; there have been changes in legal terms, through legislation, through legal interpretations, and through more informal processes. But the federal state, the division between legislative and executive branches of government, the independent judiciary, the separation of church and state, the basic rights of personal liberty, of assembly, and of property, and a variety of other features have for most purposes remained constant (1961, p. 36).

We often think of governments and other institutions as entities, as things, but they are fundamental processes of sustained social interactions and relationships, created and maintained by people as much as by buildings and legal documents. It seems to me that the "living tapestry of men and women and people" Thatcher describes is an accurate description of society from this point of view, in the sense that she recognized the nature of modern society as a tapestry of relationships. Furthermore, the term society emphasizes the connection to the concept of the social contract, and idea first popularized by the Ancient Greeks and then again by the Scottish philosophers during the Enlightenment period of the 18th century. Essentially the social contract is a tacit agreement among people that they will willingly submit to various forms of authority within society, but, in exchange, society must maintain a civil environment with policies and rules conducive to the people's own interests. This is the promise of a liberal democratic society, that the government is of, by, and for the people, securing our rights and liberties, governed by the law, and treating all citizens as equals before the law.

The framers of the Constitution wrote down their views on the purpose of government in America's foundational document: "To form a more perfect Union, establish Justice, insure domestic Tranquility, provide for the common defence, promote the general Welfare, and secure the Blessings of Liberty to ourselves and our Posterity." This sounds fairly comprehensive and clear to me and is similar in intention to the guiding principles of many European countries. But I'm reminded of President Ronald Reagan's first Inaugural address in 1981, where he declared, "Government is not the solution to our problem; government is the problem." The problem at the time was specifically with promoting the general welfare of American citizens. Republicans during the Reagan era argued, just as Thatcher's supporters did in England, that an overblown welfare state undermined the vitality of the private economy and sapped self-reliance among the poor (Murray, 1984). At the time, conservative solutions for poverty focused on reducing welfare dependency by cutting aid and encouraging self-reliance in an expanding free-market economy. Not much has changed since then, apparently, and right-wing attitudes toward welfare remain negative. The Pew study found that only about a third of Republicans say that the federal government should have a major role in helping people get out of poverty and ensuring access to health care (Pew, 2015). In contrast, almost three-quarters of Democrats support government welfare efforts, and a whopping 83% of Democrats agreed that the government should play a major role in ensuring access to health care.

The social implications of those disparities of opinion can actually be measured. Recently, for example, researchers who study the differences between American and Canadian social outcomes have pointed to the negative effects associated with America's more neo-liberal attitude toward government and the economy. One set of studies compared the lives of low-wage hotel workers on either side of the U.S./Canadian border, in the neighboring cities of Seattle and Vancouver (Zuberi, 2006). The studies found dramatic differences in both individual outcomes but also in the quality of the communities in which they lived. Canadians, they found, had higher rates of unionization and more social welfare benefits in general. Social policies including unemployment insurance, childcare subsidies, government mandated vacation, maternity leave, job training, community services and so on helped the Canadian hotel workers and their families live much more stable, middle class lives than in America. In more recent work, the Canadian professor of social policy Dan Zuberi has shown how the neoliberal reorganization of work and employment relations has negative consequences even beyond the low-wage workers, their families, and communities (2013). Specifically, Zuberi found connections between the degradation of working conditions among hospital cleaning staff and increased death rates from hospital acquired infections both in the U.S. and abroad.

Another implication of this research is that the effects of low pay and limited social services for low-wage workers in the U.S. contribute to many larger problems that can affect society in general. Low wages and investment can often lead to stressed or unmotivated workers, poor infrastructure, and inadequate safety protections. For example, according to the most recent US Centers for Disease Control and Prevention (CDC) report, in 2011, an estimated 722,000 patients contracted an infection during a stay in an acute care hospital in the US, and about 75,000 of them died as a result of it (CDC, 2016). This means that hospital-acquired infections now affect one in 25 patients and cause 205 deaths every day. Studies like these point to the many negative outcomes from an economic agenda that insists on minimal government regulation and oversight, and at the same time promotes low wages and reduced social welfare policies for the workforce.

Additionally, there is an irony inherent in the conservative position having to do with the concept of a "free-market," in which participants are successful or not based solely on merit and the

mechanisms of the market, and uninfluenced by government interference. This view is unrealistic at best and completely ignores the
idea of *corporate welfare*, which has a long and well-documented
history. For example, powerful oligopolies in the health care and
defense industries represent dominant drains on the federal budget, not entitlement spending (Ferguson, 2012). In 2015, government
spending on defense amounted to 800 billion dollars, whereas welfare spending totaled only half a trillion dollars (usgovern-
mentspending.com). According to Robert Reich, professor and
Labor Secretary under Bill Clinton, conservatives tend to view the
government as a "welfare machine doling out benefits to the poor,
some of whom are too lazy to work" (Reich, 2014). But according to
the Center for Budget and Policy Priorities, only about 10% of federal spending is on safety net programs for individuals and families
facing hardship (CBPP, 2016).

   According to Reich, increasing budget provisions in recent spending bills reward Wall Street, health insurers, food companies, and
defense contractors, as well as many other corporate stakeholders.
Often these benefits are in the form of tax loopholes, but in the case
of healthcare, corporate interests get a huge windfall because Congress has expressly forbidden government healthcare programs
from negotiating drug price. Federal spending on healthcare
represents over 20% of the entire federal budget, reaching a total of
2.4 trillion dollars in 2015. So, on the one hand, some people are
complaining about how much the government spends, yet at the
same time supporting policies that maintain those high levels of
spending by blocking the government's efforts to lower its costs.
These subsidies, tax breaks, and pro-business regulations follow the
fluid logic of neoliberalism, which assumes that less government
involvement is always better unless the government can provide
advantages. This is what the German sociologist Ulrich Beck (2007)
suggests, that the neoliberal capitalist economic system relies on a
capital-state coalition where the political system is complicit in
maintaining the power and profitability of the economic system,
but often at the expense of the public.

   It is an unfortunate fact that these realities are intruding into the
lives of everyday people and therefore trust in government in the
U.S. is at an all-time low. According to the Pew Research Center, in
2014 just 19% respondents said that they could trust the government always or most of the time, which is one of the lowest percentages in the past half-century (Pew, 2014). Only 20% agreed that

government programs are being well run, and 75% said that most elected officials put their own interests ahead of the national interests. Incidentally, this level of mistrust in government is mirrored in the public's perceptions of people in general. A recent study, for example, reported that only 32% of the public agrees with the statement, "Most people can be trusted," down from 48% in the 1970s, and the 1970s were a time of major social turmoil in the U.S. with Vietnam, Watergate, and so on (Morgan, 2014).

Democracy and the Public Sphere

The faith in the power of democracy here in America, which is as old and cherished as the country itself, is a clear example of a particular and popular social order with admirers around the world. Also, the democratic political ideal is often assumed to be in a sort of symbiotic relationship with the capitalist economic system. In fact, the sociologist Peter Berger demonstrated empirically in the 1980s that capitalism is a necessary condition for the success of democracy in societies around the world (1986). Berger's research showed that capitalism increases growth and prosperity wherever it is adopted. The resulting shared prosperity naturally leads to more democratic forms of political organization as newly prosperous citizens press for greater control of their circumstances. Berger recognized that capitalism also increases inequality as the economy takes off, but claimed that there would eventually be a leveling-off of inequality within a reasonable time.

However, the idea that democratic governments follow in the wake of market capitalism may not be as accurate or widespread as many might assume. For example, the American scholar Robert Reich has argued that the assumptions about connections between capitalism and democracy are breaking down, and capitalism is succeeding around the world even while the principles of democracy have steadily weakened (2009). He points to China as one example, the world's largest capitalist nation, where markets have begun to flourish but without being matched by any political freedom among its population. Worse, nepotism is blatant in China, where the family members and friends of political officials enjoy economic access and opportunities denied to most others. Reich suggests that many other economically successful nations, like Russia and Mexico, are also only superficially democratically governed, and that they "are encumbered by the same problems that have hobbled American democracy in recent years, allowing corporations and elites buoyed by runaway economic success to undermine the gov-ernment's capacity to respond to citizens' concerns" (2009). Unfor-tunately, the celebrated freedoms associated with open markets and entrepreneurship so revered here in the U.S. are not necessarily integrated with democratic policies elsewhere.

In fact, it is worth noting that America's historical founders were not fans of democratic government, and many of the nation's earli-est leaders spoke against it. For example, Thomas Jefferson, the third president, once wrote,

> To take from one, because it is thought that his own indus-try and that of his fathers has acquired too much, in order to spare to others, who, or whose fathers have not exer-cised equal industry and skill, is to violate arbitrarily the first principle of association, — the guarantee to every one of a free exercise of his industry, & the fruits acquired by it (Jefferson, 1905).

John Quincy Adams, the sixth President had this to say, "The ex-perience of all former ages had shown that, of all human govern-ments, democracy was the most unstable, fluctuating, and short-lived." More recently, none other than Winston Churchill, British Prime Minister and hero of the second World War, declared, "The best argument against democracy is a five-minute conversation with the average voter."

These concerns with democracy included the fear that the poor and indolent would take advantage of government by unfairly tak-ing resources away from those who are willing to work. This is couched as a moral issue, one of fairness and personal responsibili-ty. But even the largesse of the New Deal policies implemented by Roosevelt after the Great Depression here in the United States, which included the enforcement of fair labor standards, Social Security, unemployment insurance, public assistance, and public works programs, did not create the underclass of takers that Jeffer-son, and generations of modern conservatives, worried about.

In any case, many of the social welfare policies from the New Deal era have been weakened or even eliminated, especially by those leaders under the influence of neoliberal ideology. And, not surpri-singly, levels of economic inequality and the social problems asso-ciated with inequality have risen to all-time highs here in America, despite the fact the nation's Gross Domestic Product, a common measure of a country's economic strength, hit an all-time high in

2015 (World Bank, 2016). One particularly sinister social problem that results from inequality, for example, is infant mortality. The United States currently ranks 29th among the 34 industrialized nations in the Organization for Economic Cooperation and Development in terms of life expectancy for newborn girls. Thirty-six years ago, America ranked 13th. "In 1980, the infant mortality rate in the United States was about the same as in Germany. Today, American babies die at almost twice the rate of German babies" (Porter, 2015). Although to make that quote completely accurate, it should read *poor* American babies.

Here is a portion of Aristotle's discussion of democracy, written 2500 hundred years ago. It outlines a basic principle at the heart of democracy, liberty.

> The basis of a democratic state is liberty; which, according to the common opinion of men, can only be enjoyed in such a state; this they affirm to be the great end of every democracy. One principle of liberty is for all to rule and be ruled in turn, and indeed democratic justice is the application of numerical not proportionate equality; whence it follows that the majority must be supreme, and that whatever the majority approve must be the end and the just. Every citizen, it is said, must have equality, and therefore in a democracy the poor have more power than the rich, because there are more of them, and the will of the majority is supreme. (Politics, Book 2).

Who among us will recognize our current political culture in this description? What examples can we point to where "the poor have more power than the rich"? Why, when the wealthy are so outnumbered, does a democratic nation like America tolerate things like inaction on climate change, corporate tax avoidance, the environmental and human damage from industrial pollution, or the privatization of public services, when these things are clearly not in the public's interests?

These questions lead to a more fundamental question about what, exactly, democratic government is for. We recognize that collective goal attainment is one of the functional imperatives of any stable society. The larger social goals of a nation must be defined, conflicts must be resolved, and policies must be developed to regulate collective efforts, including the allocation of resources and the regulation of social behaviors for the public good. These efforts represent political activity among a country's various groups and communities, and political activity in the context of democratic social organization ideally is a product of discourse and consensus. Politics is essentially about power relations among members of society, but in a democratic and inclusive social system, the political decisions ideally should be in relative harmony with the overarching values and normative structures of the larger cultural system.

Unfortunately, discourse and consensus are not the dominant patterns of political action today. Instead, powerful economic actors in the U.S. have increased their use of political tools like lobbying, public relations campaigns, and simple monetary contributions, seeking to manipulate laws and regulations to maintain the status quo and their lofty positions in the social hierarchy. In fact, over three billion dollars is spent on lobbying in the U.S. every year, an increase of fifty percent in the last ten years alone (Opensecrets.org, 2014). Also, recent Supreme Court rulings, including the *Citizens United* (2010) and the *McCutcheon* (2014) decisions, have reinforced the notion that money is equivalent to political speech. These rulings have ushered in a new era of potential political influence by wealthy donors. According to the New York Times, for example, "fewer than four hundred families are responsible for almost half the money raised in the 2016 presidential campaign, a concentration of political donors that is unprecedented in the modern era" (Confessore, 2015). The Washington Post editorial board referred to the same facts when they claimed, that a wealthy oligarchy of donors now dominates campaign finance (2015). These factors contribute to the type of democracy that Habermas described as "formal," a type of politics where the ideal forms of democracy are maintained but not the practical realities of representation and voice.

Another reason that social policies created through democratic political action often are less than ideal is because members of the public are misinformed and distracted by the strategic efforts of corporate stakeholders to limit exposure and awareness among the public regarding their own interests. Some social theorists point to the success of political techniques that borrow from consumer marketing and advertising in confusing the distinctions between economic freedom and the more fundamental democratic principles that make American society so attractive in appearance. As sociologist Colin Crouch claims, there is a "growing incapacity of modern citizens to work out what their interests are" (Crouch, 2004, p. 28). This incapacity is leading to changes in motivations, values, and attention levels, with the result that "the consumer has triumphed over the citizen" (p. 49). He warns that modern societies are heading toward a *post-democratic state*, and that "politics and government are increasingly slipping back into the control of privileged elites in the manner characteristic of pre-democratic times" (p. 6).

Media and the Public Sphere

It seems logical that political decisions in a democratic society must be subject to public input in order to be considered legitimate. The social theorist Jürgen Habermas has written extensively about "the public sphere," which refers to the social interactions that form a society's collective mind or, in Habermas' words, "something approaching public opinion." Every meaningful conversation or debate about current events or pressing concerns contributes to a general body of shared information and opinion, and this body of shared information can be considered the *vox populi* – the voice of the public, or the public sphere.

> Citizens behave as a public body when they confer in an unrestricted fashion-that is, with the guarantee of freedom of assembly and association and the freedom to express and publish their opinions about matters of general interest... Today newspapers and magazines, radio and television are the media of the public sphere (Habermas, 1974, p. 49).

The public sphere is the idealized communication structure within a society that contains and enables critical discourses on social practices and acts as the mechanism for political self-determination. The emergence of the public sphere in the 18th century transformed political authority within European and North American societies and established an equitable relationship between the political system and the cultural wishes of the educated and land-owning classes (Habermas, 1984). According to the Canadian philosopher Charles Taylor, the revolutions of 18th century Europe "transferred the ruling power from a king onto a 'nation,' or a 'people.' In the process, they invented a new kind of collective agency" (2002). The terms *nation* and *people*, not new, now referred to a new kind of power, "an entity which could decide and act together, to whom one could attribute a *will*" (emphasis in the original) (2002).

Ideally, policies are generated, evaluated and codified based on the consensus of the governed, in an open communicative process within the public sphere through which the relevant cultural values are represented and confirmed. In this way, political power transforms cultural will into social reality and maintains social cohesion through legitimated authority. Political outcomes are recognized as products of legitimate processes, and the results are accepted even by those who are not favored by them because they are considered to be fairly and inclusively derived, and representative of the larger group's needs.

Unfortunately, this is not how political decision-making occurs in the United States. Economic interests can influence the media so that public debate and social participation are altered in problematic ways. Left-wing critics argue that the liberal public sphere that originated in the Enlightenment has been transformed into a corporate media-dominated arena where political participation has been reduced to political spectacle. In the same way that consumer capitalism has turned non-economic relations and processes into monetized and market-based exchanges, the rationalized and instrumental norms of the *systems world* have modified public discourse to fit an economically sensitized and managed system of public presentation. Consider the influence of conservative media tycoon Rupert Murdoch in Britain, a man whose employees have been convicted of crimes like phone-hacking the cell phone of a murdered schoolgirl and maintaining corrupt relations with the police. Murdoch moved to the U.K. and bought the British newspapers The Sun and News of the World in the late 1960s, and integrated them into his already worldwide media corporation, News Corp. Since then, it is claimed, no party has won a British general election without News Corp's endorsement (McNair, 2012). Silvio Berlusconi, likewise, both before and during his reign as Italy's prime minister, was able to influence political discourse in Italy because he controlled the state-run media while Prime Minister of Italy, but also controlled his own media empire of television networks that dominated Italian news cycles. He was able to propel his own interests and quash criticism first through his own and then through his and the state's outlets. The result of this type of media power is the managed presentation of information that can mislead as often as inform. This creates a situation where active citizens are reduced to passive consumers of news, information, and public affairs. The result is that the public becomes part of what Habermas called "a culture of consumers," which can only passively ingest and absorb information as spectators of commercially mediated discourse. The media largely determine public opinion, yet they are commercially motivated and politically biased. Unfortunately, these facts often remain below the public's level of awareness. "Authority formally resides 'in the people,' but power is in fact held by small circles of men," according to C. Wright Mills, "That is why even when the authority is available, men with access to it may still prefer the secret, quieter ways of manipulation" (Mills, 1956, p. 317).

Consider some important characteristics of our modern society. Beginning in the early 20th century, technological development transformed modern economic activity, making workers more productive and placing a premium on intellectual, rather than manual, labor. The rise of global markets has also reduced the once dominant U.S. manufacturing sector and shifted the U.S. economy toward the service sector, which tends to reward the most educated workers with high-paying professional positions in industries such as finance, healthcare, and information technology. At the low end of the spectrum, unfortunately, jobs in the service economy are concentrated in retail sales and entertainment, where salaries are low, unions are weak, and workers are expendable. This transformation is not simply an economic issue but also includes a great deal of social upheaval. Further, these transformations require at least tacit political approval in the form of deregulation, corporate subsidies, and so on. The social consequences of these economic trends are often underplayed or overlooked by the media, however. For example, research suggests that news reports of issues involving law enforcement or many aspects of foreign policy are likely to be shaped by a type of media bias known as "spin" (Mullainathan & Shleifer, 2002). Spin results when a media outlet attempts to tell a simple and memorable story, but the act of simplification leads to bias since some information is necessarily omitted.

> Not only do the media outlets bias news reporting, but the stories reinforce each other. As each paper spins stories it increases the incentives of later outlets to spin... Moreover, spin can exacerbate the influence of one-sided ideology. When the first news outlet that uncovers the story is ideological and later ones are not, the first one sets the tone and later ones reinforce this spin. This can explain why and how inside sources leak information to news outlets. Their principal motivation is to control how the story is eventually spun (Mullainathan & Shleifer, 2002, p. 3).

Consider the words of Treasury Secretary Henry Paulson in 2007 in response to reporters' questions about the growing economic inequality in the US. Over the previous three decades, the share of pretax national income raked in by the richest *one tenth of one percent* of Americans had more than quadrupled, accounting for about one dollar of every eight dollars earned in the country. This was partly achieved through favorable tax legislation and deregulation that were very beneficial to the richest members of society. Paulson acknowledged the trend but suggested that Americans should get used to it. Growing inequality, he declared, "is simply an economic reality" (Hacker & Pierson, 2010). There were no repercussions for Paulson at all following this bold statement, and very little attention was paid to this pronouncement by the media. It should also be noted that Paulson, a former head of the Goldman Sachs investment firm, had a net worth of around $700 million at the time of this statement.

Since then, inequality has continued to increase. Nobel Prize winning economists like Robert Shiller and Paul Krugman have warned about the dangers and the suffering associated with inequality. In fact, in 2013, President Obama declared that reversing the widening gap in income inequality was "the defining challenge of our time," and began promoting a legislative agenda aimed at reversing the trend (Hansen, 2014). Yet the pundits on Fox News media have consistently dismissed these concerns. One Fox correspondent, for example, claimed it was simply class resentment based on the fact that some people are better than others. Even worse, when they did acknowledge it, contributors claimed that it couldn't be helped and trying to fix it would lead to chronic unemployment. This is the type of media bias that pushes into the public sphere and misinforms the very people affected by these problems, convincing them, falsely, that the status quo is inevitable.

The Media and Elitism

It is naïve, of course, to assume that there were halcyon eras in the past where the common man (much less woman) had direct access to political power. Historically, the public sphere was never completely inclusive. Instead, the educated and landowning members of society influenced political action. And by the late 19th century private interests had assumed direct political functions, as powerful business interests came to control and manipulate the media and to some degree the political state. At the same time, the state began to play a more fundamental role in the private and everyday lives of the populace, thus eroding the difference between state and civil society, between the public and private spheres of influence. Nevertheless, we can still refer to the public sphere as the closest representation of public opinion that can be achieved. We can recognize that the power of the public sphere has declined significantly and that an emphasis on active citizenship has transformed into an emphasis on consumer identity, where members of society are urged to dedicate themselves to passive consumption and private concerns rather than to issues of the common good and democratic participation. This is what Habermas called the "culture of consumers," passive spectators of commercially mediated discourse.

If public opinion was ever formed purely by political debate and consensus, this is no longer the case. Now, public opinion is largely administered by political, economic, and media elites which manage public opinion as part of systems management and social control. In many mediated contexts, communicative discourse aimed at achieving consensus has been replaced by managed, strategic discussion and manipulation by the advertising and public relations industries who strive to limit public discourse to themes validated and approved by corporate sponsors. In England, for example, a recent national referendum has led to the decision that Britain will leave the European Union (known as Brexit), an action that many experts say will result in hardship for Britain and risk for the stability of the EU. In addition, many researchers argue that the national media unfairly influenced the public by promoting the "Leave" side of the argument with false and misleading information. Loughborough University's Center for Research in Communication and Culture, for example, calculated that "whilst newspaper coverage of Leave or Remain is broadly balanced, a weighted evaluation that takes circulation and strength of partisanship into consideration shows 82% circulation advantage in favour of Brexit" (CRCC, 2016). In a similar vein in America, it is widely reported that over the course of Donald Trump's campaign, he received about $2 billion worth of free media attention, about twice as much as the most expensive presidential campaigns in history (Confessore, 2016). According to experts cited by the New York Times, Mr. Trump earned $400 million worth of free media just in February 2016 alone, which equals what John McCain spent on his entire 2008 presidential campaign (Confessore, 2016). This raises many concerns about bias and influence, since, as the Federal Communication Commission itself noted, media outlets are themselves commercial enterprises that have long given up on the public service aspects of their goals (FCC, 2011). As Jürgen Habermas warned,

"Publicity loses its critical function in favor of a staged display; even arguments are transmuted into symbols to which ... one can not respond by arguing but only by identifying with them" (Habermas, 1989, p. 206).

Elitism

Two hundred and fifty years ago, the English economist Adam Smith, in *The Wealth of Nations,* described how economically powerful actors would legitimize their own special interests by convincing the public that social benefits were tied to the success of the wealthy elite: "the clamour and sophistry of merchants and manufacturers easily persuade them, that the private interests of a part, and a subordinate part, of the society, is the general interest of the whole" (1776). Recall that the perennial reemergence of the neoliberal economic paradigm as the dominant economic ideology and its acceptance as the normal "way things are" is seen as an indication that political systems are largely in thrall to the wealthy minority that dominate the economic sphere and benefit from the neoliberal agenda. As many social critics argue, under the veil of ideological legitimation, wealthy economic actors have diminished the prosperity of the middle class in the U.S. and several European nations and have been able to dominate policymaking for the better part of forty years with little opposition. Through the promotion of supportive ideologies and outright influence over political decision-making, the wealthy elite, including the heads of many large corporations, have established a de facto oligarchy within the U.S. social system.

> The American financial industry gained political power by amassing a kind of cultural capital—a belief system... The banking-and-securities industry has become one of the top contributors to political campaigns, but at the peak of its influence, it did not have to buy favors... Instead, it benefited from the fact that Washington insiders already believed that large financial institutions and free-flowing capital markets were crucial to America's position in the world (Johnson, 2009).

Unfortunately, the continuing legitimation of an economic system that favors a small segment of the population at the expense of the larger community is partly an issue of narrative control, in which solutions that would do the greatest good for the majority of

Americans are minimized, disparaged, or ignored while those that benefit powerful and wealthy economic actors are promoted, repeated, and presented as uncontested. The power to control the flow of ideas still rests in the hands of the traditional media, which are dominated by a few wealthy economic actors. Consider that only six corporations control the vast majority of commercial media in America.

> The global commercial-media system is radical in that it will respect no tradition or custom, on balance, if it stands in the way of profits. But ultimately it is politically conservative, because the media giants are significant beneficiaries of the current social structure around the world, and any upheaval in property or social relations—particularly to the extent that it reduces the power of business—is not in their interest (McChesney, 1999).

What could be better than having the ability to influence public opinion and make your own special interests seem necessary and right? The answer is doing away with the need to influence public opinion at all. If a powerful stakeholder could convince the public that the mechanisms of society are in capable hands, and no public inputs are required, then the result is legitimate but private control. And, in fact, there have been powerful arguments to the effect that genuine participation of citizens in the processes of political decision-making is actually problematic and unnecessary even in democratic societies. The social theorist Niklas Luhmann proposed such a view of social organization in the 1970s, and his ideas supported notions of elitism, exclusion, and disembeddedness that have unfortunately familiar characteristics to the modern political landscape (in Habermas, 1973). Luhmann argued that the complexity of modern industrial society necessitated the isolation of public administration from the interference of participatory politics. An autonomous administration would ideally have both the responsibility and ability to handle societal problems in such a way that society can function smoothly and would adopt a scientific and systematic approach to increase its effective management of society. To this extent, input from the public domain is not only superfluous; it undermines the effectiveness of the administration.

As Luhmann described it, suppression of general public interests in modern society results from a separation of the instrumental functions of the administrative system from the legitimating functions of the cultural system. Instead of testing political actions against the will of the public to ensure adherence to cultural values, for example, the political system provides its own legitimation by manipulating the media in a way that would draw public attention to "expressive symbols that release an unspecific readiness to follow" (in Habermas, 1973, p.70). Luhmann identified several familiar strategies that could be used to achieve this illusion of legitimacy. These strategies include the personalization of substantive issues, the symbolic use of hearings, expert opinion, and advertising techniques that "confirm and exploit existing structures of prejudice" and that manipulate the public sphere through emotional appeals, stimulation of unconscious fears, and spectacles. With these techniques, which result in directing attention to selected topical areas and "pushing other themes, problems, and arguments below the threshold of attention and, thereby, of withholding them from opinion-formation, the legitimating function of the cultural system is co-opted and the public is manipulated into acceptance" (p.70).

Luhmann's vision of an independent administrative system untethered from the cultural values of the public may be closer to the current reality here in America than the notion of vibrant and active democracy. In fact, this form of elitism has had quite a supportive history in the United States. The Austrian economist Joseph Schumpeter for example, considered one of the most influential economists of the 20th century, suggested that democratic elitism, what he called the "competitive theory of democracy," was the best solution to the problems associated with a uniformed public. Schumpeter accepted that the primary purpose of the democratic arrangement "… is to vest the power of deciding political issues in the electorate" (Schumpeter, 1950, p. 269). Electing leaders was of secondary importance. But public decisions would only be workable based "on the proposition that 'the people' hold a definite and rational opinion about every individual question," (p. 269) which Schumpeter did not accept. So, instead, Schumpeter suggested, "we reverse the roles of these two elements and make the deciding of issues by the electorate secondary to the election of the men who are to do the deciding (p. 269). His idea was that the complexity of issues confronting any modern society would overwhelm the public. The election of effective and informed representatives would thus be a much more ideal democratic configuration.

Schumpeter's point was well accepted by the mid 20th century. But even earlier, in the 1920s, science had convinced some members of the public that many issues of daily life were difficult and

complicated and that this complexity carried over into public administration. In books like Public Opinion and *The Phantom Public*,
for example, written in 1922 and 1925 respectively, the influential
American journalist Walter Lippmann outlined his views on the
superiority of the economic and political elite over the general public when it came to the administration of the state. Basically, Lippmann argued that the public was simply unable to make the important decisions about governance and that these functions must be
carried out by the elite members of society with the technical expertise to guide society.

> We must assume as a theoretically fixed premise of popular
> government that normally men as members of the public
> will not be well-informed, continuously interested, nonpar-
> tisan, creative or executive. We must assume the public is in-
> expert in its curiosity, intermittent, that discerns only gross
> distinctions, is slow to be aroused and quickly diverted; that,
> since it acts by aligning itself, it personalizes whatever it
> considers, and is interested only when events have been me-
> lodramatized as a conflict (Lippmann, 1925, p.108).

At the time, Lippmann's blatant support of elitism flew in the
face of popular notions of democratic participation and social
justice. To Lippmann and a growing group of U.S. intellectuals,
however, the public was ill-suited to the task of governance,
disinterested and uninformed, unable to meet the demands of
sophisticated and complex issues of the day. As previously mentioned, modern macroeconomic policy issues and industrial
innovations based on scientific advancements were not well
understood by the public, making the regulation of these production techniques a matter for technocratic elites rather than a
democratic populace. The public was therefore forced to increasingly rely on experts for information processing and decision-
making even though political inclusion was a necessary coun-
terbalance to this type of differentiation. Lippmann and others
viewed the public as bystanders or outsiders, however, and the
insiders were the only ones capable of making good choices:

> The burden of carrying on the work of the world, of invent-
> ing, creating, executing, of attempting justice, formulating
> laws and moral codes, of dealing with the technic and the
> substance, lies not upon public opinion and not upon gov-

ernment but on those who are responsibly concerned as agents in the affair (Lippmann, 1925, p. 73).

Lippmann and others made careers out of understanding the limitations of public opinion and developing the mechanisms by which public consent could be influenced or "manufactured." In fact, Lippmann challenged the very notion of participatory democracy:

> For when public opinion attempts to govern directly it is either a failure or a tyranny. It is not able to master the problem intellectually, nor to deal with it except by wholesale impact. The theory of democracy is not recognized this truth because it has identified the functioning of government with the will of the people. This is a fiction. The intricate business of framing laws and of administering them ... is in no sense the act of the voters nor translation of their will (Lippmann, 1925, p. 71).

Like the arguments of Lippmann, the political scientist Peter Bachrach, in his book *The Theory of Democratic Elitism: A Critique*, found that all elite theories are based on the assumption that the public is inherently incompetent and not to be entrusted with the administration of the state, and any theory of democracy that promotes the participation of the common masses in governing themselves is a dangerous anachronism (1967).

> Thus it is said that there is no alternative but to recast democracy, emphasizing the stable, constitutional, and liberal nature of the system of elite pluralism; the competitiveness of political elites, their accountability to the electorate at periodic elections; and the open, multiple points of access to elite power for those who bother to organize to voice their grievances or demands (Bachrach, 1967, p. 8).

This view is not new, of course, and has been promoted throughout history. For the ancient Greek philosopher Aristotle, the ideal political system was not democracy but some form of natural monarchy or aristocracy, the rule by one or a few of surpassing wisdom and virtue. The Scottish philosopher John Stuart Mill was also a supporter of elite governance. In his *Representative Government*, first published in 1861, he clearly outlined the necessity of an elite class of citizens or the influence of what he called the "instructed minority."

The natural tendency of representative government, as of
modern civilization, is towards collective mediocrity: and
this tendency is increased by all reductions and extensions
of the franchise, their effect being to place the principal
power in the hands of classes more and more below the
highest level of instruction in the community. But though
the superior intellects and characters will necessarily be
outnumbered, it makes a great difference whether or not
they are heard (2007, p.145).

The first element of good government, Mill claimed, was the virtue and intelligence of the community members, and the most
important purpose of any form of government is to promote those
qualities among its people. But only those who already possess
those intellectual and moral qualities can promote virtue and intelligence, and they are therefore unavoidably more valuable to the
society than the rest.

When two persons who have a joint interest in any business differ in opinion, does justice require that both opi-
nions should be held of exactly equal value? If, with equal
virtue, one is superior to the other in knowledge and intelligence — or if, with equal intelligence, one excels the other
in virtue — the opinion, the judgment, of the higher moral
or intellectual being is worth more than that of the inferior:
and if the institutions of the country virtually assert that
they are of the same value, they assert a thing which is not
(Mill, 2007, p. 172).

But a democratic public would not simply give up power in the
face of self-professed expertise. They would need convincing and
Edward Bernays, considered the father of public relations, knew
how to do just that. Bernays started as a military propagandist for
Woodrow Wilson during the World War I and then adapted his
techniques to advertising and political influence after the war.
Starting in the 1920s Bernays began to advise politicians on the use
of the media for political purposes. To avoid the negative connota-
tions associated with the word propaganda, Bernays introduced the
term *public relations.* The purpose of public relations was clear to
Bernays since he agreed with and was influenced by Walter Lippmann's views that the American public's democratic judgment was
unreliable. In his book, Propaganda, for example, Bernays claimed,

Ours must be a leadership democracy, administered by the "intelligent minority" who know how to regiment and guide the masses... Is this government by propaganda? Call it, if you prefer, government by education. But education, in the academic sense of the word, is not sufficient. It must be enlightened expert propaganda through the creation of circumstances, through the high-spotting of significant events, and the dramatization of important issues (1928, p. 127).

Bernays had no qualms about the deception involved in this type of public manipulation, declaring in the same book, "If we understand the mechanism and motives of the group mind, it is now possible to control and regiment the masses according to our will without their knowing it" (p. 71).

Knowledge and Power

Despite the deceptive nature of public relations as described by Edward Bernays, elitism in a democratic society is ultimately predicated on values such as merit and trust, and modern societies have managed to *problematize* even those seemingly innocuous ideals. The thinking that permeated the Enlightenment era and gave rise to modernity was fixated on promises of equality, liberty, and justice delivered through the application of scientific knowledge and democratic processes. Many of the administrative functions aimed at fulfilling those promises of expanding public welfare in modern societies are guided by expertise and knowledge provided by what John Stuart Mill called "the instructed minority." One problem with this elitism is that knowledge and expertise are not always objective criteria. The politicization of science, for example, is a common concern in modern societies as is the relationship between knowledge and power. Science is a source of political and economic power, and the French philosopher Michel Foucault's philosophy of science points out the co-constitutive relationship between power and knowledge, or the "internal regime of power of scientific statements." Foucault's philosophy reminds us that knowledge is never free from relations of power (Nothdurfter & Lorenz, 2010). Knowledge emerges from specific social relations between persons, domains of discourse and social institutions, and these relations constitute a framework of power. There are many examples of knowledge production, some brilliantly analyzed by Foucault, that represent the creation and legitimation of power *in an arbitrary way*. Consider the development of our understanding of abnormal psychology. Foucault pointed out that being different, being abnormal, and being sick are very different categories "but have been reduced to the same thing" by modern medicine. It wasn't that long ago that the Diagnostic and Statistical Manual for Psychiatric Disorders, the veritable Bible for identifying mental illness, included homosexuality as a disorder. Now, the idea that homosexuality is a sickness seems quaint to all but the most resolutely religious or bigoted. But this serves as a fine example of how scientific production can be not only wrong but also wrong in a way that favors some members of the community over others. Thus, "It is necessary to abandon an idea of knowledge as a neutral and hence self-legitimating procedure and product, even if it was produced with scientific rigor ..." (Nothdurfter & Lorenz, 2010).

This situation represents a tension between the obvious benefits of modern science and the power of elite political and economic actors to bend scientific evidence in favor of their own agendas. Since at least the 1960s, elected officials in the U.S. Congress have increasingly delegated technical policy decisions to regulatory agencies staffed by scientific experts. But agencies that had once addressed solely technical issues now exercise extensive policymaking authority in areas with clear society-wide moral and political implications, such as environmental protection, consumer safety standards, civil rights, worker protections, pharmaceutical approval, and so on. What's more, the assumptions about the levels of expertise or integrity within these elite agencies are often wrong, since we naively assume a level of ability and of intellectual honesty that is often lacking. Climate change, for example, is a significant scientific issue that has many social and, perhaps more importantly, economic ramifications. The 2013 Intergovernmental Panel on Climate Change (IPCC) report states with 95 percent confidence that humans have caused most, and probably all of the rapid global warming over the past 60 years, and approximately ninety-seven percent of climate experts and peer-reviewed climate science studies agree with that statement. However, a recent British survey found that the percentage of the British people who *do not* think the world's climate is changing has almost quadrupled since 2005, and a similar survey in the United States shows an even greater rise in climate skepticism (Roppolo, 2014).

Partly this discrepancy between what the vast majority of climate scientists believe and what the general public believes is due to simple misinformation from our political leaders and their wealthy supporters. In the U.S. for example, a majority of the Republican in the House of Representatives and the Senate deny climate change, and make public statements indicating that they question or reject that climate change is real, that it is happening, or that it is caused by human consumption of fossil fuels (Schulman, 2015). Generally, they oppose the climate change data either because it would require government regulation, which they oppose, or because they have been swayed by the enormous campaign contributions made by energy companies that would be economically impacted by climate change legislation. However, there are seemingly legitimate sources of expertise and knowledge that promote the same skepticism. The Heartland Institute, for example, claims to be a nonprofit "think tank" that questions the reality and import of climate change, second-hand smoke health hazards, and other issues. Environment & Climate News is a monthly publication of the Heartland Institute described as an "outreach publication for common-sense environmentalism," that consistently takes positions contrary to those of most environmental organizations. The Institute refuses to publicly disclose its corporate sponsors, but past contributors included the Koch brothers, two energy company owners, Exxon Mobil, the largest energy company in the world, and a host of other economic interests. This would seem like a clear example of the potential manipulation of science for private economic or political gain.

Even more egregious manipulations occur due to the disembedded nature of the modern economic system, however. Consider the fallout from the housing market crash, in which hundreds of thousands of mortgages were sold and resold without proper care for the paperwork. In an online Business Week article in 2011, Peruvian economist Hernando De Soto argued that the financial crisis partly was due to the destruction of economic facts (2011). Modern economic development requires a shared set of facts. "Knowledge had to be gathered, organized, standardized, recorded, continually updated, and easily accessible" (2011). The legal establishment and enforcement of private property rights, according to De Soto, was one of the pivotal developments in modern history, and this development coincided with a huge new need for public record-keeping and archive systems.

Over the past 20 years, however, De Soto claims that Americans and Europeans have been *destroying* these facts. For example, mortgages were "granted and recorded with such inattention that homeowners and banks often don't know and can't prove who owns their homes." Governments have succumbed to the "entrenched institutional problems of a failing order" and allowed economic activity to become disembedded from the legal system of facts and documentation, and so the economic system has deteriorated into "an anarchic legal space, where arbitrary interests can trump facts and paper swirls out of control" (2011). De Soto warned that the rule of law is more than a set of norms, it is an "information and management system that filters and processes local data until it is transformed into facts" organized in a coherent and comprehensive way, and its abandonment could undo centuries of progress.

In fact, during the last decade, the neoliberal global capitalist system has been tested by a series of financial crises that started within the emerging markets in the 1990s and ended with the Global Financial Crash of 2008. Every mistake made during the buildup to the Crash was supported and legitimated by numerous experts and policy makers, including economists, regulators, business experts, and even the head of the Federal Reserve Board. These events remind us that principles and practices that seem sensible and beneficial today may turn out to be terrible mistakes, even though thoughtful, intelligent people promote such practices. There is always the nagging possibility that powerful economic actors are swayed by greed to overlook or minimize risks, or that the knowledge produced by scientific communities is politicized and deformed by ideological interests, or captured and monetized by economic forces, such as by limiting the dissemination of vital knowledge through intellectual property laws. Even Aristotle warned that monarchies and aristocracies would become corrupted over time and devolve into dictatorships and oligarchies. Hence, we are bound in a dilemma: we are increasingly reliant on experts and technocrats for guidance and context even though these same people may jeopardize the stability and sustainability of our material and social environments. And, unfortunately, we ourselves cannot always evaluate the accuracy or value of these experts, nor can we police them effectively. Even worse, the powerful segments of society may intentionally mislead us in order to maintain a manufactured perception of legitimacy.

As previously mentioned, the medical industry is another area where misinformation is commonplace. Marcia Angell, an editor of The New England Journal of Medicine for over twenty years, warned that it is no longer possible to believe much of the clinical research that is published (Angell, 2009). And more recently, Richard Horton, the editor-in-chief of The Lancet, Britain's top medical journal declared that "The case against science is straightforward: much of the scientific literature, perhaps half, may simply be untrue" (2015, p.1380). He cites invalid exploratory analyses, flagrant conflicts of interest, and an obsession with fashionable trends of questionable importance as contributing factors to what he describes as science's "turn towards darkness."

These declarations by the editors of the world's top medical science journals are well supported by investigations into the clinical drug trials sponsored by the major pharmaceutical companies. Consider that scientists at the biotechnology firm Amgen tried to confirm published findings related to claims in preclinical cancer-related drug studies over the past decade and could duplicate the reported claims in only 6 out of 53 (11%) cases. In a report of these findings in the journal Nature, the authors remarked, "Even knowing the limitations of preclinical research, this was a shocking result" (Begley & Ellis, 2012). The authors also took pains to put a positive light on the original researchers by assuring us that "These investigators were all competent, well-meaning scientists who truly wanted to make advances in cancer research" (Begley & Ellis, 2012). Unfortunately, Amgen's findings are consistent with those of others in the industry. For example, researchers at Bayer HealthCare in Germany reported in 2011 that only about 25% of published preclinical studies could be validated.

Passive Democracy and Political Illusions

At this point, an assessment of the democratic system in general is necessary. I argue that not only are the mechanisms of political decision-making under elite control, but the characteristics of the system itself are flawed and misunderstood. According to critical theorists like Jürgen Habermas, formal democratic institutions and procedures are structured so that the political system permits administrative action to be independent of the specific motives of the citizens, and this is accomplished through a legitimation process that emphasizes generalized motives and a vague mass loyalty but limits active participation (Habermas, 1973). This is made possible through the creation of public institutions and procedures that are democratic *in form*, but limit political involvement to a minimum, basically the right to withhold your political support, whether or not to vote for a particular candidate or to support a particular proposal. In Bachrach's assessment of democratic elitism, the public can

still play a role in the system but the role is limited to selecting leaders and the accouterments of leadership. Self-determination and
participation are no longer "natural" to the social system, and "democracy" is no longer expected to take the generalizable interests of
all individuals into account. Democracy instead has become the
"key for the distribution of rewards and the regulator for the satisfaction of private interests" (Bachrach, 1967, p. 8). This formal but
passive democracy based on limited access to power and private
rather than public interests is not tied to ideals of political equality
in the sense of an equal distribution of political power and does not
seek to rationalize authority through the participation of citizens in
collective, communicative processes. Instead, it simply facilitates
compromises between ruling elites and makes "prosperity without
freedom," a phrase used by President Obama in a speech in Australia in 2011, possible. Only those government decisions still defined
as political are subject to the processes of democratic influence
while the majority of political action is isolated from public involvement administered by technocratic elites. In this way, political
power becomes independent of the pressures of democratic legitimation and scrutiny. According to the passive system, the democratic political system is legitimate if voters can choose between
competing elites, and the elites refrain from making their power
hereditary or blatantly domineering or obvious. Direct access to
political decision-making is rarely available to the public, however.
Instead, lobbyists and the wealthy, powerful elite are the only actors
with access to the hermetic system.

I contend that this is the actual state of American democracy. Although identified as a representative democracy, it is actually entangled with economic and elite interests, and largely unresponsive
to public concerns. It should be mentioned that, at the state and
local level in the United States, direct democratic action in the form
of ballot initiatives and referenda are allowed in 49 of the 50 states
(only Delaware does not). The purpose is to empower ordinary
citizens to participate in the making of public policy so that 'the
people' are able to circumvent state legislatures or officials that are
controlled by political or economic special interests. This has been
the case for over one hundred years. However, *soft money* loopholes
allow corporations or labor unions to make unlimited contributions
to promote or defeat various ballot measures, which means that
wealthy financial interests are able to set the agenda and assert

their privileged position through the process (Tolbert & Smith, 2006). As political scientist John Shockley pointed out, special interests have been able to influence direct democracy as easily as representative democracy for the last hundred years.

> As long as wealth is as unequally distributed as it is in American society, and political interest groups are organized around private rather than public rewards, ballot proposition campaigns, like American politics generally, will reflect the power of the best organized and wealthiest groups in society (1985, pp. 427–8, quoted in Tolbert & Smith, 2006).

In his book *A Government by the People*, the historian Thomas Goebel provided a detailed overview of the adoption and use of direct democratic processes by the states and concluded that they were ineffective overall.

> [T]he historical analysis of direct democracy since its inception a century ago makes abundantly clear that the initiative and referendum have never served, and probably never will serve, as the means to strengthen democracy in America, to truly build a government by the people (2002, pp. 198-9).

Illusions of Representation

Unfortunately, representative democracy is not a successful system either. In theory, representative democracy is based on the principal–agent relationship between voters and their elected representatives summarized by the view that "representation is authority, the right to make commitments and incur the consequences for one another" (Pitkin, 1967, p. 8). Thus, elected officials act on behalf of voters so that their political commitments represent the wishes of the voters and the extent to which elected officials faithfully represent the will of the public is the basis for evaluating the quality of political representation. This normative ideal is commonly violated in modern political systems, revealing a significant gap between actions of governments and the wishes of their citizens. For example, Powell and Vanberg (2000) have provided empirical evidence showing that the correspondence of action, the match between the actions of the legislators and their constituent voters in the U.S., is consistently inferior compared to other multi–party democracies. Elected officials in America simply do not consistently carry out the wishes of the voting public that put them in power. Other research that compared the preferences of Senate constituencies to the voting behavior of their senators shows that the Senate actions align more closely with the preferences of the rich than the poor, though the poor vastly outnumber the wealthiest constituents (Bartels, 2008).

In a similar set of findings, research shows that the affluent are far better represented than the poor in terms of federal government policy. The connection between preferences and policy shows a bias toward the status quo in policy making, but policy also is much more likely to change when the rich support the change than when the poor do (Gilens, 2009). Also, other research has shown that poor government responsiveness to public preferences relates to a "systematic disjoint" between the politician's and voter's policy preferences. This results in inefficiencies in political representation due to a systematic bias in which politicians enact policies that they themselves prefer over the preferences of the voters (Krause, 1996). Here then is the formal but non-substantive nature of modern representational democracy as practiced in the U.S.; the public has the right to vote for representatives and if representation is not provided then the public can withhold their votes for that official at the next election. In the meantime, elected officials apparently do whatever they themselves or their rich supporters want.

Furthermore, the problem is largely structural, in that there are biases built into our current system of governance. For example, while representation in the House of Representatives is distributed equally across states in terms of population, the U.S. Senate is comprised of two senators from each state, so that each state is equal in terms of political power in the Senate. But that means that California, with a population of over thirty-seven million, is represented by the same number of senators representing Wyoming, with its population of under a half million. The obvious problem is that states have varying population densities, but political representation in the Senate completely ignores these population differences, essentially shortchanging the larger states and favoring the smaller states.

Consider the fact that the ten largest states contain over 53% of the total population (almost 167 million people) and are represented by only twenty senators, while the twenty least populated states have a combined population of less than thirty million, which is far less than the population of California alone, but are represented by forty senators. Furthermore, even though the American democratic system, like any democratic system, is based on the power of the majority to enact policy, the process known as the "filibuster" allows a minority of forty senators to block any Senate action except specific budget-related bills. Therefore, until recently, senators representing a population smaller than California could block almost all legislation in the U.S. Senate, and representatives of the other 280 million Americans are rendered powerless.

Thus, we are left with two problematical issues: first, that representative democracy is not very representative of the public's wishes, and second, that the modern U.S. political system is structured in a way that reduces public political participation and minimizes the need for legitimation of the system itself. Consider the political push by administration officials such as the Secretary of Housing and Urban Development and the Secretary of the Justice Department to try to persuade the states' attorneys general to support a financial settlement with major banks over their wrongdoing associated with the mortgage-backed securities in 2011 (Cohan, 2014). Usually referred to as "improprieties" by the mainstream media, the issue centered on widespread acts of fraud like the so-called robo-signing procedures in which mortgage bank employees fraudulently signed tens of thousands of legal documents or the widespread practice of submitting apparently forged documents to the courts to hasten the foreclosure process against troubled borrowers. In response to the threat of prosecution, institutions like Bank of America, Citigroup, JPMorgan Chase and Wells Fargo agreed to pay $25 billion in exchange for broad releases protecting them from further litigation on matters relating to the "improper" bank practices.

Putting aside the fact that any member of the public who commits fraud or forgery is likely to serve time in jail or even prison while banks that engage in the same behavior are simply fined, the amount of the fine was ludicrously low; estimates ranged into the hundreds of billions of dollars in compensation owed to wrongfully foreclosed homeowners and cheated investors. Even worse, the deal barred members of the public from seeking further compensation or justice from these banks. The idea that the political system, ostensibly representing the "will of the people" would blatantly support such an unjust (both legally and financially) deal with banks engaged in criminal activity against the public shows just how independent the administration of the political system is from cultural norms and values embraced by society.

In a similar vein, after the tragic Newton school massacre in 2012, polls showed that over *ninety percent* of the public supported legislation that would require background checks for firearms purchases, yet Congress voted the legislation down and the issue quickly disappeared from media coverage. A vast majority of Americans supported it but a small group of special interests opposed it, and the legislation died. Examples like these make it clear that the public has little power to influence decisions made by the political elite for the benefit of the economic elite even when it is at the expense of the public. Justice, it appears, though the cornerstone of democratic cultures everywhere, is simply not available much of the time. Even worse, the law professor Joel Bakan warns that the diminishing role of the state in protecting citizens from corporations is offset by "the expanding role of the state in protecting corporations from citizens" (Bakan, 2004, p.154). The public sphere is unable to mount a serious defense against these practices.

Illusions of Public Participation

The nature of political participation has also changed dramatically in the last few decades, and in many ways, political power has been concentrated by the rise of special interest groups. The number of interest groups in the United States quadrupled between 1959 and 2001, according to the Encyclopedia of Associations. Part of the power that special interest groups have is the ability to utilize the necessary tools to influence political action. Generally, in the U.S. especially, voter turnout is low and political participation has waned, and the diminished public participation in the political system is partly due to the massive ideological shift that transformed citizens into consumers over the last century. In 2012, the American Idol finale, for example, drew 63 million votes, more than have *ever* been cast for a president in a U.S. election (Sweeney, 2006). Even Ronald Reagan only received 54.5 million votes in his 1984 presidential landslide.

The diminution of the power of the public sphere is also related to changes over time in the functional roles of unions, civic associations, and public interest groups. Traditionally, these types of associations combined affiliation and social engagement with community service and involvement in national affairs. For example, the AFL-CIO promotes various economic and social policies to benefit its union members; the American Farm Bureau Federation (AFBF) organizes regional farm associations to influence agricultural policies; and the National Congress of Parents and Teachers (PTA) influence educational and family issues (Skcopol, 2004). The efforts of these organizations are often very effective. In fact, the U.S. Social

Security program was the result of an organization called the Townsend Clubs. In 1933, Francis Townsend wrote a letter to a local California newspaper describing his dismay at the low state of American seniors and offering the outlines of a social insurance program in order to improve the lives of those impoverished senior citizens. The first Townsend Club was established eight months later, and by 1935 a half million Americans had joined Townsend Clubs across the country. That same year, a newly elected Congressman from Los Angeles promptly introduced legislation to implement The Townsend Plan, a precursor to our modern Social Security program. By 1936, Townsend Clubs had two million members, and by 1937 Roosevelt signed the Social Security Act into law, changing the lives o millions of senior citizens across the nation. In a similar way, the American Legion played a pivotal role in drafting and lobbying for the GI Bill of 1944, which provided millions of veterans with educational opportunities. After World War II, especially, patriotism was a dominant motivational orientation and associations sharply expanded their memberships and broadened the scope and vigor of their local and national activities.

According to the sociologist Theda Skocpol, one traditionally role of these groups was educational, to convey politically relevant knowledge and motivation to its membership. These organizations were often directly involved in legislative campaigns, but they also "taught people about parliamentary rules of discussion; about legislative, judicial, and executive functions; about elections or other forms of representative governance; and about the relationship between taxation and collective services" (Skocpol, 1999). These traditional voluntary associations were very much part of the cultural system and promoted ideals of good citizenship, community and national service, public engagement, and political participation. Many modern, professionally run associations, however, have moved away from an emphasis on public participation and the promotion of political action and instead rely on a select group of technocrats and elites to further their specific interests. The modern business groups and professionally managed public interest groups that dominate the public spectrum no longer reproduce the mass participatory and educational functions of classic civic associations. Paid experts are now much more valued than volunteer leaders for the public functions of modern public interest groups. Increasingly, civic organizations rely on responses to mailing-list solicitations to establish their "memberships" and view respondents as consumers who are purchasing a particular brand of public interest representation. Unfortunately, today's associations offer neither the social nor educational opportunities of membership, since all they are required to do as members is send a check (2004).

Even more problematical, large corporations understand that their political lobbying efforts are much more effective when delivered by what appear to be public interest groups, so they create *culturally disguised* associations to advance their economic interests. This is a clear example of modern public relations as described by Edward Bernays in the 1920s. Corporate elite has funded a network of front groups, corporate-funded think tanks and industry-funded academics to articulate their message while hiding their connections to those groups. An extreme version of this type of manipulation is the practice known as "astroturfing." An *Astroturf* group is an organization created by industry lobbyists that attempts to pose as a legitimate grassroots organization. These special interest groups advocate for industry-backed interests while pretending to promote the public good. Astroturf groups pressure legislators to support industry-friendly positions on issues such as energy policy, tax policy, and prescription drug legislation. The organizations often adopt populist-sounding names and make a practice of misrepresenting what they seek to accomplish. For example, according to Public Citizen, a watchdog organization, the Save Our Species Alliance pressured Congress to limit the Endangered Species Act to promote industry-friendly land management, and Citizens for Asbestos Reform supported legislation in 2003 that would have prevented citizens harmed by asbestos from suing asbestos manufacturers (2007). There are dozens of organizations that spend millions on Astroturf lobbying and falsely represent themselves as citizen organizations. For example, the effort to repeal the federal estate tax was led by a massive coalition of business and trade associations that were traced back to eighteen families, which include the families connected to Wal-Mart, Gallo wine, and Campbell's soup. Other national groups representing corporate interests are organizations with names like Citizens for a Sound Economy, the American Legislative Exchange Council, Americans for Job Security, the Competitiveness Enterprise Institute and the Washington Legal Foundation.

Another popular goal among wealthy and powerful families and corporations is protection against penalties that stem from the sale of defective products, medical malpractice, securities fraud, or environmental pollution. A large network of Astroturf organizations has been hard at work for decades to protect corporate interests at the expense of the public in the legal arena under the banner of "tort reform," which turns out to be code for "no penalties for corporate irresponsibility." The tax and funding information shows that many of these groups are connected to large corporate sponsors, including tobacco, insurance, energy, pharmaceutical companies, medical associations and auto manufacturers. Recall the examples of instrumental rationality that lead corporations to conduct cost-benefit analyses to determine whether life-threatening problems with their products should trigger a recall of those products. The Firestone tire corporation decided to ignore a problem involving defective tires that eventually took the lives of at least 271 people before they issued a tire recall in 2000, executives at The Peanut Corp. of America knowingly shipped products contaminated with salmonella to customers for two years before they finally agreed to a recall of their products. At least nine people died and over 700 were sickened during that two-year period. These decisions were rational only from a narrow economic perspective and one of the variables in their calculus is the cost of litigation. Therefore, these corporations are constantly striving to minimize the potential costs of that litigation, often through Astroturf groups. These groups typically give themselves names like Citizens Against Lawsuit Abuse, Lawsuit Abuse Watch, Stop Lawsuit Abuse, or People for a FAIR Legal System, and they promote an agenda of "lawsuit abuse" and "tort reform" to the media and in Congress, striving to influence legislation, the judiciary, and jurors. They represent themselves as citizens groups that want to protect consumers, but scrutiny eventually reveals that they represent major corporations seeking to escape liability for the harm they cause consumers and the environment.

As we all know from recent experiences, the functional weaknesses in the economic system often give rise to catastrophic market failures, which require state intervention in order to provide some minimum stabilization of social functionality as a whole. Consider the Troubled Asset Relief Program (TARP) bailouts of 2008. Confronted by a credit crisis in the U.S., then Treasury Secretary Hank Paulson urged Congress to provide a $700 billion dollar "bailout" to the banking sector to protect them from bankruptcy. Furthermore, along with the money, the TARP program also allowed the Securities Exchange Commission to suspend an accounting rule, the mark-to-market rule, which required banks to write down the value of their mortgage-backed securities to present-day market values. When this rule was suspended, banks were no longer required to report the market value of their assets and could thereby avoid admitting the losses associated with those bad investments made during the boom. As a result of all the free money and suspension of rules provided by the government, many banks diverted some of the TARP money to somewhat questionable purposes. For example, a 2008 Associated Press report claimed: "Banks that are getting taxpayer bailouts awarded their top executives nearly $1.6 billion in salaries, bonuses, and other benefits last year" (AP, 2008).

While the threat to social well-being represented by a financial crisis was very real, the idea that banking officials could make such horrendous investment decisions as to put their firms and the entire industry in dire risk, then receive generous bailouts from the taxpaying public, and then reward themselves with extravagant pay and bonuses, is a significant violation of the social contract, one that flies in the face of the professed values of these arch-capitalists, namely self-reliance, individual responsibility, and merit-based rewards. What ties this all together for us is the fact that both Secretaries of the Treasury, the one during the Bush administration that saw the onset of the financial crisis and the one selected by the Obama administration to deal with the aftermath, have close ties to the banking industry. In fact, as previously mentioned, Paulson, the Treasury Secretary who initiated the TARP program, had been the CEO of Goldman Sachs, one of the largest investment banks on Wall Street, and one that benefitted from special treatment during the crisis. The fact that such a close connection would not be seen as a conflict of interest reinforces the idea that there is a persistent integration of the economic system with the political system, but one that ignores the practical values and norms for the cultural system and favors the instrumental logic of the economic system.

Summary Thoughts

Dominated by the economic system, today's culture is stifled by the desire for the predictability and dependability of the status quo. Therefore, the public is often at the mercy of surreptitious social control through the political system, which attempts to mollify or at least contain political dissent and pressures for social change in ways that benefit the systems world of wealthy economic actors and elite technocratic administrators. For example, those who protest and picket at pro-business gatherings like the World Trade Forum meetings or the G20 summits are now forced into fenced pens away from the cameras and spotlights, while the news media maintain the image of smooth and frictionless gatherings for their viewers. During the 2004 Democratic National convention in Boston, for example, protesters were relegated to a cramped area a block away from the convention center, hemmed by razor wire, concrete barriers, and eight-foot high fencing. The isolation and crowding of lawful protesters was not a decision based on democratic input. It was not voted on or approved by any public forum.

Since the late 1970s, the U.S. Congress has repeatedly cut tax rates on high incomes, capital gains, and other investment income. In addition, labor policies have made it harder for unions to offset the growing power of businesses, corporate governance policies have enabled top corporate executives to earn huge incomes regardless of their companies' performance, and deregulation of financial markets has allowed banks and other financial institutions to produce risky financial instruments that enrich managers and investors while exposing homeowners and pensioners to ruinous risks. There are many other examples of laws, policies, and regulations that benefit economic special interests at the expense of the public. New laws make the photography of potential animal rights abuses and food contamination problems illegal, which has a chilling effect on the abilities of whistleblowers to reveal potential food safety problems. At the same time, food production is often outsourced to countries like China, where terrible safety standards remain a widespread problem. In fact, with the exception of baby formula, neither the Food and Drug Administration or the Dept of Agriculture (USDA), the two main regulatory agencies in the U.S. created to protect consumers, has the legal power to require a food distributor or processor to recall a product that is either adulterated or mislabeled. Again, the news media draw little attention to these issues while the advertisements for these products continue to become more and more ubiquitous.

Another persistent phenomenon in the U.S. economy is the unequal relationship between worker productivity and pay. The political system over the last forty years has aided corporations and business owners to capture most of the added income from productivity gains at the expense of American workers. Consider that productivity gains have increased by an average of two percent *every year* since 1979 yet median wages have risen just only five percent in total during that same time period (BLS, 2013). Or that the share of U.S. income for the top ten percent of earners reached more than half of the country's total income in 2012, the highest level recorded since the government began collecting the data a century ago (Saez & Piketty, 2012). Or, even worse, since the recovery from the financial crisis began in 2009 corporate profits have risen three times faster than wages in the United States. In fact, a recent investor report published by the investment bank JP Morgan made some astonishingly candid claims. First, it cited the fact that "as we have shown several times over the last two years, U.S. labor compensation is now at a 50-year low relative to both company sales and U.S. GDP" (2011). Then it makes a second astonishing admission: profit margins for major U.S. corporations "have reached levels not seen in decades" and this dramatic increase is primarily due to reductions in the wages and benefits of workers. And what were the politicians and lobbying groups that are funded by these corporations clamoring for at the same time that profits are up and wages are down, at a time when unemployment is sky high and state and federal revenues are way down? Why, lower corporate taxes and less union representation and collective bargaining power among workers, of course.

Historically this is nothing new. In 1776, Adam Smith wrote about employers who used unfair political influence to sway the legislative process in his book *The Wealth of Nations*. "We have no acts of parliament against combining to lower the price of work, but many against combining to raise it." Smith was describing the establishment of laws at the time that prohibited workers from organizing into unions yet allowed employers to organize to keep wages low. The same things continue today, despite the heyday of union power in America after WWII, and the collective power of workers is again low. As a result, wages and salaries now make up the lowest share of the nation's gross domestic product since the government began recording the data in 1947, while corporate profits have climbed to their highest share since the 1960s. In the 1970s the top one percent of earners received six percent of all wage income, by 2004 it had almost doubled to around eleven percent (Saez & Piketty, 2004). At the same time, total employee compensation in the U.S. is at its lowest since 1966. During the last four decades, the political system has enacted trade policies that allowed corporations to outsource manufacturing jobs overseas, it has reduced the amount of regulation in a number of industries despite the fact that deregulation would increase the risk of harm (banking deregulation, for example) and has continued to provide multinational corporations with new rights (for example, the recent Supreme Court ruling allowing corporations to spend unlimited amounts of money to support "their" candidates in political elections) and outright cash subsidies despite record profits. All of these policy changes originated within the political system at the request of special interests and they often occurred gradually and imperceptibly. These policy changes also had the effect of exacerbating the growing income inequalities within the country because they so blatantly help a small wealthy minority at the expense of the majority. Yet the political system maintains that these public policies represent "the will of the people." One might wonder which people they mean.

It should be noted that the political system has also produced a number of broadly beneficial policies in the last four decades. Civil rights, environmental protections, consumer safety regulations are all examples of a political system responsive to the needs of the public, yet social inequality is currently increasing, the number of people living in poverty is increasing, and many of those same beneficial public policies are being eroded. According to a recent survey by the Organization for Economic Co-operation and Development, after Mexico and Turkey, the United States has the highest inequality levels of all of the OECD countries (OECD, 2008). The countries included in the survey represent the most developed market economies in the world. Income inequality in the U.S. has increased rapidly in the last decade, continuing a long-term trend that that began the 1970s. Further, the OECD reports that rich households in America have been leaving both middle and poorer income groups behind. This is not unique, but nowhere has this trend been so stark as in the United States, partly because redistribution of income by the government (taxes and social transfers) plays a relatively minor role in the U.S. compared with other advanced countries. In fact, the level of spending on social benefits such as unemployment insurance and welfare protections in the U.S. is relatively low; equivalent to just nine percent of household income, while the OECD average is more than double that at twenty-two percent, and the effectiveness of taxes and transfers in reducing inequality here in the U.S. has eroded even further in the last ten years. Finally, it should be noted that the U.S., despite increased productivity, despite being one of the richest nations on earth, is one of the five worst nations in the OECD community in terms of child poverty and fourth worst in terms of overall poverty. Here in America, twenty-two percent of our children live in poverty compared to the OECD average of twelve percent. It is increasingly difficult to defend these developments as beneficial to the public, and easier to see how they benefit an elite few at the expense of the many. This pattern of biased legislation often promotes agendas that are counter to "public good," and can at least partly be blamed on an institutional failure to adequately provide a representative democratic political system in the U.S.

Chapter 6

Why Do These Problems Persist?

Democratic social institutions enable collective action and achieve the goals set out by members of society, especially goals of social welfare. In democratic nations today, the public has the ability to assert its political collective will by electing representatives who propose and enact regulations and policies to promote the public's interests and correct discriminatory or damaging practices or unfair distributions of resources. The linguist and social theorist Noam Chomsky reminds us that modern social institutions are the products of our collective efforts and can be changed when needed.

> There is no reason to accept the doctrines crafted to sustain power and privilege, or to believe that we are constrained by mysterious and unknown social laws. These are simply decisions made within institutions that are subject to human will and that must face the test of legitimacy. And if they do not meet the test, they can be replaced by other institutions that are more free and more just, as has happened often in the past (Chomsky, 1997).

Yet various and significant forms of injustice and inequality persist despite these democratic institutions and processes, especially in the United States. For example, the latest data from the Urban Institute shows that economic inequality based on race continues to be a significant issue, with white families on average six times as wealthy as black or Hispanic families (2013). More broadly, the gap between hourly compensation and productivity, which measures the goods and services generated per hour worked, is the highest it's been in seventy years. Productivity rose by eighty percent between 1973 and 2011, compared to less than eleven percent growth in median hourly compensation, according to the Economic Policy Institute (2014). In fact, median wages among U.S. workers were lower in 2013 than 2003 and the majority of productivity gains in the economy are captured by a small elite segment of the population, the so-called *one percent*.

The logical conclusion of these percentages is for the public to recognize the shared plight regardless of political orientation or other demographic characteristics and enact the political changes that would mutually benefit us all. We have acknowledged that conservatives often value freedom above equality, but do conservatives rationally and intentionally vote against their own economic interests? Do blue-collar Republicans intentionally elect representatives that will likely do more harm than good for them? If so, why? Why does a modern democratic society allow social inequality to expand even when the disadvantaged members of that society have the power to correct those inequalities? Why don't we create political remedies to correct imbalances such as the gap in productivity gains?

The answers are undeniably grim. Social scientists have explained that societies are the most stable "under conditions of widespread 'false consciousness,'" when the public believes in "culturally palatable principles that bolster a preference to maintain the status quo" (Hanson, 2012, p. 365). Research shows that economic or political stakeholders can and do often manipulate our frames of reference to make us more receptive to economic intrusions, political corruptions, and cultural manipulation. We have acknowledged that corporate political power and supportive ideologies like the sanctity of free markets and the superiority of rational individualism influence our attitudes about issues of fairness and equality. We recognize that powerful economic actors in the U.S. use tools like lobbying, public relations campaigns, and campaign contributions to manipulate laws and regulations that maintain the status quo and their lofty positions in the social hierarchy. But I suggest that several additional factors play a role in our present circumstances that are particular to American culture.

Educational Weakness

One factor may be the state of education in America. Education is truly fundamental and has an essential role in the maintenance of civil society. As the French sociologist Émile Durkheim explained, education is "only the means by which a society prepares, within its children, the essential conditions of its own existence" (1956, p. 72). Historically, public education since the 19th century has been justified as a means to foster a literate population necessary for democracy and on the grounds that universal education was necessary to create an adaptable work force. But education can also help people find happiness and purpose by providing students with the critical tools for understanding their lives. The psychoanalyst Erich Fromm warned that the capitalist emphasis on individual freedom and self-interests caused Americans to lose sight of the intrinsic value of "man's capacity to love his fellow men, to work creatively, to develop his reason and objectivity, to have a sense of self which is based on the experience of his own productive powers" (1955, p. 72). In 1976, in a book called "To Have or To Be?" he posited that having and being were two modes of existence available to people. *Having* focused on material possessions and power, while *being* focused on being authentic, active, and productively engaged with the world (1976). Fromm argued that the necessities of 20th century capitalism pushed the Western world in the direction of having, which benefitted the economic system, and away from an emphasis on being.

> The development of [capitalism] was no longer determined by the question: What is good for Man? but by the question: What is good for the growth of the system? One tried to hide the sharpness of this conflict by making the assumption that what was good for the growth of the system (or even for a single big corporation) was also good for the people (Fromm, 1976, p. 30).

But economic growth does not necessarily have any connection to personal development or social progress. Fromm warned that this shift towards having rather than being led people astray from their true goals, which, according to Fromm, was to "grow optimally according to the conditions of human existence and thus to *become* fully what one potentially *is*... The full humanization of man requires the breakthrough from the possession-centered to the activity-centered orientation..." (Fromm, 1992, p. 1).

Fromm's implication, then, is that education is needed to reveal the hidden biases in society, and to provide the tools to measure and evaluate the entire social system on its merits, something that corporate stakeholders might choose to avoid. Today, unfortunately, the public education system in America is subpar at best, and this is creating an enormous underclass of unprepared, unskilled workers who lack the abilities and educational background to thrive economically. Also, this situation allows bad ideas to flourish and makes the public more susceptible to economic and political manipulation. In this chapter, I review the curious characteristics of American culture regarding education, including the long-running anti-intellectualism so common in this country, the political manipulation of conservative values that results in increased social problems despite the best intentions of the public, and the perversion of traditional values for strategic purposes.

The role of education in the development and maintenance of humane and democratic social systems over these many centuries of progress cannot be underestimated. Now more than ever, the complexities of modern life require that members of the social system have a firm educational grounding in order to effectively grasp the practical aspects of our current circumstances. Social policy production, risk management efforts, economic innovations, all require an educated populace if democratic political systems are to be sustained in the face of technocratic elitism and economic manipulation. Education in a general sense is one of the primary functions of the cultural system. It is the mechanism by which children are socialized into the broader community, the path to innovation and transformation for entire societies, and the crucial ingredient for democratic political systems. On an individual level, philosophers as far back as the ancient Greeks have pointed out the essential benefits of an educated society. For example, Aristotle said, "The educated differ from the uneducated as much as the living from the dead." Epictetus claimed, "Only the educated are free." In 1778, Thomas Jefferson wrote in the preamble to *A Bill for the More General Diffusion of Knowledge*:

> Whereas ... even under the best forms [of government],
> those entrusted with power have, in time, ... perverted it into
> tyranny; and it is believed that the most effectual means of
> preventing this would be, to illuminate... the minds of the
> people at large, and more especially to give them knowledge
> of those facts... that... they may be enabled to know ambi-
> tion under all its shapes, and... defeat its purposes (Jeffer-
> son, 1905).

Modern philosophers like John Dewey wrote that education provides the social continuity of life (1916). Presaging Habermas, Dewey suggested that communication is essential for ensuring that members of a society can share the cultural understandings that bind them together in a functional and mutually beneficial community, and that education is the means of developing that shared understanding.

> Men live in a community in virtue of the things which they
> have in common; and communication is the way in which
> they come to possess things in common. What they must

have in common in order to form a community or society
are aims, beliefs, aspirations, knowledge - a common understanding (1916, p. 7).

The sociologist C. Wright Mills, in The Power Elite (1956), pointed
out that, originally, the purpose of modern public education was "to
make the citizen more knowledgeable and thus better able to think
and to judge of public affairs" (p. 317). In essence, education served
a political purpose; the production of informed citizens who could
meaningfully engage in public life. This echoes a point De Tocqueville made much earlier about the connection between education
and democracy. He recognized in 1840 that ignorance, or lack of
adequate education, would degrade the democratic potential of a
society. "The concentration of powers and individual servitude will
increase therefore among democratic nations not only in proportion to equality but also in proportion to ignorance" (De Tocqueville, 1840, p. 490).

The French demographer Emmanuel Todd identified literacy and
control of reproductive rates as the essential necessities in the establishment of a social system guided by liberal democratic ideals
(2003). Societies that have achieved these goals develop sociopoliti-
cal structures that tend to be democratic, principled, and just. Public education is at the root of both these necessities since literate
members of a society experience an expansion of consciousness
that limits the ability of autocratic rulers to maintain their power.
Education is especially anathema to the forms of power that rely on
tradition as the source of legitimation, but this is exactly where the
issue gets tricky, because education and the literacy and raised
consciousness that it creates is destabilizing to traditional social
structures. The general process of moving from a traditional, reli-
giously oriented society to a secular democratic society involves
three stages: first, the expansion of literacy, then, most significantly,
an often violent, disruptive, revolutionary period in which the tradi-
tionalist members of society resist the evolutionary pressures
created by literacy, and, finally, reproductive control (2003). The
revolutionary period is meant literally, as the "less taxing mental
routines of an illiterate world" are rendered obsolete (p. 37).

Being uprooted from one's traditional life – from the well-
trodden routines of illiteracy, pregnancy, poverty, sickness,
and death – can at first produce as much suffering and dis-
orientation as it does hope and opportunity (p. 33).

The destabilization of traditional norms and values often leads to both personal crises and ideological violence as the transformation from traditional social structures to modernity takes hold. This, according to Todd, is how we can understand the jarring violence and religious fervor in parts of the Middle East, as a process of resistance before the eventual, slow acceptance of modern values and norms brought on by education and literacy, where traditional modes of life and accompanying power structures are slowly overtaken by the demands of rational discourse, participatory politics, and just distributions of resources. The effects of education can be literally revolutionary in these cases because the functions of education include the emancipation of the public from the odious forms of social control made possible by ignorance and the emergence of democratic principles of social organization and action.

However, Mills warned in the 1950s that we were shifting the role of education away from its proper functions in ways that are indeed degrading our own chances for fulfilling our democratic ideals. Mills wrote that by the beginning of the 20th century, "the function of education shifted from the political to the economic: to train people for better-paying jobs and thus to get ahead" (1956, p. 368). The American professor of education David Larabee has written extensively on this functional shift.

> Once created to support the republic, in a time when schools were marginal to the practical business of making a living, they had become central to every citizen's ability to get a good job and get ahead socially. In the process, however, the political vision of education changed from a substantive focus on producing the citizens needed to sustain the republic to a procedural focus on providing social opportunities (2011, p. 180).

Unfortunately, an education that focuses on the skills necessary for a successful career is not the same as an education that teaches students to be actively engaged in their own emancipation through thoughtful and vibrant public discourse, personal development, and political action. Dewey warned of this as well, pointing out that "Democracy cannot flourish where the chief influences in selecting subject matter of instruction are utilitarian ends narrowly conceived for the masses, and, for the higher education of the few, the traditions of a specialized cultivated class" (1916, p. 200). In Dewey's view, the general curriculum of elementary education in modern America is "based upon ignorance of the essentials needed for realization of democratic ideals" (p. 200). The emphasis placed on work, which highlights one's economic function without providing any insight for one's political or larger cultural capacities, is a path to alienation and powerlessness.

> Getting a livelihood, "making a living," must dignify for most men and women doing things which are not significant, freely chosen, and ennobling to those who do them; doing things which serve ends unrecognized by those engaged in them, carried on under the direction of others for the sake of pecuniary reward (1916, p. 200).

Part of the problem with emphasizing vocational competence as the focus of educational efforts is that it orients the learner to a role in the capitalist economic system without providing the skills and depth of knowledge necessary to fill the void *surrounding* economic activity in a person's life experience. We are not simply workers, but also lovers, parents, citizens, dreamers, and so on, and vocational education is silent on these aspects of modern life, despite their importance. Capitalism is primarily an economic system of material production and is relatively unconcerned about the degradation of mind and spirit that is often a side effect of productive but alienated work. As the German economist Georg Simmel wrote almost a century ago,

> The product is completed at the expense of the development of the producer. The increase in psycho-physical energies and skills, which is the result of specialized activity, is of little value for the total personality, which often even becomes stunted because of the diversion of energies that are indispensable for the harmonious growth of the self" (1907, p. 454).

In today's industrialized societies, workers often have little power or control over their jobs, and the specialized nature of work requires workers to perform limited and repetitive tasks. In fact, the growing division of labor experienced by workers during the Industrial Revolution had significant negative side effects that persist today. Factory workers of the time gained little in terms of educational and cultural development from their labors. Their work, reduced to a few simple operations, provided no opportunity for creativity, problem-solving or the development of mental dexterity. The economist Adam Smith complained over two hundred years ago that the factory worker "has no occasion to exert his understanding or to exercise his invention in finding out expedients for removing difficulties which never occur" (1776, pp. 782-8). This had a stultifying effect, in which the worker "... generally becomes as stupid and ignorant as it is possible for a human creature to become." This, according to Smith, is the state into which the working classes, the "great body of the people," must necessarily fall, "unless government takes some pains to prevent it."

The education of youth at public expense was the solution that Smith recommended protecting against this degradation of mind and spirit. Scholastics would also help protect the working classes from "the delusions of enthusiasm and superstition." Educated and intelligent people "are more disposed to examine, and more capable of seeing through, the interested complaints of faction and sedition, and they are, upon that account, less apt to be misled into any wanton or unnecessary opposition to the measures of government" (1776, p. 784). This is striking since Smith writing in 1776 is essentially arguing that the working classes needed to be educated so that they wouldn't revolt against the government.

> In free countries, where the safety of government depends very much upon the favourable judgment which the people may form of its conduct, it must surely be of the highest importance that they should not be disposed to judge rashly or capriciously concerning it (Smith, 1776, p. 784).

While completion rates for secondary education (high school) hover around 82% in America, the highest on record according to the Dept. of Education, there is a clear decrease in our educational attainment levels when compared to the rest of the world. According to a recent 2010 Organization for Economic Co-operation and Development (OECD) report, for example, the U.S. still has one of most highly educated labor forces in the industrialized world, but graduation rates are not keeping up. Although 28 percent of the American population reported a bachelor's degree or higher, and 31 percent of those 25-29 years old, the U.S. graduation rate is lower in comparison to other developed nations. According to the report, the U.S. is the only country where the college attainment levels of this generation do not exceed those of the last generation. This suggests a widening gap for America in the future, and, the U.S. currently ranks 15th out of the 34 industrialized countries in post-secondary educational attainment. Further, only about 38 percent of Americans who enroll in college actually graduate, while Canada had a graduation rate of almost 60 percent, and both South Korea and Russia graduate approximately 55 percent of their students (College Board, 2010).

Part of the problem with American college graduation rates is that students are not proficient enough in reading and math for them to succeed in post-secondary education. Currently, 42 percent of 15-year-old students in the U.S. score below appropriate proficiency levels in reading, which indicates that they lack the skills necessary for post-secondary studies. If this trend continues, and there is no evidence that it is abating, it will become increasingly difficult to supply institutions of higher education with students who are able to complete their studies. Economically, these educational trends suggest increased job insecurity among workers as they compete in the global labor market against better-educated nations, and increased difficulty filling technically sophisticated or intellectually demanding positions with American workers since college graduation rates are unlikely to keep up with our competitor nations. "The implication for these countries is that the stock of skills available to them is bound to decline over the next decades unless action is taken both to improve skills proficiency among young people," the OECD wrote, referring to the U.S. and England. This is an unfortunate trend since education has traditionally been such a powerful protective factor. College graduates have the lowest unemployment rates of any segment of the population, especially in periods of difficult economic conditions.

We have already identified the ways that modernity and capitalism both lead to social inequality. The technical nature of modern bureaucratic administration of political and economic systems requires the differentiation of skills and labor, and the resulting differences in status, power, and rewards. Further, capitalism has exploitative tendencies built into its functions, for example, the tendency for economic power to concentrate itself, and reduce competition by creating oligarchies and monopolies, and thereby concentrate wealth into the hands of a small group of wealthy elite. Based on data from 2000, a study by the Global Policy Forum found that one percent of the world's adults owned 40 percent of the world's wealth, while the bottom half of adults in the world together owned less than one percent. These inequalities are partly a result of the flawed educational opportunities available to America's most vulnerable populations. It is well established that education is universally linked with poverty reduction, economic growth, and wealth creation and that illiteracy and poverty constitute a mutually reinforcing vicious cycle that is difficult to break.

> People with low levels of literacy are more likely to earn less and experience poverty or extreme poverty; moreover, their opportunities are limited in all spheres of life (work, education, housing and access to health care) and their children risk falling into the same cycle by attending poor quality schools and dropping out of school at an early stage (UNESCO, 2014).

Here in the United States, both income inequality and educational deficits among the young are the highest in the industrialized world. As of 2011, America was the only industrialized, free-market nation where the current generation is less well educated than the previous generation. Additionally, twenty-five percent of the children in America grow up without learning how to read, and this educational deficit is directly associated with poverty and crime. For example, according to statistics reported by the Nevada Dept of Corrections, nearly eighty-five percent of the juveniles in the juvenile court system and over seventy percent of inmates in America's prisons cannot read above a fourth-grade level. According to an official at the U.S. Department of Justice, "The link between academic failure and delinquency, violence, and crime is welded to reading failure" (Brunner, 1993). And the connection to poverty is also obvious. Currently, ninety percent of high school dropouts rely on some type of social welfare program.

Unhelpful Biases

One might wonder why the weaknesses of cultural institutions such as the public education system and the resulting suppression of general public interests can be maintained over generations in the United States without resolution. One answer is that the U.S., in particular, suffers from a distinct resistance to intellectual efforts to critique the status quo, and this is partly due to a conservative bias among Americans. Conservatives are more likely to support authority and the status quo than their liberal neighbors, and this may partly explain the perpetuation of social inequality in the United States. For example, researchers have consistently shown that public opinion shifts in a conservative direction in response to rising income inequality, which has been the case here in America for decades. This conservative shift in sentiment has been found to occur among both the rich and the poor (Kelly & Enns, 2010). In fact, the preferences of both the wealthiest and the poorest Americans move in tandem and respond to economic inequality similarly over time. When inequality in America rises, studies find, the public responds with increased conservative attitudes regarding redistributive policies even though this conservative response produces more economic inequality (Kelly & Enns, 2010).

One reason for this is a particular worldview popular among conservatives involving the concept of justice. A theory known as the "just world hypothesis" developed by the psychologist Melvin Lerner (1980) can help explain this phenomenon. The just world hypothesis refers to a basic belief that the world is a place where people deserve what they get, and get what they deserve. One major consequence of this belief is that people see themselves and others as responsible for the outcomes they experience. According to Lerner, all people are strongly motivated by the desire to eliminate suffering of innocent victims (1980). But if the suffering cannot be eliminated, some people will redefine the victim as deserving of the suffering. The original studies by Lerner and Simmons in 1966 found that, when presented with a victim who suffered through little fault of her own, people recognized the unfairness of the situation and were motivated to compensate the victim if they could. But when presented with the same victim and the additional expectation that the victim would continue to suffer, some people lowered their opinion of the victim's character and described her in more negative terms. This is a type of cognitive bias, a psychological rationalization of the victim's fate by reinterpreting the victim's fate as deserved and, therefore, less unfair. In essence, it is a bias to maintain the belief that we live in a world with fair and predictable consequences.

Research has found that people who have a strong tendency to believe in a just world tend to be more conservative, more likely to support existing social institutions, and more likely to have negative attitudes toward underprivileged groups (Rubin & Peplau, 1975). Americans with conservative values also tend to attribute poverty, crime, homelessness, and obesity to causes internal to persons, whereas those with liberal values tend to attribute the same phenomena more to situational or structural factors. From this perspective, problems like poverty are attributed to failures of personal responsibility, either at the individual or family level.

Furthermore, research on the allocation of resources like welfare or health care has found that people with conservative political orientations experience anger toward claimants, devalue their deservingness, and are motivated to withhold resources from those in need if the claimants' needs are perceived as "self-inflicted." In research by Skitka & Tetlock, for example, conservatives were simply more likely to withhold aid to those in need. For example, in a 1993 set of studies, they found that Conservatives typically deny help to claimants who are personally responsible for their predicament, and they do so even in life-and- death settings (1993, p. 1216). In an earlier study, the same researchers found that politically conservative participants "withheld resources from those responsible for their needs regardless of severity of need and likelihood of effective helping, even when there were sufficient resources to satisfy all claimants, whereas liberals tended to provide resources to all claimants" (Skikta & Tetlock, 1992, p. 519). The just world hypothesis is not a view exclusively held by conservatives, but it is associated with conservative values, the ideology of individualism, and the concept of personal responsibility. It may be useful to point out that in the U.S. in 2016, according to the Gallup polling company, 37% of Americans described their views as conservative, 35% as moderate, and 24% as liberal, making the conservative political ideology the dominant one in America (Saad, 2016).

The U.S. in particular also suffers from a distinct resistance to intellectualism, and this is an even bigger hindrance to solving the social problems associated with economic inequalities. It is generally accepted that modern democracy requires an educated public able to make informed choices about their lives and their larger interests. Ideally, education and socialization processes can provide the skills necessary to do that. Knowledge, in general, is empowering, and critical thinking skills can help us differentiate the sources of knowledge that are politicized or ideologically biased from those that are emancipatory and consciousness expanding. Critical thinking skills and an appreciation of scientific principles can provide answers in terms of lifestyle choices at the personal level and public policy choices at the social level. These capacities can be developed in people by an engaged public educational system. Unfortunately, America, in particular, has a strain of antipathy to knowledge and science that does not bode well for the future. As the prolific science fiction writer Isaac Asimov wrote years ago in a column in Newsweek,

There is a cult of ignorance in the United States, and there
always has been. The strain of anti-intellectualism has been
a constant thread winding its way through our political and
cultural life, nurtured by the false notion that democracy
means that 'my ignorance is just as good as your knowledge'
(Azimov, 1980, p. 19).

In 1963, the American historian Richard Hofstadter wrote a Pulitzer-prize winning book called *Anti-Intellectualism in American Life*, which traced the rise of anti-intellectualism to the earliest days of the nation. In the beginning, according to him, the relationship between intellect and power was not problematical. The leaders in control of national affairs were intellectuals, the "patrician elite" as Hofstadter put it, and "moved freely and spoke with enviable authority." In every segment of society, these men used their learning and cultivation to solve the exigent problems of their time. "No subsequent era in our history has produced so many men of knowledge among its political leaders" (1963, p. 145). Unfortunately, soon after the signing of the Constitution, however, a reputation for intellect became a political disadvantage.

It is ironic that the United States should have been founded
by intellectuals; for throughout most of our political history,
the intellectual has been for the most part either an outsider,
a servant, or a scapegoat (p. 145).

Eventually political power shifted from the patrician elite to a popular democracy, and those members of the elite, "who with notable character and courage led the way through the Revolution and with remarkable prescience and skill organized a new national government in 1787" began to quarrel amongst themselves, and lower their political standards to the point that "snarling and hysterical differences" related to the French Revolution led them to engage in a new style of politics "with little regard for decency or common sense." According to Hofstadter, the first notable victim of American anti-intellectualism was Thomas Jefferson, attacked by both the Federalist leaders and members of the clergy of New England for possessing the very qualities that made him so great, "the capacity for reflective, creative, and critical thought, finely honed argumentation, and public persuasion—talents one might other–wise assume well recommend a candidate for the office of president... which they insisted made him unfit for practical tasks" (Giroux, 2011).

Unfortunately, lowered political standards accurately describe a large swath of the current political landscape here in America. "It's like these guys take pride in being ignorant," Barack Obama remarked about his Republican challengers in 2008 as he campaigned for the American presidency. Unfortunately, there is no serious political penalty for ignorance and intolerance among the modern Right in American politics, and many members have adopted an attitude of willful ignorance to appeal to their conservative constituents and supporters.

Willful ignorance by political and economic stakeholders and the anti-intellectual stance is alive and well here and abroad. As an example, the right-wing member of parliament Michael Gove famously declared that the British public had "had enough of experts" during the discussions leading up to the Brexit (British Exit) referendum, which resulted in England voting to leave the European Union (Stewart, 2016). Gove claimed before the vote that the Vote Leave contingent knew more about economics than the economic experts who issued warnings of a financial downturn after Brexit. The actual impact of the historic vote remains to be seen, but the anti-expert sentiment continues to be popular.

Reactionary Populism

In the U.S., populist anger at the "intellectual elites" in Washington is a perennial political issue. More broadly, anxieties about racial, ethnic, and generational changes in American society have spawned political interest among older white voters across the nation. One such populist movement, the Tea Party movement, for example, emerged as a semi-coherent political force in the U.S. following the economic crisis in 2008. According to sociologists Theda Skocpol and Vanessa Williamson, the Tea Party is a particular incarnation of a longstanding type of U.S. conservatism (Williamson, Skocpol, et al., 2011). Anger about new federal social programs such as the Affordable Care Act and general resentment of perceived federal government largesse given to undeserving racial and ethnic groups coexists with acceptance of long-standing federal social programs like Social Security and Medicare, to which Tea Partiers feel legitimately entitled. Williamson and Skocpol argue that the Tea Party is a strange hybrid; a semi-coherent grassroots movement promoted by the conservative media and supported by wealthy and elite donors.

The movement seems to embrace the ideas that underpin the neoliberal economic perspective; that we are rational, autonomous agents without connection or obligation to other individuals or institutions, and they reject the technocratic institutions and "elites" who attempt to manage or interfere with individual liberties and engagement with the free market. These ideas are popular with economic entities that desire an end to regulation and oversight, entities like the energy, food, and financial industries, but these ideas have also found fertile soil in the blue-collar regions of modern society as well.

Unfortunately, movements like the Tea Party perpetuate the anti-intellectual biases so popular here in America. In an essay titled "The Tea Party Jacobins," published in The New York Review of Books, for example, the American political scientist Mark Lilla describes the angry coalition of the aggrieved, what he calls the "libertarian mob," as the latest, and strangest, populist uprising in some time.

> Many Americans, a vocal and varied segment of the public at large, have now convinced themselves that educated elites— politicians, bureaucrats, reporters, but also doctors, scientists, even schoolteachers—are controlling our lives. And they want them to stop. They say they are...tired of being told what their children should be taught, how much of their paychecks they get to keep, whether to insure themselves, which medicines they can have...which guns they can buy...which foods they can eat...the list is long (Lilla, 2010).

Lilla makes the point that the Tea Party is not a setting out a list of political grievances in the conventional sense. The Tea Party rhetoric of taking back the country is based on a repudiation of what they see as social entanglement and forced dependency, and they are not seeking political power as much as they are trying to neutralize it. This critical attitude may be seen as a repudiation of the rationalized, technocratic, and elite control of the mechanisms of modern society, and is echoed in many places around the world, as in Britain and their having "had enough of experts." Unfortunately, these critical responses to modern society are easily co-opted by economic forces, since the media have an oversized influence on public perceptions. Of course, Fox News is well understood as a source of bias, but currently, even stalwarts like CBS are in on the game. According to Fortune magazine, Leslie Moonves, the chairman of CBS, was quoted at a conference in San Francisco talking about the cable news outlet's intense coverage of presidential candidate Donald

Trump, "It may not be good for America," Moonves said, "but it's damn good for CBS" (Huddleston, 2016).

The reason the extreme segments of the Republican Party like the Tea Party are so popular, according to the American political analyst Thomas Frank, is the "class animus" that blue-collar, working-class people feel about the cultural values and liberal policies promoted by "the wealthy, powerful, and well-connected – the liberal media, the atheistic scientists, the obnoxious eastern elite" (2004, p. 7). In fact, Frank, in his book, *What's the Matter with Kansas?* (2004), claims that the Republican political machine has persuaded working class people to vote against their own economic interests by convincing them that the Republican Party will defend traditional cultural values against radical liberal elites. Socially conservative cultural values are often seen as *moral* when compared to the liberal views that support gay rights, abortion, and so on. So blue-collar conservatives support the Republican Party candidates in the hope that morality can be maintained.

Their efforts were misguided, however, because the working class generally does not benefit from Republican policies, especially an economic agenda of tax cuts for the wealthy, deregulation, and corporate welfare. Furthermore, the defense of traditional cultural values has never been successful at the national level. Thus, there is a tragic irony when working-class cultural conservatives provide the crucial political support for cultural protections that never materialize and economic policies that directly harm them.

> All they have to show for their Republican loyalty are lower wages, more dangerous jobs, dirtier air, a new overlord class … and, of course, a crap culture whose moral free fall continues, without significant interference from the grandstanding Christers whom they send triumphantly back to Washington every couple of years (2004, p.136).

Worse, some scholars have suggested that the primary philosophical orientation of the majority of Tea Party members is basically nihilism. The philosopher JM Bernstein had an interesting view on this. During the worst of the financial crisis that began in 2008, Bernstein argued that the idea of a free and autonomous citizen "is an artifact created by the practices of modern life: the intimate family, the market economy, the liberal state," and "these social arrangements articulate and express the value and the authority of the individual; they give to the individual a standing she would not have without them" (2010). However, the results of the financial crisis, especially the sudden unemployment and recessionary pressures, "demonstrated the depths of the absolute dependence of us all on government action," and have "undermined the deeply held fiction of individual autonomy and self-sufficiency that are intrinsic parts of Americans' collective self-understanding." In other words, state institutions supporting modern life were politically acceptable as long as they could be rendered invisible, and people could maintain the fictional belief that they were autonomous and self-sufficient. But recent economic and political developments have forced people to acknowledge their dependencies, and this makes many people angry and destructive in ways that include self-harm. As Mark Lilla put it,

> Now an angry group of Americans wants to be freer still—
> free from government agencies that protect their health,
> wealth, and well-being; free from problems and policies too
> difficult to understand; free from parties and coalitions; free
> from experts who think they know better than they do; free
> from politicians who don't talk or look like they do... They
> don't want the rule of the people, though that's what they
> say. They want to be people without rules—and, who knows,
> they may succeed (2010).

Social Conservatism & Nostalgia

There is an argument to be made in support of traditional notions of freedom and morality, and morality, in general, is representative of human interests in ways that cross national and cultural boundaries. Charles Taylor, Canada's foremost philosopher, for example, contends that moral decisions are rooted in what he calls "strong evaluations" (1989). These evaluations, or intuitions, involve discriminations of right and wrong that are independent of our own desires or choices. As he describes it, "We are dealing here with moral intuitions which are uncommonly deep, powerful, and universal. They are so deep that we are tempted to think of them as rooted in instinct" (p. 4).

In Taylor's model, morality can be objectively approached as a component of human ontology. Morality is "inextricably bound" to selfhood. Respect for life, the quest for meaning, freedom, and human dignity are all universally recognized as "good," and Taylor contends that we cannot help but orient ourselves and our lives "in relation to the good" (1989, p. 54). In fact, according to Taylor, any

claims of moral relativism or accusations that these moral discriminations are simply subjective are *themselves* situated within a moral
framework, as in the case of existentialism or hedonism. There is no
way for anyone, whether social critic or empirical scientist, to stand
in a position of objectivity regarding moral frameworks. No matter
what claim one makes, insists Taylor, it is made from within some
moral framework. "Living within these frameworks is not an op-
tional extra, something we might just as well do without, they provide a kind of orientation essential to our identity" (p. 78).

On the other hand, calls for a "return to morality," or what Habermas calls "dogmatic provincialism," are often based on a nostalgic view of the past in which society was more simple and homogenous, a view that overlooks many glaring weaknesses (Smart,
1999). Social conservatism embodies the tension between newly
imagined freedoms relating to lifestyle and identity and the traditional conceptions of social order related to a stable, stratified, social structure. The promises made by Donald Trump in 2016 to
"make America great again" are eerily similar to the rhetoric used
by Rick Santorum during his presidential campaign in 2012 and
used by Senator Bob Dole over twenty years ago, for example in
their pledge to "take this country back" to a past where family values dominated our collective culture. Although popular, the possi-
bilities to fulfill such pledges are problematical due to the increasing fragmentation and complexity of modern society. The professor
of higher education Harland Bloland uses the term "politics of nostalgia" to describe the attempt to "pull back to an ideal time, a period when the country's values were homogenous, where hierarchy
reigned, distinctions between high and low culture were ironclad
and backed by money, government, tradition, and a belief in experts" (1995, p. 266).

However, most social critics generally agree that this nostalgic
view refers to a community dominated by a power elite of white
males who consistently marginalized minorities and women, over-
reached in international affairs, and jeopardized the global financial
system with risky and often illegal actions. These images of a "golden age" of normalcy overlook the brutal and unjustifiable oppression of others necessary to support this elite power hegemony.
Ultimately, however, as the civil rights champion Martin Luther
King, Jr. once said, "The arc of the moral universe is long, but it
bends towards justice." Tea Party supporters, along with other
members of the social conservative faction of the Republican Party

may see expanded civil rights, women's rights, and gay rights as political failures, but these new policies actually represent failures of the old, white power hegemony.

The nostalgia for that "golden age" before things got so complicated, however, makes many persist in their support of political parties antithetical to their own interests. Thus, Frank claims, we see a version of Marx's false consciousness among these blue-collar conservatives,

> [S]turdy blue-collar patriots reciting the Pledge while they strangle their own life chances; ... small farmers proudly voting themselves off the land; ... devoted family men carefully seeing to it that their children will never be able to afford college or proper health care; ... working-class guys in Midwestern cities cheering as they deliver up a landslide for a candidate whose policies will end their way of life, will transform their region into a 'rust belt,' will strike people like them blows from which they will never recover (Frank, 2004, p. 10).

Concluding Thoughts

It is an unfortunate fact that many of our current social and environmental problems are related to evolutionary advances that have brought so much benefit to the world, developments like the economic advances of the Industrial Revolution, the power of science and technology, and the increased efficiencies associated with bureaucratic forms of social organization. From a historical standpoint, it is *not* universally accepted that economic development will necessarily lead to better lives and stronger, more vibrant societies. For example, in the 1960s, the historian Carroll Quigley pointed out that civilizations pass through a predictable process of evolution: every civilization is born in some fashion and eventually begins a period of vigorous expansion, increasing its size and power (1966). Eventually, a crisis of organization develops and forces the civilization to reorganize itself at the expense of some of its vigor and morale. Continued stability eventually leads to stagnation, and internal crises again arise, but the civilization has become morally and physically weak so that, as new challenges arise and internal conflicts persist, "the civilization grows steadily weaker until it is submerged by outside enemies, and eventually disappears" (p. 15).

In his study of twenty historical civilizations, Quigley found that periods of expansion (demographic, geographic, economic) are always followed by periods of conflict (1966). The periods of conflict are marked by four chief characteristics: a declining rate of expansion; growing tensions and class conflicts; increasingly frequent and violent imperialist wars; and growing irrationality, pessimism, and superstitions. Social classes and political groups within the civilization try to compensate for the lack of expansion through violence against the other groups. However, claimed Quigley, the beginning of the end for any civilization is when one political unit eventually triumphs and begins what Quigley called *the Age of the Universal Empire*. The triumph of one political group over the rest creates a stratified power structure that leads to economic and cultural oppression if unchecked. Personally, I fear that the ascendency of neoliberalism as a global political-economic force may represent the universal empire that Quigley describes.

From a different perspective, the historian Arnold Toynbee suggested that the causes of societal disintegration are related to political failure to resolve internal social conflicts when addressing large-scale challenges (1965). The failure to maintain cultural integrity within a society results in a loss of cohesive motivation among members of society and can result in the alienation of the "creative minority," the technocratic elite that directs the society's problem-solving processes, resulting in a breakdown of the existing social order. The differentiation of creative elite from "parasitic" minority becomes a cultural problem in that two distinct cultures may emerge. This can lead to the exploitation of the majority by the elite minority and cause an eventual decline and collapse of the society. This type of alienation is already developing in America and other Western nations, as evidenced by the rising popularity of radical political groups like the Tea Party here and abroad.

Democracies around the world are predicated on a few basic principles. For example, almost all countries in the world respect the rule of law According to the World Justice Project (WJP), the rule of law guarantees that governments, individuals, and private entities are all equally accountable under a common set of laws, which are clear, publicized, stable, and protect the security of persons and property and certain core human rights. Also, the processes by which the laws are enacted, administered, and enforced should be accessible, fair, and efficient; and justice delivered by competent, ethical, and independent representatives. But we have already documented that the United States has real problems with institutionalized racism and the tendency to soften the enforcement of the law in cases of white-collar crime, among other weaknesses. For reasons like these, the World Justice Project Rule of Law Index ranks the U.S. 19th out of the 31 richest nations of the world in 2015 (WJP, 2016). Secondly, democratic governments are by their very natures for the public and exist to protect and serve the population, yet we have documented the many ways that the U.S. political system allows and even promotes predatory practices that take advantage of poor and marginalized members of society. Finally, all democracies require that information is provided to the public as a public good, and is accurate and timely. Unfortunately, we have documented the many ways that vital information can be distorted or misrepresented in pursuit of special interests.

According to Michael Ignatieff, former leader of the Canadian Liberal Party and now a scholar at Harvard, "Slowly, painfully, we do seem to be shaking ourselves awake, rediscovering what Adam Smith told us all along, that markets are public institutions that only function efficiently when regulated in the public interest" (2014). Many futurists suggest that the current economic ideologies that emphasize the profit and wealth generated by the "markets" as ultimate ends are unlikely to thrive in the technological future because the incentives are likely to be less appealing to future technocratic leaders. Instead, they say, cultural values having to do with social welfare and creativity are likely to determine the success or failure of tomorrow's societies.

Furthermore, the economic gap between knowledge workers and non-knowledge workers is likely to become increasingly significant and there can be no realistic expectation that this gap can be closed by economic means alone, for example through growth in the productivity of the non-knowledge workers.

> That is why the market economy as the framework for [society] would most likely fail. It would offer only "income-based" creativity circles, tie dignity and status to the level of income, and in this way permanently exclude the non-knowledge workers (DESA, 2005).

A transformation of social institutions will be necessary to create opportunities for non-knowledge workers and manage the social impact of those workers who are tied to communities out of necessity and are therefore "captive taxpayers." Without these changes, the inequalities of socioeconomic disparity will worsen and the resulting social problems will be more severe. A 2004 UN study found that the key element of global competition will be the creative capacities of nations and their ability to attract creative talent from other regions of the world (DESA, 2005). The future leaders of the global economy "will be those nations that are best able to attract, retain and develop creative talent and harness their creative assets and capabilities." Cultural values cannot be overestimated as a catalyst for success in this global economy.

According to futurist Peter Drucker (1994), modern societies currently rely on a traditional mindset that emphasizes the primacy of capital and the financier, 'while bribing knowledge workers to be content to remain employees by giving them bonuses and stock options." But this is unlikely to be a successful strategy because key knowledge workers in the industries of the future will expect to share in both leadership and profits. "The central tension is based on values, not on wealth" (Florida & Tinagli, 2004). Drucker criticizes the current economic order for emphasizing economic values rather than social values and suggests that the reliance on appeals to workers' greed, in the form of bonuses and salaries, or insecurities, in the form of steady versus precarious work, will not be effective in the future. Industries will have to satisfy the *values* of their workers by giving them social recognition and social power, effectively "turning them from subordinates into fellow executives, and from employees… into partners" in order to maintain and motivate them (1994). As Peter Drucker predicted twenty years ago,

> Knowledge workers will not be a majority in the knowledge
> society, but in many if not most developed countries they
> will be the largest single population and work-force group.
> And even where outnumbered by other groups, knowledge
> workers will give the emerging knowledge society its charac-
> ter, its leadership, its social profile… And in their characte-
> ristics, social position, values, and expectations, they differ
> fundamentally from any group in history (1994).

The anger of conservatives here and abroad, especially those in groups like the Tea Party movement, is likely due in part to the tremendous transformations that are slowly but surely altering the socio-cultural landscape around the world. In an interconnected world of technocratic elites who manage the global systems of commerce, politics, and information, there will be those who cannot adapt or are hindered from taking part in the process. The processes of functional differentiation ensure that inclusion and exclusion will continue to divide communities around the globe into the haves and have-nots. People are being left behind, and they are often made aware of this fact, like in the aftermath of the financial crises here in the U.S. and the ongoing sovereign debt crisis in Europe. The result of this awareness is likely to be anger and social conflict. Especially here in the U.S., the poor quality of our education system almost guarantees that many of our citizens will not have the tools to adapt. Many people around the world will not be participating in the culture of life, whereby those with wealth and knowledge will live longer while the poor majorities see their life spans diminish. We can already see this phenomenon in the United States. A study in the journal Health Affairs in 2013 found that in almost half of the nation's counties, women are dying at rates higher than before. The counties where women's life expectancy is declining typically are in the rural South and West, and wealth inequality is a major factor (Stobbe, 2013). Similarly, a study in England found that the life expectancy for people living in England's most deprived areas is up to 20 years lower than those in affluent areas (Bingham, 2014).

On the one hand, our problems are too complex and sensitive to leave to the uneducated segments of the public sphere for the evaluation and selection of potential solutions. On the other hand, educational failures, including the creeping misinformation in our media, and cultural colonization will make it more true tomorrow than today that vast numbers of people simply don't understand what is going on. Risks will continue to be borne by the people who can least protect themselves, political policies will continue to favor the elite and wealthy at the expense of the poor and weak among us. The transformation of modern culture is one where we will soon no longer have moral qualms about human life; in an economic system, everything can be quantified and commoditized, including life and death. Organ trafficking, slavery, the perverse industries of for-profit prisons and the pharmaceutical industry, where incarceration and illness are profit sources, these are not threats looming in our future, they are already here. The business of war is big business, the fraud and corruption that run rampant in the financial industry are largely ignored, while civil liberties and privacy are stripped away. These problems are the result, at least in large part, to the disembedded economic systems that dominate the political functions of even the most democratic nations. The transformations are part of a juggernaut, a secular trend that will run its course unless massive collective action is taken. But here in the U.S, it would seem that half the voting population celebrates the economic colonization of American culture, even as it becomes increasingly apparent that those voters are working against their own well-being and future survival. It is reminiscent of the Thanatos, the death wish, that Freud said pushed men into violence and destruction that was a hidden desire for self-destruction and oblivion.

Keynes wrote in the mid-1920s that the single biggest political problem faced by humanity is how to combine economic efficiency, social justice, and individual freedom. Neoliberal capitalism assumes that only the free market can provide a solution, yet free market systems have failed over and over again, resulting in unequal distributions of welfare, subordination, and exclusion. The "double movement" described by Polanyi can be seen in the strengthening of a state-capitalist system in response to the failures of liberal and neoliberal economic systems here in the U.S. and abroad after World War II. While under almost constant attack by supporters of the neoliberal agenda, the state-capitalism system has managed to maintain most of the public policies needed to ensure at least a minimum level of public welfare. Yet the current system is by no means ideal, and practically every day we see failures of state intervention to curb economic risks and imbalances. Scholars have found ample evidence for the effectiveness of social welfare policies by comparing relatively free-market economies that have low rates of taxation and social outlays (countries include Australia, Canada, Ireland, New Zealand, the U.K. and the U.S) with social-welfare states that have high rates of taxation and social outlays (the Nordic social democracies, including Denmark, Finland, Norway and Sweden) (Sachs, 2006). The low-tax, high-income countries, mostly English speaking, economically neoliberal, tend to favor private spending over public spending. The Nordic social democracies, on the other hand, combine market-based economies with a strong commitment to public antipoverty programs. Budgetary outlays for social purposes average around twenty-seven percent of gross domestic product (GDP) in the Nordic countries and just seventeen percent of GDP in the English-speaking countries. Also, even though Australia, Canada, and New Zealand all have low levels of public spending on social welfare, a relatively high proportion of their spending goes to programs that are means tested so that the money goes to the most needy. More than a third of direct public spending goes to means-tested programs in Australia, and almost a quarter in Canada and the United Kingdom (Morgan, 2013).

In the United States, however, only about *seven percent* of direct public spending goes to means-tested benefit programs (Morgan, 2013). Furthermore, according to the Center on Budget and Policy Priorities, in 2010 fifty-eight percent of entitlement spending went to middle-income households, and only thirty-two percent went to the poorest twenty percent of households. Indirect benefits like tax breaks and employer-based benefit packages like retirement benefits and paid sick leave in the United States also flow disproportionately to those in the middle and at the top of the income ladder.

The conclusion is that social welfare spending is not directed primarily at the poor in America, so *by design* it will fail to solve the problems of poverty or inequality. The United States ranks fourth from the bottom among OECD countries in terms of its poverty rate, above only Israel, Mexico, and Chile. The United States also has one of the most unequal distributions of income of the advanced industrial democracies, and these trends are not counteracted by political action. Taxes and social spending are the mechanisms by which the political system distributes the country's wealth. It is the Robin Hood part of the social equation, where the government takes from the rich and gives to the poor to maintain basic standards of living for the populace and limit the economic and political power of the elite. Every developed nation has such a transfer system. However, in the U.S. those taxes that would limit the concentration of wealth, taxes like the capital gains tax on investment income for private individuals, corporate earnings taxes, or even more importantly the estate taxes that limit intergenerational concentration of wealth within families, have been reduced over time and are now no longer effective mechanisms of wealth distribution. Furthermore, the spending part of the equation is also consistently attacked and often undermined by politically powerful wealthy interests through their political surrogates. The result is predictable – more and more wealth concentrated in fewer and fewer hands and less and less social welfare.

Worse still, in addition to the subtle legitimation of the social inequalities inherent in our system of state-regulated capitalism, there is a constant and powerful pressure on the political system to drift more toward the neoliberal models of capitalism (see Gilens & Page, 2014). Around the world, governments provide subsidies and tax breaks to multinational corporations and thus contribute to the consequences of investment decisions made by globalized capital, despite the tendency of economic actors to externalize risks, destabilize markets, disrupt access to vital commodities, and contribute to the uncertainty of modern economic life. Neoliberal capitalism has been increasing global risks in the form of climate change, pollution, economic disruption and so on for many years, and externalizing the costs of those risks downward onto less powerful peripheral parts of the global system. At the same time, neoliberal economic actors attempt to optimize and legitimize the interests of capital worldwide and surround themselves with an aura of self-regulation and self-legitimation.

Just as Wallerstein described in 1974, capitalism is based on "the constant absorption of economic loss by political entities, while economic gain is distributed to 'private' hands." Present circumstances allow corporate special interests to externalize risks, damages, and costs onto the social system, largely the political system, in a way that increases corporate profits while at the same time degrading the social fabric and material environment. Because capitalism as an economic system operates within an arena larger than that which any political entity can totally control, capitalists are structurally unrestrained. Unregulated capital moves around the globe at will seeking increased profit and accumulation, and, in the process, often disrupts established labor patterns, thereby disrupting and straining the lives of the working classes. Yet the costs of these labor disruptions are left for the political system to manage, which is itself strained by growing limitations and crises. In essence, the economic systems are offloading their responsibility for the social problems they create onto the backs of those most affected, pushing risk down to the level of the individual while manipulating the political system to reduce or eliminate any penalties for "white collar" crime or mismanagement. In a variation on this theme, the sociologist Ulrich Beck (2007) suggests that the current neoliberal capitalist economic system consists of a global capital-state coalition where the political system is complicit in maintaining the power and profitability of the economic system, and this coalition is powerful and often successful.

I have been arguing in this work that the integrative power of cultural institutions is waning in the face of technological and economic evolutionary pressures. The power of the cultural system to develop, instill, and enforce its norms is increasingly usurped by "alien systems." Processes like socialization and identity formation are traditional functions of the cultural system, enabled by institutions such as the family, religious organizations, and the school system, but economically oriented and disembedded processes are now pushing into these cultural realms and greatly influencing their functions. These disembedded economic processes minimize the influence of the traditional social interactions that make up the cultural system and reduce the processes that create, legitimize and integrate the values that are at the core of the system, the human values that form the bedrock for the norms and sanctions that create social order. The modern patterns of cultural innovation are reflective of growing diversity, but diversity may easily lead to a continued atomization of the public sphere and in any event, is a challenge to the maintenance of social cohesion. Further, a fragmented and isolated public may be inadequate to meet the cultural needs for integration and solidarity within the larger cosmopolitan social system.

> Integration… is almost universally understood in terms of human bonds formed through common interests … or through normative consensus and shared values (as in the tradition of Parsons and Durkheim). But these forms of integration appear to become less and less effective given the increased cultural and other diversity of the respective populations, increased detraditionalization, and the "waning" of social authorities that symbolize value integration (Knorr-Cetina & Breugger, 2000, p. 167).

It seems that the concerns of the early modern theorists have been realized, and we continue to deal with the worsening effects of bureaucratic and technocratic development predicted by Weber and Habermas, the mechanized petrification and colonization of culture resulting from the domination of the alien *systems world* of economic and political administration. While new technologies provide efficiencies they also create and increase complexities, and the reliance on computer and telecommunications-based systems are not only inherently susceptible to failure (think of a major power grid failure and the resulting telecom and data blackouts) but are already at the point of being "unknowable" to all but the few technocratic experts in the public sphere. We are increasingly relying on systems and objects that we do not understand.

Also, the social inequalities inherent to capitalist enterprise continue to create problems for millions of people and antagonize the most universal of our cultural values like fairness, reciprocity, and merit. Labor crises disrupt the lives of workers around the world, and the alienating characteristics of modern life pose a special problem for the traditional social institutions such as community and education. Further, there is a rapid increase in the number and extent of risks associated with modern life, including everything from terrorism, to environmental degradation, global warming, and nuclear threats. Public policies are actually creating risk, including the risks associated with social inequalities and poverty, and modern society is ill-equipped to deal with the increasingly significant consequences, partly due to the pressure of elite actors who create risk to control the public discourse and their ability to push consequences downward onto those who are neither responsible for nor able to control those risks. Perhaps an increased emphasis in public discourse on the ideological drivers of economic inequality and oppression will help us avoid a legitimation crisis here in America and the potential for upheaval or even revolution.

References

ACLU (2013). *How Ohio's Debtors' Prisons Are Ruining Lives and Costing Communities.* Retrieved from http://www.acluohio.org/wp-content/uploads/2013/04/TheOutskirtsOfHope2013_04.pdf.

Action on Smoking and Health (ASH) (2016). Retrieved from http://ash.org/resources/tobacco-statistics-facts/.

Adorno, T. W. (1991). *The Culture Industry: Selected essays on mass culture.* London: Routledge.

Adorno, T. W. & Horkheimer, M. (1991; 1947). *Dialectic of Enlightenment.* London: Verso, 1979, (originally published as: Dialektik der Aufklärung. Amsterdam: Querido, 1947.

Aldrick, P. (2012). King attacks 'deceitful' banking culture. *The Telegraph.* Retrieved from http://www.telegraph.co.uk/finance/economics/9364187/King-attacks-deceitful-banking-culture.html.

AFL-CIO (2008). Retrieved from http://www.aflcio.org/Press-Room/Press-Releases/Statement-by-AFL-CIO-President-John-Sweeney-on-the12.

Alexander, M. (2010). *The New Jim Crow: Mass Incarceration in the Age of Colorblindness.* New York: The Free Press.

Anderson, R. (2016). Debtors prison a thing of the past? Some places in America still lock up the poor. *LA Times.* Retrieved from http://www.latimes.com/nation/la-na-debtors-prison-20160607-snap-story.html.

Angell, M. (2009). Drug Companies & Doctors: A Story of Corruption *New York Review of Books.* Retrieved from http://www.nybooks.com/articles/2009/01/15/drug-companies-doctorsa-story-of-corruption/.

American Psychological Association (APA) (2004). *Television Advertising Leads to Unhealthy Habits in Children; Says APA Task Force.* Retrieved from http://www.apa.org/news/press/releases/2004/02/children-ads.aspx.

American Psychological Association (APA) (2007). *Sexualization of Girls is Linked to Common Mental Health Problems in Girls and Women--Eating Disorders, Low Self-Esteem, and Depression; An APA Task Force Reports.* Retrieved from http://www.apa.org/news/press/releases/2007/02/sexualization.aspx.

Applebaum, B. (2011). As U.S. Agencies Put More Value on a Life, Businesses Fret. *New York Times.* Retrieved from http://www.nytimes.com/2011/02/17/ business/economy/17regulation.html. Accessed on May 12, 2016.

Applebaum, B. (2014). How Disney Turned 'Frozen' Into a Cash Cow. *New York Times.* Retrieved from http://www.nytimes.com/2014/11/23/magazine/how-disney-turned-frozen-into-a-cash-cow.html

Ariely, D. (2008). *Predictably Irrational: The Hidden Forces That Shape Our Decisions.* New York: Harper Collins.

Aristotle. (Unknown). *Politics.* Tufts Digital Library. Retrieved from http://www.perseus.tufts.edu/hopper/text?doc=Perseus%3Atext%3A1999.01.0058%3Abook%3D1%3Asection%3D1252a

Associated Press (AP) (2008). $1.6B Of Bank Bailout Went To Execs. *CBS News.* Retrieved from http://www.cbsnews.com/news/16b-of-bank-bailout-went-to-execs/.

Atkinson S. & Gilkeson J. (1998). Unusual Investments: A Look at Viatical Settlements. *AAII Journal/July 1998,* 17-19.

Azimov, I. (1980). A Cult of Ignorance. *Newsweek,* January 21, 19. Retrieved from http://media.aphelis.net/wp-content/uploads/2012/04/ASIMOV_ 1980_Cult_of_Ignorance.pdf

Bachrach, P. (1967). *The Theory of Democratic Elitism: A Critique.* New York: Little Brown & Company.

Baker, D. (2013). *Fighting Corruption in the Pharmaceutical Industry With a Water Pistol.* Retrieved from http://cepr.net/blogs/beat-the-press/fighting-corruption-in-the-pharmaceutical-industry-with-a-water-pistol.

Bakan, J. (2004). *The Corporation: The Pathological Pursuit of Profit and Power.* London: Constable.

Bartels, L. M. (2008). *Unequal Democracy: The Political Economy of a New Gilded Age.* Princeton, NJ: Princeton University Press.

Baudrillard, J. (1970). The Consumer Society: Myths and Structures. London: Sage.

Bauman, Z. (2013). *150 Years of German Social Democracy.* Social Europe Occasional Paper. Retrieved from https://www.socialeurope.eu/wp-content/uploads/2013/10/OccPap2.pdf.

Baumeister, R.F. (2010). *The New Science of Morality.* Paper presented at the Edge Conference, Washington, D.C., July 23, 2010.

BBC (2015). Bank of England liquidity auctions probed by fraud office. Retrieved from http://www.bbc.com/news/business-31739051.

BBC (2014). Tanzania arrests 23 over killing of seven 'witches.' Retrieved from http://www.bbc.com/news/world-africa-29572974.

Beck, U. (1992). *Risk Society - Towards a New Modernity.* London: Sage.

Beck, U. (2007). *World at Risk.* New York: Polity Press.

Becker, A.E., Burwell, R.A., Herzog, D., Hamburg, P. & Gilman, S. (2002). Eating behaviours and attitudes following prolonged exposure to television among ethnic Fijian adolescent girls. *British Journal of Psychiatry, 180,* 509-514.

Belk, R., (1988), Possessions and the Extended Self. *Journal of Consumer Research, 15,* 139-168.

Berger, P. (1986). *The Capitalist Revolution: Fifty Propositions About Prosperity, Equality, and Liberty.* New York: Basic Books.

Berger, P. and Luckmann, T. (1966). *The Social Construction of Reality.* Garden City, N.Y.: Doubleday & Company, Inc.

Bernays, E. (1928). *Propaganda.* New York: Horace Liveright.

Bernstein J.M. (2010). The Very Angry Tea Party, *New York Times.* Retrieved from http://opinionator.blogs.nytimes.com/2010/06/13/the-very-angry-tea-party/?_r=0. Accessed on January 4, 2014.

Bingham, J (2014). Rich will live life to the full 20 years longer than poor, official figures show. *The Telegraph.* Retrieved from http://www.telegraph.co.uk/ news/politics/10699077/Rich-will-live-life-to-the-full-20-years-longer-than-poor-official-figures-show.html.

Bloland, H.G. (1995). Postmodernism and higher education. *Journal of Higher Education, 66,* 521-550.

Bourdieu, P. (2005). *The Social Structures of the Economy.* Translated by C. Turner. Cambridge, UK: Polity.

Buchanan, M. (2013) Why Homo Economicus Might Actually Be an Idiot. *Bloomberg News.* Retrieved from https://www.bloomberg.com/view/articles/2013-08-04/why-homo-economicus-might-actually-be-an-idiot.

Bureau of Labor Statistics (BLS). (2011). *The compensation-productivity gap: a visual essay.* Retrieved from http://www.bls.gov/opub/mlr/2011/01/art3full.pdf.

Bureau of Labor Statistics (BLS). (2012). *Manufacturing: NAICS 31-33.* Retrieved from http://www.bls.gov/iag/tgs/iag31-33.htm

Bradsher, K. (2000). Ford Says Firestone Was Aware of Flaw In Its Tires by 1997. *New York Times.* Retrieved from http://www.nytimes.com/2000/08/14/business/ford-says-firestone-was-aware-of-flaw-in-its-tires-by-1997.html.

Callard, C. (2010). Follow the Money. *Tobacco Control, 19,* 285–290.

Capps, C. (2009). T*he approximate effect of hospital consolidation on national healthcare expenditures.* Presentation at the Institute of Medicine Workshop Series, May 22, 2009.

Castillo, J.C. (2011). Legitimation and justice ideologies in contexts of extreme economic inequality. *Social Justice Research, 24,* 314–340.

Center on Budget and Policy Priorities (CBPP) (2016). *Federal Budget.* Retrieved from http://www.cbpp.org/topics/federal-budget

Centers for Disease Control and Prevention (CDC). (2012). *2012 National Conference on Health Statistics.* Retrieved from https://www.cdc.gov/nchs/events/2012nchs/.

Centers for Disease Control and Prevention (CDC). (2013). *Economic Trends in Tobacco.* Retrieved from https://www.cdc.gov/tobacco/data_statistics/ fact_sheets/fast_facts/index.htm.

Centers for Disease Control and Prevention (CDC). (2016). *HAI Data and Statistics.* Retrieved from https://www.cdc.gov/hai/surveillance/

Centre for Research in Communication and Culture (CRCC) (2016). *Media coverage of the EU Referendum.* Retrieved from https://blog.lboro.ac.uk/crcc/eu-referendum/uk-news-coverage-2016-eu-referendum-report-5-6-may-22-june-2016/.

Cerni, P. (2007). The Age of Consumer Capitalism. *Cultural Logic: An Electronic Journal of Marxist Theory and Practice.* Retrieved from http://clogic.eserver.org/.

Chandy & Gertz, (2011). With Little Notice, Globalization Reduced Poverty. *Yale Global.* Retrieved from http://yaleglobal.yale.edu/content/little-notice-globalization-reduced-poverty.

Chomsky, N. (1997). *The Common Good.* Speech delivered at the Progressive Challenge, Capital Hill, January 9, 1997.

Cohan, W. (2014). Jamie Dimon's $13 Billion Secret: The inside story of JPMorgan Chase's landmark mortgage settlement. *The Nation.* Retrieved from https://www.thenation.com/article/jamie-dimons-13-billion-secret/.

Cohen, L. (2004). A consumers' republic: The politics of mass consumption in postwar America. *Journal of Consumer Research, 31,* 236-239.

Confessore, N. (2016). $2 Billion Worth of Free Media for Donald Trump. *New York Times.* Retrieved from http://www.nytimes.com/2016/03/16/upshot/measuring-donald-trumps-mammoth-advantage-in-free-media.html.

Confessore, N. (2015). Small Pool of Rich Donors Dominates Election Giving. *New York Times.* Retrieved from http://www.nytimes.com/2015/08/02/us/small-pool-of-rich-donors-dominates-election-giving.html.

Crandall, C. S., Eidelman, S., Skitka, L. J., & Morgan, G. S. (2009). Status quo framing increases support for torture. *Social Influence, 4,* 1-10.

Crouch, C. (2004). *Post-Democracy.* Polity Press, Cambridge.

Council of Economic Advisors (CEA). (2016). *Benefits of Competition and Indicators of Market Power.* Council of Economic Advisors Issue Brief. Retrieved from https://www.whitehouse.gov/sites/default/files/page/files/20160 414_cea_competition_issue_brief.pdf.

Dafny, L., Duggan M., and Ramanarayanan, S. (2012). Paying a Premium on Your Premium? Consolidation in the US Health Insurance Industry. *The American Economic Review, 102,* 1161-1185.

Darby, P. (2007). African Football Labour Migration to Portugal: Colonial and Neo-Colonial Resource. *Soccer & Society, 8,* 495-509.

De Soto, H. (2011). The Destruction of Economic Facts. Bloomberg *BusinessWeek.* Retrieved from https://www.bloomberg.com/news/articles/2011-04-28/the-destruction-of-economic-facts.

De Tocqueville, A. (1840). *Democracy in America, Volume 2.* New York: J. & H.G. Langley.

Department of Social and Economic Affairs (DESA) (2005). *Understanding Knowledge Societies.* UN Report. Retrieved from https://publicadministration.un.org/ publications/content/PDFs/E-Library%20Archives/2005%20Understanding%20Knowledge%20Societies.pdf.

Diamond, J. (1987). The Worst Mistake in the History of the Human Race. *Discover Magazine, May 1987,* 64-66.

Durkheim, E. (1897; 1951). *Suicide: A study in sociology.* New York: Free Press.

Durkheim, E. (1956). *Education and Sociology.* New York: Free Press.

Drucker, P. (1994). The Age of Social Transformation. *The Atlantic.* Retrieved from http://www.theatlantic.com/past/docs/issues/95dec/chilearn/drucker.htm.

Epstein, B. (2015). *The Ant Trap: Rebuilding the Foundations of the Social Sciences.* Oxford University Press.

Epstein, J. (2011). Kyl's flap comes full circle. *Politico.com.* Retrieved from http://www.politico.com/story/2011/04/kyls-flap-comes-full-circle-053214

Escalas, J. & Bettman, J. (2005). Self-Construal, Reference Groups, and Brand Meaning. *Journal of Consumer Research, 32,* 378-389.

Evans-Pritchard, A. (2015) Defiant Tsipras threatens to detonate European crisis rather than yield to creditor "monstrosity. *The Telegraph.* Retrieved from http://www.telegraph.co.uk/finance/economics/11642260/Defiant-Tsipras-threatens-to-detonate-European-crisis-rather-than-yield-to-creditor-monstrosity.html.

Fairness and Accuracy in Reporting (FAIR) (2012). *Right and Early!* Retrieved from http://fair.org/extra/right-and-early/.

Federal Communications Commission (FCC) (1996). *Telecommunications Act.* Retrieved from https://www.fcc.gov/general/telecommunications-act-1996.

Federal Communications Commission (FCC) (2011). *Information Needs of Communities.* Retrieved from https://www.fcc.gov/general/information-needs-communities.

Ferguson, C. (2012). *Inside Job.* Oxford: Oneworld Publications.

Ferrara, P. J. (2012). *The Overwhelming Entitlement Crisis.* Cato Institute. Retrieved from https://www.cato.org/publications/commentary/overwhelming-entitlement-crisis.

Festinger, L. (1957). *A theory of cognitive dissonance.* Evanston, IL: Row & Peterson.

Fields, R. (2011). Ohio corrections system sells one prison to private operator, reorganizes four others. *Cleveland.com.* Retrieved from http://www.cleveland.com /open/index.ssf/ 2011/09/ohio_state_prison_system_sales.html.

Fiske, A. P. (1992). The Four Elementary Forms of Sociality: Framework for a Unified Theory of Social Relations. *Psychological Review, 99,* 689-723.

Florida, R. & Tinagli, I. (2004). Europe in the Creative Age. *Demos: Europe.* Retrieved from http://www.creativeclass.com/rfcgdb/ articles/Europe_in_the_Creative_Age_2004.pdf.

Foley, S. (2011). What price the new democracy? Goldman Sachs conquers Europe. *The Independent.* Retrieved from http://www.independent.co.uk/news/business/analysis-and-features/what-price-the-new-democracy-goldman-sachs-conquers-europe-6264091.html.

Frank, T. (2004). *What's the Matter with Kansas? How Conservatives Won the Heart of America.* New York: Henry Holt and Company.

Fraser, S. & Freeman, J.B. (2012). Locking down an American workforce. *Le Monde Diplomatique.* Retrieved from http://mondediplo.com/openpage/locking-down-an-american-workforce.

Freud, S. (1963). *Therapy and Technique.* New York: Collier Books.

Fromer, J. E. (2008). *A Necessary Luxury: Tea in Victorian England.* Athens, OH: Ohio University Press.

Fromm, E. (1976). *To Have or to Be?* New York: Bantam.

Fromm, E. (1991). *The Sane Society.* New York: Henry Holt.

Fromm, E. (1992). *The Art of Being.* New York: Continuum.

Froud, J., Johal, S., Leaver, A., Williams K. (2005). Different worlds of motoring: Choice, constraint and risk in household consumption. *The Sociological Review 53,* 96-128.

Galbraith, J. K. (1967). *The New Industrial State.* Houghton Mifflin Company: New York.

Galbraith, J. K. (1958). *The Affluent Society.* Houghton Mifflin Company: New York.

Garfinkle, N. (2007). *The American Dream vs. The Gospel of Wealth.* New Haven: Yale University Press.

Giddens, A. (2003). *The Runaway World.* New York: Routledge.

Gilens, M. (2009). Preference Gaps and Inequality in Representation. *Political Science & Politics, 42*, 335-341.

Gilens, M. and Page, B. (2014). Testing Theories of American Politics: Elites, Interest Groups, and Average Citizens. *Perspectives on Politics 12*, 564-581.

Geyelin, M. (1999). Lasting Impact: How an Internal Memo Written 26 Years Ago Is Costing GM Dearly. *Wall Street Journal*. Retrieved from http://www.wsj.com/articles/SB9385366607816889.

Giroux, H.A. (2001). *Stealing Innocence: Corporate Culture's War on Children*. New York: Palgrave.

Giroux, S. (2011). *Between Race and Reason: Anti-Intellectualism in American Life*. Stanford University Press.

Goebel, T. (2002). *A government by the people: Direct democracy in America, 1890–1940*. Chapel Hill, NC: University of North Carolina Press.

Gomstyn, A. (2009). Why Bank of America's Ken Lewis Will Take Home More Than Peers. *ABC News*. Retrieved from http://abcnews.go.com/Business/bank-america-ceo-ken-lewis-retirement-pay-higher/story?id=8775299.

Granovetter, M. (1985). Economic Action and Social Structure: The Problem of Embeddedness. *The American Journal of Sociology, 91*, 481-510.

Habermas, J. (1970). *Toward A Rational Society*. Boston: Beacon Press.

Habermas, J. (1973). *Legitimation Crisis*. Boston: Beacon Press.

Habermas, J. (1974). The Public Sphere. *New German Critique, 3*, 49-55.

Habermas, J. (1984). *The Theory of Communicative Action*. translated by Thomas McCarthy, Cambridge, Mass: Polity Press.

Habermas, J. (1989). *Structural Transformation of the Public Sphere*. Cambridge, Mass: MIT Press.

Hacker, J. & Pierson, P. (2010). *Winner Take All Politics*. New York: Simon & Schuster.

Haines, E.L., & Jost, J.T. (2000). Placating the powerless: Effects of legitimate and illegitimate explanation on affect, memory, and stereotyping. *Social Justice Research, 13*, 219-236.

Hansen, T. (2014). Fox Doesn't Believe In Income Inequality But Still Blames Obama For It. *Media Matters*. Retrieved from http://mediamatters.org/blog/2014/01/16/fox-doesnt-believe-in-income-inequality-but-sti/197621.

Hanson, J. (Ed.) (2012). *Ideology, Psychology, and Law*. New York: Oxford University Press.

Harris, M. (1968). *The Rise of Anthropological Theory: A History of Theories of Culture*. New York: Thomas Y. Crowell Company.

Harris, M. (1977). Cannibals and Kings: The Origins of Cultures. New York: Vintage.

Hartzband, P. and Groopman, J. (2014). How Medical Care Is Being Corrupted. *New York Times*. Retrieved from https://www.nytimes.com/2014/11/19/opinion/how-medical-care-is-being-corrupted.html?_r=0.

Harvey, B. (1993). *The Fifties: A Women's Oral History*. New York: HarperCollins.

Havinghurst, J. (2011). The Provider Monopoly Problem in Health Care. *Oregon Law Review, 89*, 847-884.

Hegewisch, A., Williams, C., & Drago, R. (2011). *Pay Secrecy and Wage Discrimination*. Institute for Women's Policy Research. Retrieved from http://www.iwpr.org/publications/pubs/pay-secrecy-and-wage-discrimination-1/.

Held, D. and Thompson, J.B. (1989). *Social theory of modern societies: Anthony Giddens and his critics*. Cambridge University Press.

The Hindu (2011). Concentration of economic power widen inequalities. *The Hindu Online*. Retrieved from http://www.thehindu.com/news/states/tamil-nadu/article1571875.ece.

Horton, R. (2015). What is medicine's 5 sigma? *The Lancet, 385*, 1380.

Huddleston, T. (2016). CBS Chief: Trump's Success Is 'Damn Good' For the Network. *Fortune*. Retrieved from http://fortune.com/2016/03/01/les-moonves-cbs-trump/.

Ignatieff, M. (2014). *Sovereignty and the crisis of democratic politics*. Retrieved from http://www.michaelignatieff.ca/assets/pdfs/Sovereignty%20and%20the%20crisis%20of%20democratic%20politics_Demos%20Quarterly.pdf.

Intergovernmental Panel on Climate Change (IPCC) (2013). C*limate Change 2013: The Physical Science Basis*. Retrieved from http://www.ipcc.ch/report/ar5/wg1/.

Institute for Justice (IFJ) (2016). *Civil Forfeiture*. Retrieved from http://ij.org/issues/private-property/civil-forfeiture/.

Iyengar, S. & Simon, A. (1993). News Coverage of the Gulf Crisis and Public Opinion: A Study of Agenda-Setting, Priming, and Framing. *Communication Research, 20*, 365-383.

James, P. & Szeman, I. (2010). *Globalization and Culture, Vol. 3: Global-Local Consumption*. London: Sage Publications.

Jefferson, T. (1905). *The writings of Thomas Jefferson*. Definitive ed. / Washington, D.C.: Issued under the auspices of the Thomas Jefferson memorial association of the United States.

Johnson, S. (2009). The Quiet Coup. *The Atlantic*. Retrieved from http://www.theatlantic.com/magazine/archive/2009/05/the-quiet-coup/307364/.

Jost, J. T., & Banaji, M. R. (1994). The role of stereotyping in system-justification and the production of false consciousness. *British Journal of Social Psychology, 33*, 1-27.

Jost, J.T., Federico, C.M. & Napier, J.L. (2009). Political ideology: Its structure, functions, and elective affinities. *Annual Review of Psychology, 60*, 307-333.

Jost, J.T., & Major, B. (Eds.) (2001). *The psychology of legitimacy: Emerging perspectives on ideology, justice, and intergroup relations*. New York: Cambridge University Press.

Jost, J.T., Pelham, B., Sheldon, O. & Sullivan, B. (2002). Social inequality and the reduction of ideological dissonance on behalf of the system: evidence of enhanced system justification among the disadvantaged. *European Journal of Social Psychology, 33*, 13–36.

Justice Policy Institute (JPI) (2011). *Gaming the System*. Retrieved from http://www.justicepolicy.org /uploads/justicepolicy/documents /gaming_the_system.pdf.

Kadirov, D. & Varey, R. (2006). *Transcending consumption system's self-closure: Systems redefinition of consumer identity beyond individual self*. Paper presented at the Australian and New Zealand Marketing Academy (ANZMAC) 2006 Conference, Brisbane, Australia.

Kasser, T. (2002). *The High Price of Materialism*. Boston: MIT Press.

Kasser, T. (2014). What Psychology Says About Materialism and the Holidays. *American Psychological Association*. http://www.apa.org/news/press/releases/2014/12/materialism-holidays.aspx.

Kelly, N.J. & Enns, P.K. (2010). Inequality and the Dynamics of Public Opinion: The Self-Reinforcing Link Between Economic Inequality and Mass Preferences. *American Journal of Political Science, 54*, 855–870.

Knorr-Cetina, K. (1997). Sociality with objects. Social relations in postsocial knowledge societies. *Theory, Culture & Society, 14*, 1–30.

Knorr-Cetina, K. & Bruegger, H. (2000). The Market as an Object of Attachment: Exploring Postsocial Relations in Financial Markets. *Canadian Journal of Sociology 25*, 141-168.

Krause, G. A. (1996). The institutional dynamics of policy administration: Bureaucratic influence over securities regulation. *American Journal of Political Science. 40*, 1083–121.

Krugman, P. (2009). *The Return of Depression Economics and the Crisis of 2008*. New York: Norton.

Kuttner, R. (2008). Market-Based Failure - A Second Opinion on U.S. Health Care Costs. *New England Journal of Medicine, 358*, 549-551.

Labaree, D. F. (2011). *Citizens and consumers: Changing visions of virtue and opportunity in U.S. education, 1841-1954*. In Tröhler, Popkewitz, and Labaree (Eds.), *Schooling and the making of citizens in the long nineteenth century* (pp. 168-183). New York: Palgrave Macmillan.

Lakoff, G. (1996). *The Metaphor System For Morality.* In Goldberg, A. (ed.) *Conceptual Structure, Discourse, and Language I.* Cambridge University Press.

Lakoff, G. (2006). *Thinking Points: Communicating Our American Values and Vision.* New York: Farrar, Straus and Giroux.

Lakoff, G. and Johnsen, M. (2003). *Metaphors we live by.* London: University of Chicago Press.

Langer, B. (2005). Consuming anomie: children and global commercial culture. *Childhood, 12,* 259–271.

Lasch, C. (1977). *Haven in a Heartless World: The Family Besieged.* New York: Basic Books.

Lasch, C. (1991). *The True and Only Heaven: Progress and its Critics.* New York: Norton.

Lasch, C. (1995). *The Revolt of the Elites and the Betrayal of Democracy.* New York: W. W. Norton.

Leach, W. (1993). *Land of Desire: Merchants, Power, and the Rise of a New American Culture.* New York: Pantheon.

Lears, J. (1981). *Salvation to self-realization: Advertising and the therapeutic roots of the consumer culture, 1880-1930.* In Fox, R. and Lears, T.J., (Eds.), The Culture of Consumption: Critical Essays in American History, 1880-1980. New York: Pantheon Books, 1-38.

Leydesdorff, L. (2001), *A sociological theory of communication: the self organization of the knowledge-based society.* Parkland, FL: Universal Publishers.

Lerner, G. (1986). *The Creation of Patriarchy.* New York: Oxford University Press.

Lerner, M. J. (1980). *The Belief in a Just World: A Fundamental Delusion.* New York: Plenum Press.

Levin, D. & Carlsson-Paige, N. (2006). *The War Play Dilemma: What Every Parent and Teacher Needs to Know* (2nd Ed.). New York: Teachers College Press.

Levin, D. & Kilbourne, J. (2009). *So Sexy So Soon: The New Sexualized Childhood and What Parents Can Do to Protect Their Kids.* New York: Ballantine Books.

Lilla, M. (2010). The Tea Party Jacobins. *The New York Review of Books.* http://www.nybooks.com/articles/2010/05/27/tea-party-jacobins/.

Linn, B. (2010). *Cornered: The New Monopoly Capitalism and the Economics of Destruction.* New York: Wiley.

Lippmann, W. (1922). *Public Opinion.* New York: Harcourt, Brace and Company.

Lippmann, W. (1925). *The Phantom Public.* New York: Harcourt, Brace and Company.

Marx, K. and Engels, F. (1970). *The German Ideology.* International Publishers Co.

Mazzarella, W. (2003). *Shoveling Smoke: Advertising and Globalization in Contemporary India.* Durham: Duke University Press.

McAdams, D. P. (1996). Personality, modernity, and the storied self: A contemporary framework for studying -persons. *Psychological Inquiry, 7,* 295-321.

McChesney, R. W. (1999). The New Global Media; It's a Small World of Big Conglomerates, *The Nation.* Retrieved from http://www.hartford-hwp.com/archives/29/053.html.

McNair, B. (2012). The truth about Rupert Murdoch's empire of control emerges blinking into the light. *The Conversation.* Retrieved from https://theconversation.com/the-truth-about-rupert-murdochs-empire-of-control-emerges-blinking-into-the-light-6731. Accessed on Sept 23, 2016.

Mead, G. H. (1934). *Mind, Self, and Society.* Chicago: University of Chicago Press.

Memoli, M. A. (2011). Fox News viewers less informed about current events, poll shows. *LA Times.* Retrieved from http://articles.latimes.com/2011/nov/21/news/la-pn-fox-news-poll-20111121.

Mill, J. S. (2004). *Principles of Political Economy With Some of Their Applications to Social Philosophy,* Stephen Nathanson (Ed.). Hackett Publishing Company.

Mill, J. S. (2007). Utilitarianism, Liberty & Representative Government. Wildside Press.

Mills, C. W. (1951). *White Collar: The American Middle Classes.* New York: Oxford University Press.

Mills, C. W. (1956). *The Power Elite.* Oxford University Press.

Mills, C. W. (1959). *The Sociological Imagination.* Harmondsworth, UK: Penguin Press.

Mischel L. & Sabadish, N. (2013). *CEO pay in 2012 was extraordinarily high relative to typical workers and other high earners.* Economic Policy Institute, Issue Brief 367. Retrieved from http://www.epi.org/publication/ceo-pay-2012-extraordinarily-high/.

Moisse, K. (2011). 10-Year-Old Model's Grown-Up Look: High Fashion or High Risk? *ABC News.* Retrieved from http://abcnews.go.com/health/w_mindbodyresource/ 10-year-models-grown-high-fashion-high-risk/story?id=14221160.

Morgan, J. (2014). The Decline of Trust in the United States. *Medium.* Retrieved from https://medium.com/@slowerdawn/the-decline-of-trust-in-the-united-states-fb8ab719b82a#.p7b9bouex. Accessed April 27, 2016.

Morgan, K. J. (2013). America's Misguided Approach to Social Welfare. *Foreign Affairs.* Retrieved from https://www.foreignaffairs.com/articles/united-states/2012-12-03/americas-misguided-approach-social-welfare.

Moynihan, R., Heath, I., & Henry, D. (2002). Selling sickness: the pharmaceutical industry and disease mongering. *British Medical Journal, 324,* 886–891.

Mullainathan, S. & Shleifer, A. (2002). *Media Bias.* Harvard Institute Research Working Paper No. 1981. Retrieved from https://papers.ssrn.com/sol3/papers.cfm?abstract_id=335800.

Murray, C. (1984). *Losing ground: American social policy, 1950-1980.* New York: Basic Books.

NAACP (2013). *Fact Sheet.* http://www.naacp.org/criminal-justice-fact-sheet/. Accessed April 2, 2013.

Nothdurfter, U. & Lorenz, W. (2010). Beyond the Pro and Contra of Evidence-Based Practice: Reflections on a Recurring Dilemma at the Core of Social Work. *Social Work and Society, 8.* Retrieved from http://www.socwork.net/sws/article/view/22/62.

O'Cass, A. & McEwen, H. 2004. Exploring consumer status and conspicuous consumption. *Journal of Consumer Behaviour 4,* 25-39.

OECD (2008). *Growing Unequal? Income Distribution and Poverty in OECD Countries.* Retrieved from http://www.oecd.org/els/soc/41527936.pdf.

OECD (2013). *OECD Health Statistics 2013.* Retrieved from http://www.oecd.org/health/healthdata.

Okazaki, S. (2006). Excitement or sophistication? A preliminary exploration of online brand personality, *International Marketing Review, 23,* 279-303.

Opensecrets.org. (2014). Accessed Mar 23, 2015.

Orwell, G. (1943). *Mark Twain - The Licensed Jester. Reprinted in The Collected Essays, Journalism and Letters of George Orwell.* Martin Secker & Warburg Ltd., 1968.

Parsons, T. (1951). *The Social System.* New York: Free Press.

Parsons, T. (1961). *An Outline of the Social System.* In Talcott Parsons, Edward A. Shils, Kaspar D. Naegle, and Jesse R. Pitts (eds.), *Theories of Society.* New York: Simon & Schuster.

Pew Research Center (2015). *Beyond Distrust: How Americans View Their Government.* Retrieved from http://www.people-press.org/2015/11/23/beyond-distrust-how-americans-view-their-government/.

Pew Research Center (2014). *Millennials in Adulthood: Detached from Institutions, Networked with Friends.* Retrieved from http://www.pewsocialtrends.org/2014/03/07/millennials-in-adulthood/.

Pitkin, H. (1967). *The Concept of Representation.* Berkeley, CA: University of California Press.

Polanyi, K. (2001). *The Great Transformation: The Political and Economic Origins of Our Time.* Boston: Beacon Press.

Porter, E. (2015). Income Inequality Is Costing the U.S. on Social Issues. *New York Times.* Retrieved from http://www.nytimes.com/2015/04/29/business/economy/income-inequality-is-costing-the-us-on-social-issues.html.

Powell, G. & Vanberg, G. (2000). Election Laws, Disproportionality and Median Correspondence: Implications for Two Visions of Democracy. *British Journal of Political Science, 30*, 383-411.

Prasad, P.H. (1996). Dynamics of Neo-Colonial Exploitation. *Economic and Political Weekly, 31*, 719-722.

Public Citizen (2007). *Organizing Astroturf: Evidence Shows Bogus Grassroots Groups Hijack the Political Debate*. Retrieved from https://www.citizen.org/documents/Organizing-Astroturf.pdf.

Pullella, P. (2014). Financial, commodities speculation is "intolerable," Pope says. *Reuters Africa*. Retrieved from https://www.yahoo.com/news/pope-says-food-commodity-speculation-hurts-fight-against-120100342--sector.html?ref=gs.

Quigley, C. (1966). *Tragedy and Hope: A History of the World in Our Time*. New York: The Macmillan Company.

Ramzy A. (2010). Chinese Factory Under Scrutiny As Suicides Mount. *Time*. Retrieved from http://www.time.com/time/world/article/0,8599,1991620,00.html#ixzz1PAiOo9tH.

Rawls, J. (1971). *A Theory of Justice*. Cambridge, MA: Harvard University Press.

Reese, S. D. & Lewis, S. C. (2009). Framing the War on Terror: The internalization of policy in the US press. *Journalism, 10*, 777–797.

Reese, S. D. (2007). *Finding frames in a web of culture: The case of the War on Terror*. In P. D'Angelo and J. Kuypers (eds.) *Doing News Framing Analysis: Empirical, Theoretical, and Normative Perspectives*. New York: Routledge.

Reich, R. (2014). *The Government Problem*. Retrieved from http://robertreich.org/post /106010799435.

Reich, R. (2009). How Capitalism Is Killing Democracy. *Foreign Policy*. Retrieved from http://www.foreignpolicy.com/articles/2009/10/12/how_capitalism_is_killing_democracy.

Rideout, V. & Jamel, E. (2006). *The Media Family: Electronic Media in the Lives of Infants, Toddlers, Preschoolers and Their Parents*. Menlo Park: CA.: Kaiser Family Foundation.

Rideout, V., Foehr, U., & Roberts, D. (2010). *Generation M2: Media in the Lives of 8-18-Year-Olds*. Menlo Park, CA: Kaiser Family Foundation.

Rogoff, K. (2012). Coronary Capitalism. *Project Syndicate*. Retrieved from https://www.project-syndicate.org/commentary/coronary-capitalism?barrier=true.

Rokeach, M. (1973). *The Nature of Human Values*. New York: The Free Press.

Roppolo, M. (2014). Americans more skeptical of climate change than others in global survey. *CBS News*. Retrieved from http://www.cbsnews.com/news/americans-more-skeptical-of-climate-change-than-others-in-global-survey/.

Rosenthal, E. (2013). The Soaring Cost of a Simple Breath. *New York Times*. Retrieved from http://www.nytimes.com/2013/10/13/us/the-soaring-cost-of-a-simple-breath.html?pagewanted=all&_r=0.

Rubin, Z. and Peplau, L.A. (1975). Who Believes in a Just World. *Journal of Social Issues, 31*, 65-89.

Saad, L. (2016). Conservatives Hang On to Ideology Lead by a Thread. *Gallup*. Retrieved from http://www.gallup.com/poll/188129/conservatives-hang-ideology-lead-thread.aspx.

Sachs, J. (2006). The Social Welfare State, beyond Ideology. *Scientific American*. Retrieved from https://www.scientificamerican.com/article/the-social-welfare-state/.

Saez, E. & Piketty, T. (2004). *Income Inequality in the United States, 1913-2002*. Retrieved from http://eml.berkeley.edu/~saez/piketty-saezOUP04US.pdf.

Saez, E. & Piketty, T. (2012). *Top Incomes and the Great Recession: Recent Evolutions and Policy Implications*. Paper presented at the 13th Jacques Polak Annual Research Conference, Washington, DC. November 8–9, 2012

Sandel, M. J. (2012). *What Money Can't But: The Moral Limits of Markets*. New York: Farrar, Straus and Giroux.

Schor, J. B. (2004). *Born to buy: The commercialized child and the new consumer culture*. New York: Scribner.

Schulman, J. (2015). 72 Percent of Republican Senators Are Climate Deniers. *Mother Jones*. Retrieved from http://www.motherjones.com/blue-marble/2015/01/republican-climate-denial-caucus.

Schumpeter, J. (1950). *Capitalism, Socialism, and Democracy*. New York: Harper & Row.

Schwartz, N. D. (2013). Recovery in U.S. Is Lifting Profits, but Not Adding Jobs. The *New York Times*, March 4, 2013, A1.

Scott-Samuel, A., Bambra, C., Collins, C., Hunter, D. J., McCartney, G., & Smith, K. (2014). The effects of Thatcherism on Health and Wellbeing in Britain. *International Journal of Health Services, 44*, 53–71.

Seife, C. (2015). Research Misconduct Identified by the US Food and Drug Administration: Out of Sight, Out of Mind, Out of the Peer-Reviewed Literature. *JAMA Internal Medicine, 175*, 567-77.

Sidanius, J. & Pratto, F. (1999). *Social Dominance: An Intergroup Theory of Social Hierarchy and Oppression*. London: Cambridge University Press.

Sidanius, J., Levin, S., Federico, C. M. & Pratto, F., (2001). *Legitimising ideologies: A social dominance approach* In Jost, J. T. and Major, B. (Eds), *The psychology of legitimacy* (pp. 307-331). NY: Cambridge University Press.

Simmel, G. (1907; 1978). *The Philosophy of Money*, translated by Tom Bottomore and David Frisby. Boston: Routledge.

Simmel, G. (1903; 1971). *The Metropolis and Mental Life*. In D. Levine (Ed.), On *Individuality and Social Forms: Selected* Writings (pp. 324-339). University of Chicago Press.

Singer, T. (2013). Beyond Homo Economicus. *Project Syndicate*. Retrieved from https://www.project-syndicate.org/commentary/a-new-model-of-human-behavior-by-tania-singer?barrier=true.

Skitka, L. J., & Tetlock, P. E. (1992). Allocating scarce resources: A contingency model of distributive justice. *Journal of Experimental Social Psychology, 28*, 491-522.

Skitka, L. J., & Tetlock, P. E. (1993). Providing Public Assistance: Cognitive and Motivational Processes Underlying Liberal and Conservative Policy Preferences. *Journal of Personality and Social Psychology, 65,*1205-1223.

Skocpol, T. (1999). Associations Without Members. *The American Prospect*. http://prospect.org/article/associations-without-members.

Slater, D. (1997) *Consumer Culture and Modernity*. Cambridge: Polity Press.

Small, M.L., Harding, D.J., and Lamont, M. (2010). Reconsidering Culture and Poverty. *The Annals of the American Academy of Political and Social Science, 629*, 6-27.

Smart, B. (1999). *Facing modernity: Ambivalence, reflexivity, and morality*. London: Sage Publications.

Smith, A. (1776; 2001). *An Inquiry into the Nature and Causes of the Wealth of Nations*. Hayes Barton Press.

Stewart, D. (2016). Inside the Week That Broke British Politics. *Time Magazine*. Retrieved from http://time.com/4389464/boris-johnson-michael-gove-brexit-vote/.

Stearns, P. (2001). *Consumerism in World History: The Global Transformation of Consumer Desire*. London & New York: Routledge.

Stille, A. (2006). Silvio's Shadow. *Columbia Journalism Review*. Retrieved from http://cjrarchives.org/issues/2006/5/Stille.asp.

Stobbe, M. (2014). Study finds declining life span for some women. *USA Today*. Retrieved from http://www.usatoday.com/story/news/nation/2013/03/04/study-life-span-women/1963093/.

Stromberg, P. (1990). Elvis Alive?: The Ideology of American Consumerism. *Journal of Popular Culture, 24*, 11-19.

Suskind, R. (2004). Faith, Certainty and the Presidency of George W. Bush. *New York Times Magazine*. Retrieved from http://www.nytimes.com/2004/10/17/magazine/ faith-certainty-and-the-presidency-of-george-w-bush.html?_r=0.

Sweeney, M. (2006). American Idol outvotes the president. *The Guardian*. Retrieved from.

https://www.theguardian.com/media/2006/may/26/realitytv.usnews.

Taibbi, M. (2014). The $9 Billion Witness: Meet JPMorgan Chase's Worst Nightmare. *Rolling Stone*. Retrieved from http://www.rollingstone.com/politics/news/ the-9-billion-witness 20141106?page=6.

Tavernise, S. & Hurdle, J. (2011). Former Judge Is on Trial in 'Cash for Kids' Scheme. *New York Times*. Retrieved from http://www.nytimes.com/2011/02/ 09/us/09judge.html.

Taylor, C. (2002). Democratic Exclusion (and Its Remedies?). *Eurozine Magazine*. Retrieved from http://www.eurozine.com/articles/2002-02-21-taylor-en.html.

Taylor, C. (1989). *Sources of the self: The making of modern identity*. Cambridge, UK: Cambridge University Press.

Thatcher, M. (1987). Interview for Woman's Own ("no such thing as society"). Retrieved from http://www.margaretthatcher.org/document/106689.

Thompson, J. B. (1995). *The Media and Modernity: A Social Theory of the Media*. Cambridge: Polity.

Tolbert, C. J. & Smith, D. A. (2006). Representation and Direct Democracy in the United States. *Representation, 42*, 26-44.

Toynbee, A. (1965). *A Study of History*. London: Oxford University Press.

Triandis, H C., Bontempo, R., Villareal, M J, Asai, M, & Lucca, N. (1988). Individualism and Collectivism: Cross-Cultural Perspectives on Self-Ingroup Relationships. *Journal of Personality and Social Psychology, 54*, 323-338.

Twitchell, J.B. (2000). In Praise of Consumerism: When the going gets tough, the tough go shopping. And sometimes even get happy. *Reason Magazine*. Retrieved from http://reason.com/archives/2000/08/01/in-praise-of-consumerism.

United Nations Development Program (UNDP) (1998). Human Development Report 1998. Retrieved from http://hdr.undp.org/sites/default/files/reports/259/hdr_1998_en_complete_nostats.pdf.

United Nations Educational, Scientific and Cultural Organization (UNESCO). (2014). *Teaching And Learning: Achieving quality for all*. Retrieved from http://unesdoc.unesco.org/images/0022/002256/225660e.pdf.

usgovernmentspending.com. (2016). Accessed May 23, 2016

Vardi, N. (2013). The 40 Highest-Earning Hedge Fund Managers And Traders. *Forbes Magazine*. Retrieved from http://www.forbes.com/sites/nathanvardi/2013 /02/26/the-40-highest-earning-hedge-fund-managers-and-traders/#477b168a3037.

Veblen, T. (1934). *The Theory of the Leisure Class: An Economic Study of Institutions.* New York: The Modern Library.

Waldman, S. (2011). *The Information Needs Of Communities: The changing media landscape in a broadband age.* Steven Waldman and the Working Group on Information Need, Federal Communication Commission. Retrieved from www.fcc.gov/infoneedsreport.

Wallerstein, I. (1974). *The Modern World-System, vol. I: Capitalist Agriculture and the Origins of the European World-Economy in the Sixteenth Century.* New York/London: Academic Press.

Weber, M. (1905). *The Protestant Ethic and the Spirit of Capitalism.* Translated by Talcott Parsons. Los Angeles: Roxbury.

Weber, M. (1946). *From Max Weber: Essays in Sociology,* translated by H.H. Gerth and C. Wright Mills. New York: Oxford University Press.

Wen, P. A. (2010). Legacy of Unintended Side-Effects: Call It the Other Welfare. *The Boston Globe.* Retrieved from http://archive.boston.com/news/local/massachusetts/articles/2010/12/12/with_ssi_program_a_legacy_of_unintended_side_effects/.

Williams, J. (2011). Fox style newscasting a "NO" in Canada. *Examiner.* Retrieved from http://www.examiner.com/article/fox-style-newscasting-a-no-canada.

Williamson, V., Skocpol, T. & Coggin, J. (2011). The Tea Party and the Remaking of Republican Conservatism. *Perspectives on Politics, 9,* 25-49.

Wilson, E. O. (1998). *Consilience: The Unity of Knowledge.* New York: Knopf.

World Bank (2016). GDP in US$. Retrieved from http://data.worldbank.org/indicator/NY.GDP.MKTP.CD?locations=US.

World Justice Project (WJP) (2016). World Justice Rule of Law Index. Retrieved from http://worldjusticeproject.org/publication/rule-law-index-reports/rule-law-index-2015-report.

Zhang, J. and Jargon, J. (2009). Peanut Corp. Emails Cast Harsh Light on Executive, *Wall Street Journal.* Retrieved from http://www.wsj.com/articles/SB123436949588473457.

Zimmerman, F.J., Christakis, D.A., & Meltzoff, A.N. (2007). Associations between Media Viewing and Language Development in Children Under Age 2 Years. *The Journal of Pediatrics, 151,* 364-368.

Žižek, S. (2015). Slavoj Žižek on Greece: This is a chance for Europe to awaken. *The New Statesman.* Retrieved from http://www.newstatesman.com/politics/2015/07/ Slavoj-Zizek-greece-chance-europe-awaken.

Zuberi, D. (2006). *Differences that Matter: Social Policy and the Working Poor in the United States and Canada.* Ithaca and London: Cornell University Press / ILR Press.

Zuberi, D. (2013). *Outsourced: Neoliberalism and the Fate of our Hospitals, Health Care Systems, and Societies.* London: ILR Press.

Index

www.ingramcontent.com/pod-product-compliance
Lightning Source LLC
Chambersburg PA
CBHW050708280326
41926CB00088B/2873

9781622732449